Transformative Philosophy

Transformative Philosophy

A STUDY OF ŚAṄKARA, FICHTE, AND HEIDEGGER

JOHN A. TABER

UNIVERSITY OF HAWAII PRESS
Honolulu

MANUFACTURED IN THE UNITED STATES OF AMERICA

Library of Congress Cataloging in Publication Data

Taber, John A., 1948–
Transformative philosophy.

Bibliography: p.
Includes index.
1. Śaṅkarācārya. 2. Fichte, Johann Gottlieb, 1762–1814. 3. Heidegger, Martin, 1889–1976. I. Title.
B133.S5T27 1983 181'.483 83-4993
ISBN 0-8248-0798-7

For my parents

Every thinker is prone to claim that his conclusions are the only logical ones, that they are necessities of universal reason, they being all the while, at bottom, accidents more or less of personal vision which had far better be avowed as such; for one man's vision may be much more valuable than another's, and our visions are usually not only our most interesting but our most respectable contributions to the world in which we play our part. What was reason given to men for, said some eighteenth-century writer, except to enable them to find reasons for what they want to think and do?—and I think the history of philosophy largely bears him out. "The aim of knowledge," says Hegel, "is to divest the objective world of its strangeness, and to make us more at home in it." Different men find their minds more at home in very different fragments of the world.

William James, *A Pluralistic Universe*

alaṃ sukumārahṛdayopadeśyajanavairasyadāyinībhiḥ kathābhiḥ. citśaktyarthibhiḥ pratyabhijñā parīkṣyā.

Kṣemarāja, *Spandanirṇaya*

Contents

Acknowledgments

THE PRESENT WORK was submitted in August 1979 to the Universität Hamburg as a Ph.D. dissertation in Philosophy (Fachbereich Philosophie und Sozialwissenschaften) under the title "On the Relation of Philosophical Knowledge and Self-Experience in the Philosophies of Śaṅkara and J. G. Fichte: A Study in Transformative Philosophy." It is being published after considerable revision.

I owe thanks above all to my Ph.D. advisers: Prof. L. Schmithausen of the Seminar für Kultur und Geschichte Indiens, Universität Hamburg, and Prof. R. Wiehl of the Philosophisches Seminar, Universität Heidelberg. Without their learned and patient guidance and encouragement this work would not have been possible.

Many others have contributed in various ways. The late Prof. Bernard Martin of Case Western University carefully read earlier drafts of the manuscript and made many helpful suggestions toward improving its style and argument. Professor T. Vetter of the Kern Institut, Leiden, offered trenchant criticisms of the material relating to Śaṅkara. Comments made by Harvey Alper, Eliot Deutsch, Jürgen Dünnebier, Kenneth Inada, and Karl Potter have also been taken into account. I am, more generally, indebted to Prof. A. Wezler of Hamburg for introducing me to Indian philosophy and showing me its analytic-philosophical worth. I am grateful, finally, to Maharishi Mahesh Yogi, who originally suggested the theme of the work—namely, in his words, that "knowledge is structured in consciousness." It is necessary to add that perhaps none of these men will be in total agreement with the method or outcome of this study, whereas I alone am responsible for any errors it may contain.

During the period that I was revising the manuscript I was supported by a grant from the Andrew Mellon Foundation. Prior to that I was supported by my wife, Marianne Cramer. I offer my thanks to both. I owe special thanks too to Eliot Deutsch for leading me to my publisher and, finally, to my editor, Stuart Kiang, who encouraged me to expand the work.

Transformative Philosophy

Introduction

IN THE HISTORY OF PHILOSOPHY there have been certain figures for whom philosophy has been not so much a quest for true ideas as a search for higher states of consciousness. Such thinkers tell us that ordinary experience is a dream, an illusion, a faint reflection of what is truly real, and that if we are to know the truly real we must awaken from the dream, enliven slumbering faculties, make a transition to a new state of awareness. Plato is a prime example of this type of philosopher. He exhorts us in his *Republic* to turn our faces toward the Good which shines like the sun in resplendent self-evidence. But this can be done only by tearing ourselves loose from the shackles that bind us in darkness, that is, by overcoming delusion. Thus Plato does not—indeed, he cannot—demonstrate the truth *for us.* He cannot deliver it to us in the form of a finished logical proof, but he does detail a program for cultivation of the spirit which, if followed, will enable one eventually to *see* the truth, not excogitate it, by employing dialectic as an instrument. Spinoza similarly resolves to improve and purify the understanding at the outset, so that he may apprehend things without error before attempting to realize human perfection in the form of recognizing the unity of man and nature.

Although the practical, soteriological outlook of these thinkers has been acknowledged, resistance to investigating them under this aspect has been great. Scholars continue to deplore the mystical interpretation of Plato. The emphasis of modern research, rather, has been on his theory of knowledge, his theory of truth, the Third Man Argument, and so on—matters which are more or less contiguous with contemporary philosophical concerns and can be dealt with in a formal, analytical way. We are wont to study Plato by rearranging his ideas according to rules with which we are familiar or replacing them with concepts we already know. Thus, on the profoundest of available interpretations, Plato's works are a textbook for extrapolating from the seen to the unseen—a soul, immortality, the forms. But, clearly, Plato means to inspire us to open our eyes so that the unseen will cease to be so. The formal approach to holistic thinkers such as Plato or Spinoza entirely misses the point. Not by shuffling ideas, but by altering our way of perceiving ideas, do we gain an appreciation of what they have to say.

Fichte and Śaṅkara, the two thinkers with whom the present study is primarily concerned, are philosophers of this same breed. Indeed, the purpose of this investigation is to show precisely that—that they are "transformative philosophers," as I shall call them, philosophers intent on effecting a total transformation of consciousness, the basic relationship between the knower and the things he knows. Full cognizance is here taken of their practical, soteriological outlook. In this respect, too, one must go against the mainstream of interpretive tradition. For, as in the case of Plato, scholars have refused to consider Fichte a mystic; and, although most regard Śaṅkara a mystic, some have made his mysticism seem completely dependent on formal knowledge *(epistēmē)*, as if for him a vision of Unity were to emerge miraculously out of philosophical ratiocination. But both thinkers emphasize in their works the necessity of a special spiritual faculty for understanding their philosophies, and they recommend programs of religious practice (Śaṅkara) or education (Fichte) to cultivate it.

The comparison of Fichte and Śaṅkara was first attempted by Rudolf Otto in an appendix to his famous study of Śaṅkara and Meister Eckhart, *West-östliche Mystik (Mysticism East and West)*. Otto, however, concentrates on doctrinal parallels between the two, concerning himself with the question whether Śaṅkara and Fichte deal, ultimately, with "the same experience." In the case of completely different cultural traditions, such a question may well be meaningless, since, in that case, the concepts and categories used to talk about experience will diverge drastically. That the content of an experience may be somehow divorced from its formulation in concepts is by no means a gratuitous assumption. Nevertheless, general similarities having to do with the methods of philosophers of different cultures, or with the overall structure of their systems, can be meaningfully observed. We are thereby able to ascertain *types* of philosophical systems, and by contrasting systems of the same type from different cultures we are often better able to understand them. By seeing what a certain philosophy is *not*, we see more clearly what it is. Similarity—not identity—established by means of comparison, is the ground for contrast, which in turn aids comprehension. Thus, with a view to achieving a deeper comprehension of the philosophies of Fichte and Śaṅkara, I compare them here with regard to their method.

Apart from this comparative or evaluative purpose, however, I wish to establish the transformative pattern as a distinct type of philosophy, casting Śaṅkara and Fichte as outstanding examples, and to explore some of its unique problems and advantages. Frederick Streng, in his pioneering study *Emptiness: A Study in Religious Meaning*, calls transformation the mark of the religious; I aim to show that it is the mark of the philosophical as well. Under the heading of "problems" comes the mystical or subjective attitude of the transformative philosopher. How can a system of thought which is intelligible to only a gifted few claim to be a viable contribution to science, which is necessarily objective and accessible to everyone? How can transformative philosophy claim to be philosophy at all, which is necessarily—or, at least, ideally—scientific? On the other hand, the advantage of transformative philosophy lies precisely in its appeal to intuitive knowledge—mystical experience—which provides it with a certificate of authenticity that traditional, formal metaphysics, in its attempt to extend reason beyond its proper scope, does not have. These issues will emerge naturally in the course of elucidating the systems of Fichte and Śaṅkara as transformative philosophies.

The plan of the work is therefore as follows. In Chapter 1 I make the case for viewing Śaṅkara as a transformative philosopher, underlining his acceptance of religious practice as an aid in engendering a kind of spiritual purity which is to be transformed into supreme knowledge by philosophical understanding. The complexity of the matters dealt with requires that we start *in medias res*; unfortunately, a general introduction to Śaṅkara's philosophy cannot be offered here. Nevertheless, I have tried to keep the argument as comprehensible as possible for readers who are unacquainted with Indian philosophy; technical points are pursued in the notes. In Chapter 2 the correctness of the interpretation offered in the first chapter is confirmed by seeing that Śaṅkara's system would be egregiously incoherent if he did not himself consider it transformative in the sense described. In this context the problem of the restricted intelligibility, hence restricted validity, of transformative philosophy is introduced. That problem is provisionally solved in connection with a discussion of the psychological mechanism of transformation. Here, too, some technical, philological matters must be given attention; but—perhaps inevitably to the dissatisfaction of Indologists—they are treated lightly. Chapter 3 is a straightforward exposition of the principles gleaned from the investigation of Śaṅkara in relation to Fichte's philosophy. At the conclusion of that chapter transformative philosophy is distinguished from metaphysics, and in considering its immunity to a Kantian critique of metaphysics the discussion of the validity of transformative philosophy is carried forward. In Chapter 4 I demonstrate the scope of the concept of transformative philosophy by applying it to another figure in Western philosophy: Martin Heidegger. Although Heidegger does not develop a full-fledged transformative system, his concern to introduce a new mode of "authentic thinking" expresses the essential spirit of transformative philosophy. And insofar as he identifies authentic thought as the original impetus of Greek speculation he assigns transformative philosophy a central role in the Western philosophical tradition. In a final effort to clarify the notion of transformative philosophy I contrast it to Richard Rorty's concept of "edifying philosophy." My study concludes with a general defense of transformative philosophy, drawing, once again, on Fichte.

The Transformative Structure of Śaṅkara's Advaita Vedānta

INDIAN SYSTEMS OF PHILOSOPHY are commonly divided into different "paths" to salvation: the path of knowledge *(jñānamārga)*, the path of devotion *(bhaktimārga)*, the path of action *(karmamārga)*, and, sometimes, the path of yoga. This scheme of classification goes back to the *Bhagavadgītā*,[1] but it was made popular by certain Neohinduistic thinkers (such as Vivekananda) who have much influenced contemporary scholars. Śaṅkara's Advaita Vedānta—a radically monistic interpretation of the mystical texts of the Veda, the Upaniṣads—besides being generally regarded the greatest of the Hindu philosophical systems is also typically characterized as the path of knowledge *par excellence.*[2] By this path, it is claimed, one can attain liberation or enlightenment—salvation—solely by means of the cognition of the true nature of the self and its relation to the world without the least dependence on religious practice, such as the performance of sacred ritual, the worship of a personal god, or the practice of yoga.

In the present chapter I wish to challenge, or at least qualify, this idea. It will be argued that, far from rejecting religious practice, Śaṅkara presupposes it as a necessary means for establishing a higher state of consciousness, on the basis of which his philosophy first becomes comprehensible and is able to effect the profound transformation he alleges it should cause. In other words, Śaṅkara's philosophy is transformative. It is meant primarily to structure religious experience and thus depends on the presence of the experience in question, or the seed thereof, in an unexpressed form. This experience, it will be argued, is to be brought about by means of traditional religious observances—at least, so Śaṅkara believes. In demonstrating this thesis my procedure will be as follows. First, the passages in Śaṅkara's writings which suggest that his Vedānta system is exclusively a path of knowledge will be examined. Next, that interpretation will be critically assessed from a strictly philosophical, as opposed to a philological, point of view. Third, other textual evidence will be brought forward which will suggest that Śaṅkara indeed accepts a variety of religious and "spiritual" disciplines as an essential part of his system. Finally, the apparent conflict between Śaṅkara's denial of religious practice and his acceptance of it will be resolved.

It should be noted at the outset that the present inquiry takes its place among numerous attempts, both ancient and modern, to view Advaita Vedānta holistically. Later systems of Advaita Vedānta, such as that of Vidyāraṇya, attempt to reconcile the approaches of karma, knowledge, worship *(upāsana)*, and yoga,[3] while in systems prior to Śaṅkara (that described by Bhavya in his *Mādhyamakahṛdaya*,[4] Gauḍapāda's *Māṇḍūkyakārikā*) yoga already plays a significant role. Even the *Bhagavadgītā*, from which we have the notion of distinct paths to liberation, declares that the paths of yoga and Sāṃkhya are compatible (the latter is generally considered a *jñānamārga*),[5] while the *Nyāyasūtra*, which states that liberation results from the knowledge of reality *(tattvajñāna)*, also says that the purification of the self through yoga is for that same purpose.[6]

In general, the various Hindu philosophical systems do not, on the face of it, seem to recommend one path to salvation to the exclusion of all others; rather they tend to recommend several, if not all, traditionally recognized approaches simultaneously while putting emphasis on a particular one. Whether this tendency is a reflection of the original intentions of the author of a system or whether it was introduced by later philosophers of the school in order to give the system broad appeal is in an individual case often unclear. In any case—regardless of what can be said about Hindu philosophy in general in this respect—some modern interpreters have viewed Śaṅkara's system as a *jñānamārga* which at the same time upholds and unites the various social, ethical, and ritual aspects of Hinduism, indeed, as is supposed, in an effort to preserve that religion in the face of the challenge of Buddhism, which enjoyed a vigorous renaissance during Śaṅkara's lifetime (eighth century).[7] Although the present study does not share all the assumptions of this view,[8] it may be seen as an attempt to establish one of its principal contentions in a rigorous fashion.

1. *Is Śaṅkara's Advaita Vedānta Exclusively a Path of Knowledge?*

In most of his works Śaṅkara can be found polemicizing against karma and *upāsana* as means for achieving liberation, usually at the very beginning. Karma means "work" or "action," but especially the performance of ritual acts, some of which are obligatory for the Hindu by virtue of his caste. *Upāsana* is meditation on the deeper meaning of the Vedic sacrifice or on Brahman, prescribed in various forms in the Upaniṣads and the Brāhmaṇas, the Vedic treatises on sacrifice; it is apparently considered by Śaṅkara a particular type of karma—namely, mental karma.[9]

The first step in achieving the proper perspective on Śaṅkara's attitude toward karma and *upāsana* is to see that he does not deny them categorically but in fact feels obliged to do so by the conventions of the literary genre he has chosen. For most of Śaṅkara's known writings are commentaries on the Upaniṣads; his *Brahmasūtrabhāṣya* and *Bhagavadgītābhāṣya* are commentaries on what he takes to be summaries of Upaniṣadic doctrine.[10] Since an Upaniṣad usually comprises the final chapters of a Brāhmaṇa, Śaṅkara often feels compelled to show at the outset of his work that the matters he is about to discuss have not been exhaustively dealt with in the Brāhmaṇa. Thus he distinguishes what is to be attained through the means prescribed in the Brāhmaṇa—meditation and sacrifice—from the goal of the Upaniṣad. According to Śaṅkara in his *Bṛhadāraṇyakopaniṣadbhāṣya*, identification with Prajāpati, the firstborn among all beings and creator of the universe, is the highest attainment to be expected from engaging in meditation and sacrifice.[11] A somewhat less spectacular achievement than this is the attainment of the world of the fathers *(pitṛloka)*, or heaven *(svarga)*, from which the soul eventually returns to earth to be reborn after having enjoyed there the fruits of its pious deeds.[12] But higher than either of these—and what the Upaniṣads teach about—is *mokṣa*, liberation, the highest good *(paraṃ śreyas)*, the highest end of man *(paramapuruṣārtha)*. And that, Śaṅkara argues, can have no possible connection with karma or *upāsana*.

The most complete and best-known presentation of the rationale for this last statement is given by Śaṅkara at *BrSūBh* I.1.4. Indeed, his argument there is so thorough and emphatic that one tends to forget it is not the final word he has to say on the subject. Liberation, Śaṅkara points out, is a state of existence in which the self is neither an agent of action nor the enjoyer of the fruits of action. It is a disembodied state *(aśarīratva)* untouched by pleasure or pain. As such, it cannot possibly be the result of karma, which leads to higher or lower embodied states of existence suited for the enjoyment of its fruits, depending on whether the karma is meritorious or evil.[13] Moreover, liberation is eternal in the highest sense: it is all-pervading like space, devoid of all change, eternally satisfied, without parts, and self-luminous in essence.[14] Therefore it cannot in any way be effected *(kartavya)*, that is, brought into being by the performance of some deed. Nor is liberation something to be attained. It is simply the state of the self, and the self can be neither striven after nor avoided.[15] Nor is it a special condition of the self to be brought about through ritual purification. For the self, which is Brahman, is eternally pure.[16]

Numerous scriptural passages suggest that *mokṣa* follows immediately upon the knowledge of Brahman without any intervening action: thus, *Muṇḍaka Upaniṣad* III.2.9, "He who knows Brahman becomes Brahman"; *TU* II.9, "He who knows the bliss of Brahman fears nothing."[17] Knowledge of Brahman is not in turn a kind of action, the superimposition of an idea on a thing;[18] it is simply seeing Brahman as it is. Finally, Śaṅkara states that self-knowledge is not concerned with some other thing to be done; it is not for the purpose of avoiding or attaining something else, "for this is our glory, that once the self is known to be Brahman every notion of something yet to be done is relinquished and what was to be done is accomplished."[19]

These and related arguments are to be found in the introduction to the *Aitareya*, *Taittīriya*, *Kena*, *Īśā*, and *Bṛhadāraṇyaka Upaniṣad* commentaries. Thus *Īśopaniṣadbhāṣya* I: "The mantras [of the Upaniṣad] do not refer to ritual acts, for they reveal the nature of the self which is not an adjunct to [any] action. That the nature of the self is purity, freedom from evil, oneness, eternity, unembodiedness, and all-pervasiveness will be stated [by the Upaniṣad itself]. . . . The nature of the self being such, it cannot be effected, transformed, attained, or purified. . . ."[20] A particularly interesting presentation of this same thought occurs at *BĀUBh* I.4.7., where Śaṅkara, with characteristic rigor, explains that when he talks of the "attainment of self" *(ātmalābha)*—for, indeed, he must sometimes refer to the transition from the state of bondage to the state of liberation—he means simply knowledge of the self:

> The attainment of the self does not involve, as in the attainment of what is not the self, the obtaining of something not obtained before, because

> there is no difference between the attainer and what is to be attained. Indeed, when one has something to attain that is not the self, then the self is the attainer and what is not the self is the thing to be attained. And the latter, insofar as it is unattained, is separated from oneself by actions as, for example, [the action implied by the fact that it] has to be effected. . . . But this self is just the opposite of that. Because it is the self, it is not separated [from itself] by actions. . . .[21]

I am already who I am, namely, the eternally pure, enlightened Brahman, and no effort of mine will make me more of what I am than I have always been. If anything can be said to separate the self from itself, Śaṅkara continues, it is ignorance. But ignorance is completely insubstantial. That one imagines, say, mother-of-pearl to be silver when one must be able to *see* that it is mother-of-pearl (when one is looking directly at it) is what we refer to as "error" or "ignorance," a situation without any apparent explanation.[22] One comes to realize that one is actually seeing not silver but mother-of-pearl not through a process involving actions and means—as if the false idea of silver had a concrete cause that had to be removed—but simply by being told that one is really looking at mother-of-pearl. Similarly, "the attainment [of the self] is simply the removal [of ignorance] by knowledge; it comes about in no other way. Therefore we shall declare that any other means besides knowledge [such as karma or *upāsana*] is useless with regard to attaining the self."[23]

It is in this same context that Śaṅkara provides his most unambiguous denial of yoga as a cause of liberation.[24] After denying the possibility that the Upaniṣad, in saying "Let one meditate [on the self] as the self," enjoins a meditation in the Vedāntic sense (that is, *upāsana*), Śaṅkara has an opponent suggest that yogic concentration *(nirodha)* is another possibility.[25] "Since the suppression of the fluctuations of the mind is something different than the knowledge of the self arising from the Vedic texts and since in other systems [such as the yoga system] it is known as something to be done [for the sake of liberation], let it be enjoined." Śaṅkara replies: "No; for it is in fact *not* known as a means to liberation. In the Upaniṣads nothing is considered a means to the attainment of the highest end of man except the knowledge of the identity of Brahman and the self."[26]

From such passages as these one easily arrives at the conclusion that Śaṅkara believed that karma, *upāsana*, and yoga have no bearing whatever on the attainment of liberation. This view has received support from certain modern scholars.[27] It has found its way into popular Vedānta as well. Hence this statement from a tract of a modern Indian movement devoted to the dissemination of Advaita Vedānta as a philosophy for the masses: "Ātman being one's very self, one needs only to be told so, and at the very instant of the teaching of the Śruti or the preceptor about its nature, one sees the Self in himself, giving up all other delusory notions that one is something else."[28]

Yet it is clear that there must be more to it than this. Indeed, according to Śaṅkara, the hearer of a discourse on Vedānta—such as the dialogue between Uddālaka and Śvetaketu in the sixth chapter of the *Chāndogya Upaniṣad* or that between a Vedānta master and his disciple in the second prose chapter of the *Upadeśasāhasrī*—ought to have attained liberation, "the highest end of man," by the end of the discourse. But what does that mean? It evidently means more than possession of some kind of propositional knowledge. It means, rather, that one has undergone a profound change in one's relationship to oneself and to the world—to one's own perceptions and emotions as well as to other persons and things. One is no longer *of* the world, affected by the pain and pleasure the body undergoes; one is no longer a participant in the process of striving for better states of existence. For one has done away with the notion that one is one's body: Just as it cannot be imagined that a rich householder, who might have once grieved over the loss of his wealth, could so grieve after having renounced his home and become a wandering mendicant, "it cannot be imagined that one who was formerly seen to be subject to misery and fear insofar as he thought he was the body could after that misconception has ceased . . . still be subject to misery and fear."[29]

Moreover, the liberated man has no longings. Liberation means absolute fulfillment. "For once the oneness, eternity, and purity of the self have been comprehended, no further expectation arises, because one is aware that the end of man has been achieved. Thus (*Īśā Upaniṣad* VII): 'What trouble, what sorrow, is there when one sees that oneness?' . . ."[30] But besides this inner, psychological detachment, to which Śaṅkara refers as the state of being the eternal "witness" *(sākṣin)* of one's actions and experiences[31] (as opposed to the agent himself or the experiencer himself)—beyond this, liberation is a state of union with the absolute. This is simply and elegantly expressed in the

Upaniṣad phrase that Śaṅkara quotes so often (*Muṇḍaka Upaniṣad* III.2.9): "He who knows Brahman becomes Brahman."[32] And this is something truly extraordinary. For Brahman is the substance of the universe, its material cause.[33] It is *everything*; everything is dependent on it, identical with it. Individual things appear independent of it only by an illusion, as spaces inside waterpots and jars appear different from Space.[34] Brahman is the "inner ruler" *(antaryāmin)* of all beings;[35] it is the source of scripture.[36] In fact, viewed under a particular aspect, Brahman is the omniscient, omnipotent Lord.[37] Finally, when liberation has been reached, all of this is revealed in an intuition to the enlightened soul. It is not merely felt on an emotional plane or believed, but directly cognized and lived. The hearing of the Vedic word, Śaṅkara says, results in a confirming intuition;[38] the repetition of the Vedānta texts has a visible purpose, "like the beating of husks has the purpose of extracting grain."[39] In short, there should be no wondering whether the Vedānta discourse has had the desired effect; the effect should emerge, rather, as self-evident and indubitable.

Now I submit that very few who have listened to a Vedānta discourse or studied the Upaniṣads or Vedānta treatises such as Śaṅkara's have ever experienced the psychological change Śaṅkara describes or had a clear vision of themselves as identical to God. And this failure renders invalid the thesis that hearing the Vedic word is alone sufficient for that transformation to occur. For many have fulfilled that condition—I for one—without any such thing happening. In other words, it must be admitted that, on the view that Śaṅkara's philosophy is exclusively a path of knowledge which promises a sublime transformation through *formal* philosophical knowledge alone, Śaṅkara's philosophy simply does not work. Taking this to be an unacceptable consequence—for the great interest shown in Śaṅkara's philosophy for over a thousand years would be difficult to explain if this were true—we are compelled to look for other conditions that must be fulfilled.

To be sure, the hearing of the Vedic texts *(śravaṇa)* is traditionally associated with other factors: reflection *(manana)* and intense contemplation *(nididhyāsana)*. Maṇḍanamiśra, an important successor of Śaṅkara, makes it appear that *śravaṇa* is incomplete without these elements; one cannot be said to have truly comprehended the Vedānta teaching unless one has reflected and contemplated as well.[40] Śaṅkara in fact acknowledges these factors. *Manana*, for him, is the employment of reason in support of scripture. Basically, the manifold considerations that make up his commentaries are what he regards as *manana*—the reconciliation of apparently conflicting scriptural passages and the elucidation of certain metaphysical ideas which supplement scriptural doctrines.[41] *Nididhyāsana* he does not specifically define. Nevertheless, it is plain that he considers neither it nor reflection an exercise which can bring about anything not already in principle supplied by the texts themselves. This conviction comes out in his discussion of whether *śravaṇa*, *manana*, and *nididhyāsana* are actions to be repeated or performed only once. Śaṅkara admits their repetition, but only up to a point: the repetition of hearing and reasoning is admissible for those for whom the meaning of words of the scripture is obscured by ignorance, doubt, and confusion. That repetition, however, is merely antecedent to the full realization of the self based on the discernment of the meaning of the individual words of the sentence "That thou art."[42]

In other words, *śravaṇa*, *manana*, and *nididhyāsana* do not automatically yield understanding; rather, understanding is based on *insight* into the meaning of the scripture. But whence this insight?[43] Indeed, it seems that most will share the doubt that Śaṅkara's explanation is meant to dispel: "If a sentence like 'That thou art' does not produce the cognition that the self is Brahman when heard once, what hope is there that it will do so when repeated?"[44] And what hope is there that reasoning, if it cannot yield the desired cognition the first time, will do so when gone through again? The fact that after considerable mental effort one may still not comprehend the true significance of the scripture in the fullest sense—so that a transformation, a total restructuring of consciousness, is effected—suggests that more is involved here which Śaṅkara, for some reason, does not care to reveal in this context but presupposes.

It would be especially wrong to suggest in any way that for Śaṅkara one's state of consciousness subsequent to hearing the Vedānta discourse is that of liberation *by necessity*—that just because these means are sufficient in themselves to produce enlightenment, for the Veda says so, one who employs them *in fact* becomes infinite, immortal, untouched by pleasure or pain, and so on. We find a modern preacher of Hinduism, Swāmī Prabhavānanda, approaching this misconception when he writes:

> He who chooses the path of knowledge must maintain a consciousness of his identity with the Ātman. By analysis he must know: "I am not the body, nor the mind, nor the ego—I am beyond all these. I am the Ātman —one with Brahman." Such a man, by constantly living in this consciousness, soon frees himself of all bodily desires. The activities of this body and mind will continue, but through them all he remains completely detached and unaffected.[45]

This remark suggests that the aspirant, upon hearing from the Veda that he is *buddha* (enlightened), *mukta* (liberated), and so on, makes out of his ordinary thoughts and feelings the exalted thoughts and feelings of the *jīvanmukta*, the living, truly liberated being, because he now "knows" that to be his true state. Whether or not such an exercise actually brings results, it cannot be said to derive from Śaṅkara. For it confuses "knows" with "believes." The aspirant here actually persists only in the *belief* that he is Brahman, which, somewhat paradoxically on this account, leads to the onset of the actual condition which one is confident already exists. But Śaṅkara emphasizes that liberation is to follow upon correct, unambiguous, self-verifying knowledge *(saṃyagjñāna)* for which there is no gap between one's expectations and actuality and in which imagination plays no role.[46]

We conclude from the foregoing that the mere hearing of the Vedic texts, whether accompanied by reflection or not, is insufficient to provide understanding—in the fullest sense—of the unity of the self, according to Śaṅkara's description of the consequences of such understanding. We are therefore obliged to inquire if there are other elements contributing to the rise of *mokṣa* to which Śaṅkara refers, if only indirectly, despite his initial denial that there are. Indeed, we need not look very far.

2. *Śaṅkara's Prerequisites*

At the beginning of the *Brahmasūtrabhāṣya* we find Śaṅkara discussing the prerequisites for *brahmajijñāsā*, the investigation into Brahman. After discarding the inquiry into dharma, religious duty, as one of these—for reasons akin to those according to which karma is irrelevant, for dharma involves karma—he lists several spiritual or psychological qualities: the discrimination of the eternal and the noneternal *(nityānityavastuviveka)*, the absence of passion with regard to the enjoyment of things present or remote *(ihāmutrārthabhogavirāga)*, the perfection of tranquility, self-command "and the other means" *(śama-damādisādhanasaṃpat)*, and the desire for release *(mumukṣutvam)*. "These being present," he continues, "Brahman may be inquired into and known either before or after the inquiry into dharma, but not otherwise."[47]

These elements certainly appear to be the result of, or steps involved in, spiritual practice. *Nityānityavastuviveka* at first sight suggests a philosophical exercise. Yet it reminds one of the discriminating cognition of the mind *(sattva)* and the self *(puruṣa)* discussed in the *Yogasūtra*.[48] Dispassion *(vairāgya)* is central to yoga as one of the two causes of *samādhi*.[49] The yoga system even specifies, as does Śaṅkara, that dispassion should apply to things in this life as well as to things beyond one's experience known about only through the Veda (heaven and the like).[50] Calmness, *śama*, appears as a concept in yoga philosophy in various forms—once, for example, as the tranquil steadiness of the mind which is to be brought about through the repeated practice of meditation.[51] Control, *dama*, seems equivalent to the withdrawal of the senses from their objects *(pratyāhāra)*, which is to be effected spontaneously by *samādhi* and is called "the supreme control." Finally, being desirous of release, *mumukṣutva*, may be the sign of approaching *kaivalya*, the final state of the self in isolation from the constantly changing dispositions of nature, mentioned at *YSBh* IV.25.[52] Although it would be unwarranted to say that Śaṅkara had the *Yogasūtra* specifically in mind when he listed these items, a scheme of concepts similar to that of classical yoga is evident.[53]

Śaṅkara obtains the terms "calmness" and "control" from the *Bṛhadāraṇyaka Upaniṣad* passage, "Therefore one who knows thus becomes calm, controlled, abstinent, enduring, and collected and sees the self in himself."[54] From the explanation Śaṅkara gives of these terms in his *BĀUBh* it is even more evident that he believes yoga, in some sense, has a place. While he, somewhat in conflict with the letter of the yoga texts, takes "calm" and "controlled" to refer to the senses and the mind respectively,[55] the yoga system does admit of assigning either concept to either aspect of the concentrated psyche.[56] "Abstinent" Śaṅkara explains as being turned away from all desires or being a renunciate, which points to sexual continence, *brahmacarya*—one of the yogic "restrictions" *(yamas)*. "Enduring" refers to austerity, *tapas* —one of the yogic "observances" *(niyamas)*.[57] Śaṅkara regards "collected" as being in conformity with the concept *samādhi*.[58] Faith, *śraddhā*, traditionally included among the spiritual means of Vedānta, is not mentioned in the Upaniṣad or in Śaṅkara's comment. But it is to be found listed at *YS* I.20 as one of the aids for developing the higher "seedless" *(nirbīja)* form of concentration.[59]

Śaṅkara's explanation of these terms, which in fact amounts to no more than a gloss here, is embedded in an extremely complex and extensive discussion of karma and its relevance (or lack thereof) to liberation. It is only by taking this whole discussion into account that one begins to gain insight into the complex theory of spiritual preparation that lies behind the casual mentioning of the prerequisites of the inquiry into Brahman at *BrSūBh* I.1.1. and, at the same time, realizes that Śaṅkara's original rejection of the utility of karma and the like is not so simple as it first appears. In what follows I shall present only the gist of the matter, drawing on statements from Śaṅkara's *TUBh* in addition to his *BrSū* and *BĀU* commentaries.

Certainly the thesis that karma has no bearing on liberation remains one of the firm pillars of Śaṅkara's doctrine throughout his works. He never relinquishes this idea. Yet it is so qualified in certain contexts as to mean something quite other than what one would expect. At *BĀUBh* IV.4.22, for example, the section immediately preceding the reference to abstinence and self-control, Śaṅkara interprets the Upaniṣad sentence, "Aspiring to that world [of the self] alone, those who are disposed to renunciation renounce,"[60] as an injunction requiring the seeker after liberation to renounce all action, even those rites considered obligatory in Hindu sacred law. This injunction appears as a prescription of means to *attain* liberation. But it is clear from the rest of his comment that Śaṅkara considers it to apply to those who have *already*, to a certain degree, achieved self-knowledge. Knowing the self —he continues in paraphrase of the Upaniṣad—let one be a sage, not a performer of sacrifices *(karmin)*. For when the self is known—that is, when the whole universe is seen as the self—then what thing different from oneself can one see to accomplish? Action being impossible, let there be only absorption in self-knowledge.[61] Śaṅkara summarizes this idea as he interprets the continuation of *BĀU* IV.4.22: "It is said that ancient sages did not desire children, saying, 'Of what use are children to us who possess this self, this world?' "[62]

> The sages asked, "Of what use are children to us?" who are the beholders of truth, "who possess this self," which is free from hunger, and so forth,

and is not to be altered by good or bad [works], who possess "this world" [of the self], the desired goal. For they realized: no means is to be sought for [attaining] the self, which is devoid of all transmigratory attributes such as ends and means. A search for means is made if there is some end to be attained. If means were sought for that which is unattainable, that would be like swimming on land under the delusion that it is water or looking for the footprints of birds in the sky. Thus, *having known the self*, Brāhmans ought to renounce the householder's way of life; they should not engage in rites.[63]

Śaṅkara's rejection of *upāsana* at *BĀUBh* I.4.7, which we have already noted, is also a qualified one. He denies that the phrase *atmety upāsīta*, "Let one meditate [on the self] as the self," is an *apūrvavidhi*—that is, according to the ancient Indian science of Vedic exegesis, an original injunction of an action not previously referred to in a text. Yet he admits, in agreement with the actual grammar of the phrase, that it is an injunction to choose a known alternative *(niyamavidhi)*.[64] Here Śaṅkara is involved in a dispute with a school of philosophy—the Mīmāṃsā—which held that the sentences of the Veda have meaning only insofar as they directly or indirectly move us to undertake proper karma. Thus all its sentences must ultimately be construed as injunctions or prescriptions—*vidhis*. The point of Śaṅkara's statement is that whether we must regard the phrase, "Let one meditate [on the self] as the self," as a *vidhi* or not, the knower of Brahman, for whom the prescription is apparently intended, need not *do* anything. Absorption in the self is automatic for him. Why, then, any prescription at all? Because the habit (over many lifetimes) of being active, of resorting to means to accomplish ends, still lingers. An abstinent, quiescent attitude should therefore be maintained. Śaṅkara clarifies the issue:

How is contemplation an alternative when the chain of remembrance issuing from self-knowledge is declared to be inevitable because no other possibility remains? [That is to say: Why does meditation on the self need to be enjoined by the Upaniṣad when, as a result of self-knowledge, everything is seen to be the self and nothing other than the self can be thought of?] Indeed, that is correct! [Meditation on the self is inevitable!] Since the past work that led to the formation of the present body must bear fruit, however, the functioning of speech, mind, and body persists even after correct knowledge has been acquired. Karma that has begun

> to operate is stronger [than knowledge], like the momentum of an arrow that has been released. The [relative] weakness of the efficacy of knowledge is therefore an alternative [which might unfortunately ensue]. Hence the chain of remembrance relating to self-knowledge is to be favored by recourse to the strength that comes from renunciation, passionlessness, and other means.[65]

Once the self is known, the carrying out of karma becomes irrelevant, even an obstacle, to liberation; *for those who have already grasped the essential truth* of the identity of Brahman and the self, the renunciation of mundane activity and the avoidance of spiritual exercises is enjoined "as the chief and most direct means of attaining the world of the self"[66] to consolidate that knowledge. Śaṅkara emphasizes the antecedents of these statements. But that would seem to imply that fulfilling one's duty and engaging in spiritual exercises have some relevance until knowledge is attained!

In fact, we find in the *BĀUBh* injunctions to take up the spiritual path—and all the work it implies—often in close conjunction with the same apparent denials to which I have drawn attention. Just prior to his discussion of renunciation at IV.4.22 Śaṅkara works out an interpretation of the phrase of the same verse: "Brahmans endeavor to know that [great, unborn self] by means of Vedic recitation, sacrifice, gifts, austerity, and fasting. Knowing it alone, one becomes a sage."[67] Although the Upaniṣad states that the condition of the self is in truth neither improved nor degraded by the performance of good or bad works, Śaṅkara contends that it means to indicate here that the portion of the Veda concerned with obligatory karma *(nityakarma)* has, in fact, ultimately the knowledge of Brahman in view. He argues against an interpretation of "by means of Vedic recitation" as signifying the recitation or study only of the Upaniṣads to the exclusion of the sacrificial texts. The carrying out of prescribed rites effects a purification which makes it possible for one to know the self clearly, without impediment: "Those who have been purified by works, whose self is pure, are able to know the self revealed by the Upaniṣads without obstruction. Thus in the *Atharvaveda* it is stated, 'One whose mind is pure sees the partless one when he meditates,' and the tradition *(smṛti)* teaches, 'Knowledge arises for men from the destruction of evil work.' "[68]

Moreover, Śaṅkara continues, it is taught in all scriptural texts that obligatory karma leads to purity. Thus Brahmans seek to know the self by sacrifice, by giving and the other practices mentioned in the Upaniṣad verse. "By the words 'Vedic recitation,' 'sacrifice,' 'giving,' and 'austerity' all obligatory karma is indicated. Thus the whole body of ritual works, except those done for a desired end,[69] is deemed a means to liberation insofar as it gives rise to knowledge."[70] When one has realized the self in this manner, one becomes a sage, that is, according to Śaṅkara's gloss, a yogin.

Again elsewhere, shortly before his treatment of the injunction of *BĀUBh* I.4.7, Śaṅkara discusses the suggestion made at I.4.2 that the god Prajāpati attained enlightenment spontaneously, simply by being born. Śaṅkara has someone object that this implies that faith, worship, devotion, and so on are not the causes of knowledge. But Śaṅkara denies this. For, he points out, in ordinary experience we see that a causal effect can be produced in various ways—by any one of several alternative causes or by many causes in combination. Regarding the perception of a color, for example, among animals that see in the dark the cause is the mere proximity of the color to the eye. In the case of yogins, the mind itself is sufficient for the perception of color. In the case of humans, however, several causes are combined, including the proximity of the eye to the colored object and an external source of light. The latter, moreover, may be more or less efficacious depending on whether it is a strong or weak source of illumination—whether it is, say, the sun or the moon. In precisely the same way, Śaṅkara continues,

> work done in previous lives is sometimes the cause of the knowledge of the unity of the self, as it was for Prajāpati. Sometimes austerity is the cause, as it is according to the scriptural passage, "Endeavor to know Brahman by means of austerity." Sometimes [devotion, faith, and so on are thought to be] the sole cause of the attainment of knowledge, as we gather from such *śruti* and *smṛti* passages as: "He knows who has got a teacher"; "One who has faith attains knowledge"; "Know it by means of prostration"; "Verily [knowledge received] from a teacher is best"; "The self is to be seen, to be heard." For faith, and so on, remove the causes of demerit and the like; and the hearing, thinking, and meditating on the Vedānta texts are concerned with the object of intuitive knowledge [namely, the truth "That thou art"] and are by nature the causes of true knowledge when the hindrances of the mind and the body, such as sin,

have been destroyed. Therefore faith, devotion, and the like by no means cease to be the causes of knowledge.[71]

Thus a threefold scheme for liberation is suggested in Śaṅkara's *BĀU* commentary: first is preparation, involving a combination of spiritual disciplines and the observance of religious duties, resulting in the removal of demerit; second is insight or realization based on hearing and contemplating the Vedic word, which informs the well-prepared, purified intellect as the blow of a hammer confers shape to heated metal; third is consolidation or resolution (the cooling of the forged object?), consisting in the refraining from all activity, both overtly, in the sense of withdrawing from socioreligious obligation, and inwardly.

We receive a more thorough, systematic, and straightforward presentation of these matters in Śaṅkara's *TUBh*—a generally less polemical, if less mature, work than his *BĀUBh*. We now turn to that discussion. At *TUBh* I.1 Śaṅkara sets out to show, once again, in accordance with the need to distinguish the topic of the Upaniṣad from that of the Brāhmaṇa, that *mokṣa* does not follow automatically from the omission of prohibited and selfish acts, on the one hand, and from the exhaustion or "enjoyment" *(bhoga)* of works done in previous lives and the observance of obligatory rites on the other.[72] His arguments, which focus mainly on the last point, are much the same as those already discussed and need not be repeated here. Later in the same chapter, however, Śaṅkara takes up this issue in connection with some Upaniṣad verses which clearly teach various moral and religious duties (*TU* I.9,11). In this context he systematically considers whether "the highest good results from karma alone, from karma aided by knowledge, from karma and knowledge together, from knowledge aided by karma, or just from knowledge."[73]

As one would expect, all these alternatives but the last are rejected. Liberation proceeds only from knowledge *(vidyā)*. Knowledge and action can in no way be combined, because they are contradictory; knowledge is concerned with a reality for which the distinction of factors of action such as the agent is invalid.[74] But Śaṅkara lets it be asked whether this thesis—that knowledge and work cannot be combined—does not itself imply a contradiction: a contradiction of scripture. For it is scripture that both prescribes the observance of sacraments and rites and exhorts one to know the self. In reply Śaṅkara reminds us that scripture speaks on different levels according to the purpose it has in view. Although it may concern itself with karma at one place and supreme knowledge at another, it does not do so to the same end nor on the basis of the same assumptions. Only insofar as scripture has in view the removal of the ignorance that keeps man bound in the cycle of rebirth is it concerned with transcendental knowledge. As it is restricted to this specific purpose when it teaches the truth about the self, no conflict arises when it advocates elsewhere the carrying out of rites. In particular, no conflict is to be seen in the fact that the ritual portions of the scripture assume the self to be an agent which performs sacrifices. For

> insofar as the sacred science enjoins karma as a means of destroying accumulated sins for those who aspire to liberation or as a means for achieving [certain worldly and heavenly] ends for those who desire such ends, it assumes the existence of the elements of action [such as an agent] merely according to custom but does not concern itself directly with the existence of these elements. For the rise of knowledge is inconceivable for one who is hindered by accumulated evil karma. When that has been destroyed, knowledge ought to arise, whence ignorance is destroyed, whereupon the absolute cessation of transmigration follows.[75]

In other words, karma and the assumptions on which it is based are valid for all worldly, practical purposes. But this is not to deny the opposition between karma and *vidyā*. Indeed, Śaṅkara reemphasizes it: only one who does not know the self is impelled to act by yearning for some object outside the self. But desire does not arise for one who sees the self—that is, one who sees no object distinct from the self. Śaṅkara concludes:

> It is precisely because of this conflict [between karma and knowledge] that knowledge does not depend on karma as far as *mokṣa* is concerned. With respect to its own attainment, however, we have said that obligatory karma becomes the *cause* of knowledge insofar as it removes previously accumulated hindrances. . . . Thus there is no contradiction of those scriptural passages that enjoin karma. Hence, that the highest good is a consequence of knowledge alone is proved.[76]

This discussion goes further toward clarifying the distinction between the applicability and inapplicability of karma than any to be found in the *BĀUBh.* Karma gives rise to knowledge. But knowledge, not karma, gives rise to *mokṣa.* It is of particular interest here that Śaṅkara refuses to admit that karma is even an indirect cause of liberation. In all expressions in which karma is referred to as a cause, a *hetu*, it is only a *vidyāhetu*, never a *mokṣahetu.* When it comes to *mokṣa*, it would seem, the causal relation between karma and *mokṣa* via knowledge is forgotten! There are two possible sources of this attitude. One source, I suspect, is Śaṅkara's Pūrvamīmāṃsā heritage, his grounding in the traditional method of Vedic exegesis. Although he continually upbraids the philosophical orientation of the Mīmāṃsā for its emphasis on karma, especially sacrifice, as the sole means of salvation, he in fact relies on Mīmāṃsā vocabulary and techniques of textual analysis in his commentaries.[77] Śabara in his *Mīmāṃsāsūtrabhāṣya*, for example, states that the subsidiary *(guṇa)* acts of a sacrifice are not the cause of the beneficial effect to be brought about by the sacrifice, referred to as *apūrva.* Not from all acts, but only primary acts, does *apūrva* result.[78] Acts are subsidiary when they relate to the preparation *(saṃskāra)* of a material substance, such as the husking of rice.[79] Thus, on this view, the spiritual purification achieved by karma, seen as analogous to the preparation of an offering, would not, strictly, produce *mokṣa.*[80]

Another source of this attitude is, more clearly, the idea that the true state of the self is, in Śaṅkara's opinion, an eternal condition that is not susceptible to the sort of transformations that an agent undergoes in the process of acting. The Vedānta master must move the student toward this realization without engendering in him the false idea that he is *accomplishing* something, even if getting to the point where he is *ready* to have it involves doing certain things. As if to preserve the innocence of his reader Śaṅkara rarely mentions this crucial methodological point. But on occasion he hints at it. In his discussion of the repetition of the sentence "That thou art" in the *BrSūBh*, Śaṅkara insists that although repetition is in some cases required, it is not to be construed as the object of an injunction:

> For the person for whom the intuition [of the identity of Brahman and the self] does not emerge immediately [upon hearing the sentence], repetition is assumed admissible for the purpose of giving rise to that intuition. But in that case also the student should not be moved toward repetition

> in such a way as to divert him from the [true] meaning of the sentence "That thou art." For one does not marry off his daughter in order to kill her husband.[81] One who is motivated to perform this repetition by an injunction *(niyukta)* necessarily gets the notion, "I am an agent; I *ought* to do this," which is opposed to the correct idea of Brahman.[82]

Supreme knowledge is of the whole, partless self. The notion that one obtains such knowledge by *doing* something can only interfere with it. Although one may appear to be involved in karma in the process of becoming liberated, one must finally come to see that it is just that—a mere appearance, ultimately unreal.

Elsewhere in the *BrSūBh* Śaṅkara holds to his basic qualification of the causality of the elements of liberation, as worked out in *TUBh* I—which now begins to appear somewhat strained. Knowledge is dependent on karma and other means "with regard to its origin" *(utpattiṃ prati)*, but once it has arisen, it is independent of all factors "with regard to the attainment of its fruit" *(phalasiddhiṃ prati)*—that is, *mokṣa*.[83] "The statement that works . . . serve as the cooperating cause of knowledge *(vidyāsahakāra)* is not made with the fruit of knowledge in mind . . . for knowledge is not enjoined and the fruit of knowledge is not something to be attained. . . . Only insofar as these are means for bringing about the *origin* of knowledge *(utpattisādhanatve)* is the statement that they are cooperative causes valid."[84] Thus, Śaṅkara continues, a means of knowledge might, perhaps, according to its particular strength, impart a higher or lower degree to *its* result—knowledge—but not to the result of *knowledge*—release. In reality, though, even knowledge does not admit of higher or lower degrees. If it were low, it would not be knowledge at all. Nevertheless, one can speak of degrees of knowledge insofar as it originates after a long or short time. But one cannot speak of degrees of liberation.[85]

We note, finally, the wide variety of disciplines and observances that Śaṅkara recommends at *TUBh* I.12, where he also takes account of their differing efficacy, much as he does at *BĀUBh* I.4.2. Although the *rise* of knowledge is occasioned by karma, *(karmanimittatvād vidyotpatteḥ)*, the householder phase of Hindu life, during which one has the means to perform sacrifices, is not the only one of the *āśramas*, the traditional stages of Hindu life, that is relevant to liberation. Again, this issue harks back to the dispute between the Vedāntin and the

Mīmāṃsā philosopher about renunciation. The Mīmāṃsaka, stressing the indispensability of performing sacrifices, wishes to declare illegitimate the traditionally recognized *āśrama* of mendicancy or renunciation, during which stage sacrifices are not performed. Śaṅkara resists this proposal because karma is manifold:

> The *agnihotra* [and other sacrifices] are not the only works there are. But there is continence, austerity, right speech, calmness, control, and nonviolence, too—the well-known works of other *āśramas*, which are the most effective in giving rise to knowledge because they are not mixed [with ulterior motives, such as the desire to go to heaven]—as well as those works known as meditation *(dhyāna)* and concentration *(dhāraṇā)*. And the Upaniṣad itself will say, "Endeavor to know Brahman by means of austerity." Moreover, since knowledge can emerge as a result of works done in previous lives . . . the acceptance of the householder's way of life becomes meaningless in some cases—namely, when the knowledge which was to be brought into being by karma is already present.[86]

The Veda puts great emphasis on sacrificial karma, Śaṅkara goes on to say, because the results of such work—sons, heaven, spiritual eminence, and the like—are incalculable and the desires of those who undertake them innumerable.[87] Nevertheless all karma, sacrificial as well as spiritual, serves as a means *(upāya)* with regard to knowledge, and more attention should be initially paid to the means than to the end. Coming back to the Mīmāṃsaka claim stated at the very beginning of the Upaniṣad—that there is no sense in making a special effort to achieve knowledge, such as that of hearing and contemplating the Upaniṣads, if knowledge arises simply as a result of the destruction of past sins by virtue of the performance of obligatory works—Śaṅkara says in conclusion:

> That is false . . . for there is no stipulation that knowledge emerges simply from the wearing away of hindrances but not from divine grace, austerity, study, and so forth. For nonviolence, continence, and so forth are helpful *(upakārakatvāt)* with regard to the emergence of knowledge, while hearing, thinking, and meditating [on the meaning of the sentences of the Upaniṣads] are its direct cause *(sākṣād eva kāraṇatvāt)*.[88]

This discussion leaves little doubt that Śaṅkara conceives of religious practice as an important aid in achieving *mokṣa*, even if it is not, strictly speaking, its cause. (As we have seen, religious practice is for

Śaṅkara the cause of *knowledge*, which in turn is the cause of *mokṣa*.) Moreover, Śaṅkara evidently has a multifaceted scheme of spiritual discipline, such as that expounded in the *Yogasūtra*, in mind; indeed, meditation, concentration, continence, austerity, right speech, and nonviolence—all mentioned at *TUBh* I.12—are central yoga practices. We are given to understand, finally—and this is especially important—that religious practice operates as an aid in the rise of knowledge on a preliminary or preparatory level. It produces a state of inner purity, an enlivened state of consciousness, which crystallizes into knowledge upon the receipt of the truth in the form of the Vedic word. Accordingly we discern a distinction in Śaṅkara's use of the term "knowledge," *vidyā*. In one sense it signifies alertness, brightness, wakefulness—the general capacity of the mind to see distinctions and to appreciate fully and evaluate data provided by the senses. In this sense religious practice creates or stimulates *vidyā*. In another sense *vidyā* signifies the organization of consciousness according to a proposition. It is in this latter sense that knowledge is caused by the hearing of scripture and is itself the cause of liberation by eliminating false notions about the self.

3. *The Quest for Liberation and Levels of Discourse*

Summarizing the findings of our investigation we can say: Not just by hearing the Upaniṣad discourse does one become enlightened. Certain conditions, amounting to a higher state of consciousness, must be fulfilled first if the Upaniṣad is to have its effect. Śaṅkara himself provides an apt summary of this point at the opening of the first prose chapter of his *Upadeśasāhasrī*:

> The [direct] means to liberation, that is, knowledge, should be imparted again and again until it is firmly grasped—to a Brāhman disciple who is pure, indifferent to everything that is transitory and achievable through worldly means, who has given up the desire for a son, for wealth, and for this world and the next, who has adopted the life of a wandering monk and is endowed with control over the mind and senses as well as with the other qualities of a disciple well known in the scriptures, and who has approached the teacher in the prescribed manner and has been examined with respect to his caste, profession, conduct, learning, and parentage.[89]

Śaṅkara continues:

> If the teacher realizes from certain signs that the knowledge has not been grasped by the disciple, then he should remove the causes of noncomprehension: past and present sins, negligence, want of firm knowledge regarding the distinction of the eternal from the noneternal, vanity, pride relating to caste, and so on, through means contrary to those causes, enjoined by the *śruti* and *smṛti*, such as the [yogic] restrictions relating to nonviolence and avoidance of anger and the [yogic] observances [such as austerity], so long as they do not inhibit knowledge.[90]

The path of knowledge is sometimes referred to as the path of sudden enlightenment. This name suggests that simply by hearing the truth one spontaneously becomes enlightened. I believe that this account indeed squares with Śaṅkara's writings, in which he insists again and again that *mokṣa* is caused directly by knowledge alone. But we must keep in mind what is—and what is not—implied by the word "sudden." When we say that a volcano erupts "suddenly" or "spontaneously" we do not forget that heat and lava have been building up for thousands of years.[91]

It remains for us to account for those denials of religious practice—karma, *upāsana*, yoga—which stand in direct opposition to what I have tried to show. Their explanation has to do with the fact, already alluded to, that Śaṅkara talks on two different levels throughout his works.[92] One level pertains to the path to enlightenment, as one might put it, while the other level pertains to the goal. Religious practice is valid as a means for someone who is progressing on the path. But for someone who has arrived at the goal or, perhaps, has arrived at the end of the path and is about to take the last step to the goal, religious practice is no longer a means. Indeed, the enlightening knowledge, which is the immediate and direct cause of enlightenment—*the* cause in the sense that we call the wind that shakes the branches of an apple tree *the* cause of the apples falling, ignoring the whole process of ripening that made them ready to fall—consists precisely in realizing that there can be no means to enlightenment, for one is already enlightened and always has been. "There is actually no difference," Śaṅkara says, "between being liberated and not being liberated. For, indeed, the self is always the same. However, ignorance about it is removed by the knowledge that arises from the teachings of the scripture. *But until one receives that knowledge an effort toward realizing mokṣa is valid.*"[93] Since the purpose of Śaṅkara's philosophy is to provide in its completeness that knowledge which removes ignorance, which among other things annihilates any distinction between doer and what is done, or between knower and what is known, religious practice, which depends on such distinctions (in particular, on that between God and devotee), is ultimately to be rejected. From the highest *(paramārtha)* perspective, karma, *upāsana*, and yoga make no sense. And yet they are the means by which one arrives at the point where one is able to comprehend fully that they make no sense! Thus Śaṅkara acknowledges—although almost clandestinely—that religious practice is basic to his system.[94] He is able to do this, no doubt, because karma and yoga were familiar features of his religious milieu—that is to say, he could take them largely for granted—and because he is addressing students who have passed beyond the phase of spiritual training. Spiritual purity is, after all, the prerequisite for *brahmajijñāsā.*

In conclusion, we see that Śaṅkara propounds a system of ideas for those who are fit to live up to them. His philosophy does not stand as an edifice isolated from experience; it exists only insofar as it is realized in experience. That is to say: Śaṅkara is a transformative philosopher. Let this suffice as an initial assertion of my thesis based on prima facie textual evidence. While certain objections could be raised against the foregoing analysis from a philological point of view,[95] I shall not go into them here. Instead, in the next chapter I present another argument, of an altogether different sort, which I believe will show even more decisively that Śaṅkara's Advaita Vedānta is a system of transformative philosophy—namely, *if we do not view it as such it becomes hopelessly incoherent.* This argument may be referred to as the argument from respectability. It assumes that a philosophy which has been held in high esteem for centuries cannot be completely absurd. Since this argument is relevant not only to Śaṅkara but to Fichte as well, it forms the heart of the present inquiry.

Indian Philosophy, Western Philosophy, and the Problem of Intelligibility

AFTER MORE THAN A HUNDRED YEARS of research in Indian philosophy by Western philologists, the prevailing attitude toward Indian philosophy among Western philosophers—I mean especially Anglo-Saxon philosophers—is still one of disregard. The following remarks by A. J. Ayer, though perhaps intended as off-the-record, are typical: "[Eastern philosophies] have some psychological interest, but nothing more than that. . . . For the most part they are devices for reconciling people to a perfectly dreadful earthly life. I believe there were one or two seventh-century Indians who contributed a few ideas to mathematics. But that's about all."[1]

This outlook was summed up by a distinguished contemporary American philosopher who said, when a student once expressed a desire to study Indian philosophy, "Is Indian philosophy worth a damn?" Of the factors contributing to such an attitude, two have been crucial: the inaccessibility of Indian philosophy—for Sanskrit, the principal scholarly language of classical India, is difficult and Indologists are often daunted by the challenges of translation—and the abundance of misinformation about Indian philosophy perpetrated by the myriad popular books on the subject.

Only in recent years, it seems, have Indologists become aware of this situation and taken effective steps to correct it. Realizing that Indian philosophy is appreciated least by those who ought most to esteem it, they have intensified their efforts to communicate to the professional philosopher the value of Indian philosophy in his terms. The first step in doing so has been to recognize that there are in fact certain doctrines of Indian philosophy which, even to the sincere investigator, appear at first sight obscure, unpalatable, even outright paradoxical, and whose coherence can be legitimately questioned. Such, for example, are the Buddhist doctrine of the tetralemma *(catuṣkoṭi)* and the Jaina doctrine of relative truth *(syādvāda)*, both of which appear to deny the law of contradiction, and other, typically Hindu, theories about the nature of reality as consciousness, which contradict direct experience. In recent studies scholars have attempted to show, at least, that the rules of Indian logic do not involve a transgression of fundamental logical principles such as the law of contradiction.[2] There has been, moreover, an attempt to draw attention to sophisticated discussions in Indian linguistics and epistemology of issues relevant to contemporary analytical philosophical concerns.[3] The treatment of metaphysics and soteriology, however, the roots of practically all Indian philosophical endeavor, has so far been left out of this program. The present chapter, besides elucidating the concept of transformative philosophy, is meant as a contribution to the analytical understanding of an important theory of Indian metaphysics in the context of Western skepticism about it.

The theory under consideration is Śaṅkara's theory of the self and self-consciousness. This theory is certainly of interest to Western philosophers, who since Kant have realized that the self plays a central role in the process of knowing and yet have not been able to say exactly what the self is or even decide whether we *can* say what it is. I shall be particularly concerned with the intelligibility of this theory. Śaṅkara's idea of consciousness at first sight seems to be an utter anomaly, an idea which does not extend our usual ideas about consciousness but simply goes against them. Does this anomaly, quite real on one level, in fact destroy the validity of his theory, or can it somehow be resolved? We shall find that it is resolved when one correctly interprets Śaṅkara's theory as transformative philosophy. Thus it is hoped that in elucidating the notion of transformative philosophy—which remains my primary concern throughout this chapter—the most serious charge to be directed against Śaṅkara's metaphysics, and Indian metaphysics in general, will be dispelled.

By "intelligible" I mean "makes sense" and "is not paradoxical." By "unintelligible" I mean "does not make sense" or "goes against the only rules of thought and meaning that we know." In recent philosophical literature on mysticism there has been much discussion of "ineffability" but not of "unintelligibility."[4] Mystics often claim that their experience of the ultimate reality is in one way or another ineffable or inexpressible, and this casts in an uncertain light the statements which they do make about what they experience. A more serious problem arises, however, when the mystic talks about his experience in a paradoxical or self-contradictory way. That is much more disturbing to the philosopher, who may be willing to tolerate tacit nonacceptance of the laws of discourse and semantics but not their flagrant violation. Wittgenstein's dictum that one must be silent about that of which one cannot speak is indeed a reflection on this situation: to refrain from misusing words one should not use them at all. Unintelligibility can perhaps sometimes be seen as a result of ineffability—without appropriate words at their disposal, mystics resort to inappropriate terms in order to express themselves at all (at the same time drawing attention to the imperfection of their expression—see Section 3). But unintelligibility is a more serious cognitive flaw than avowed inexpressibility and is more likely to evoke repugnance;[5] therefore, it deserves closer attention.

In elucidating Śaṅkara's theory of consciousness, about which questions of intelligibility can legitimately be raised, I shall focus on passages from his *Brahmasūtra* and *Bṛhadāraṇyaka Upaniṣad* commentaries. I shall then define in what way his theory is prima facie unintelligible—namely, it is self-contradictory when one understands its basic terms according to everyday usage. In developing that view it will be useful to draw on the theories of consciousness of two fathers of the analytical Anglo-Saxon philosophical tradition—William James and G. E. Moore—who helped introduce into modern philosophy the method of taking words to mean what they usually mean. I shall then show that the view according to which Śaṅkara's theory is self-contradictory is mistaken (more precisely, it does not apply), but that his theory remains unintelligible in another sense—that is, it fails to convey any positive meaning, or it is problematic. In this regard Śaṅkara's theory will be briefly contrasted to that of J. G. Fichte in the first version of his *Wissenschaftslehre* (1794), which I believe to be unintelligible in the first way—self-contradictory and therefore untenable. I shall, finally, attempt to resolve the problem of unintelligibility of Śaṅkara's theory by defining special conditions under which it is intelligible. In this last phase of the discussion the material relating to Śaṅkara's theory of salvation in the first chapter will be especially relevant.

1. *Śaṅkara's Theory of Consciousness*

Śaṅkara's *Brahmasūtrabhāṣya* has been treated so often in a piecemeal fashion that one may well think the work has no order of its own but is a mere hodgepodge of ideas. In fact, Śaṅkara does tend to reiterate important ideas in various contexts throughout the work; if one wishes to discuss his philosophy systematically according to topics, therefore, one must draw together passages from different chapters. A thesis may appear once explicitly as a thesis, elsewhere as a reason among many reasons for a different thesis, still elsewhere as a valid assumption contained in an objection, and so on. But I think that one is usually able to perceive in this occurrence and recurrence of an idea in the *BrSūBh* an ordered buildup of its connotations and ramifications, so that a continuous philosophical argument can be discerned beneath the sequence of topics having to do, ostensibly, with Vedānta exegesis. This is true, in any case, for the notion of the essential consciousness of the self.

The first step in the development of this notion is a discussion of the cause of the universe (*BrSūBh* I.1.5). Śaṅkara proposes that Brahman is the cause, which according to scripture must be omniscient and omnipotent. Against this a Sāṃkhya philosopher argues that the *pradhāna*, unconscious prime matter, is the cause. By properly interpreting certain Vedic passages, the Sāṃkhya maintains, the *pradhāna* can be seen as omnipotent insofar as the world is its transformation; and although the *pradhāna* is unconscious, omniscience can be attributed to it insofar as it possesses goodness *(sattva)*, of which knowledge is actually a property.[6] In attempting to establish his position, the Sāṃkhya philosopher brings forth specific objections against Śaṅkara's alternative: Brahman, if it were all-knowing, would have to be so by virtue of a capacity to know everything *(sarvajñānaśaktimattvena)* rather than by being always engaged in the act of knowing. For if it always actively knew, then it would lack independence with regard to that activity; its knowing would not be a deliberate act which it could start or stop at will. (And if Brahman were all-knowing by virtue of a capacity, it would be no better than the *pradhāna*, the omniscience of which is potentially vested in its *sattva*.) Moreover, Brahman could not possibly be said to know anything prior to the creation of the universe. (It cannot be *always* actively knowing.) For at that time there are no instruments of action (nor any objects to be known). And without instruments such as the body and the senses, knowledge cannot arise.[7]

Śaṅkara rejects the Sāṃkhya's arguments primarily by appealing to Vedic authority—namely, *Chāndogya Upaniṣad* VI.2.3, which says in effect that the first principle (being, *sat*, or the self, *ātman*) sent forth the elements after having thought.[8] This statement seems to indicate, however, Śaṅkara's *conscious* first principle—that is, Brahman rather than the *pradhāna*. It is, however, Śaṅkara's replies to the specific objections of the Sāṃkhya that have particular philosophical relevance. In essence Śaṅkara argues that if Brahman were always actively involved in knowing, then that would have to count in favor of its omniscience rather than against it. Precisely when knowledge is not permanent and one sometimes knows and sometimes does not, there is a lack of omniscience.[9] Yet this poses no problem about Brahman being independent, for we indicate the independence of the sun when we say "it burns" or "it shines," even though its heat and light are continuous.[10] To the objection that the sun may be said to burn or shine because it stands in relation to an object to be illumined or an object to be burned, whereas Brahman prior to creation does not, Śaṅkara replies that even in the absence of any particular object one says of the sun that it shines; so too it might be said of Brahman in the absence of any objects that it "thinks." If there must be an object about which it thinks, however, that might be considered to be Name and Form in their unevolved state, which are to be characterized as neither "real nor unreal."[11] With regard to the objection that Brahman could not be said to know anything without the requisite instruments (the organs of perception), Śaṅkara says that the origin of knowledge is in fact dependent on the body and perceptual faculties for the individual soul subject to ignorance and so forth but not for God—that is, Brahman—who is free from all instruments which are actually impediments to knowledge.[12] Dependence on the means of knowledge is inappropriate for Brahman, whose essence is knowledge as light is that of the sun.[13]

Thus Śaṅkara establishes that Brahman is essentially conscious and that this consciousness may or may not be object-directed. The latter point receives further clarification in the first book of the *BrSūBh*. At *BrSūBh* I.4.19–22 Śaṅkara discusses the teaching of *BĀU* II.4 (= *BĀU* IV.5). Yājñavalkya, about to renounce the householder's way of life, is asked by his wife Maitreyī what will make her immortal. His answer, which constitutes one of the best-known Upaniṣad discourses on the self, begins with the words: "It is indeed, my dear, not for the sake of the husband that the husband is loved, but the husband is loved for the sake of the self. It is, indeed, my dear, not for the sake of the wife that the wife is loved, but the wife is loved for the sake of the self. . . ." Here Śaṅkara's concern, in accordance with the general topic of the first book of his *BrSūBh*, is whether the "self" that is referred to is the lower self—that is, the self viewed under the aspect of certain attributes or limiting conditions *(upādhi)*—or whether it is the highest self, Brahman free of all limiting conditions (see I.1.11). Śaṅkara, drawing on the opinions of previous Vedāntins in the course of his argument, contends that it is the highest self that is intended here. The opponent, who maintains that the individual transmigrating soul is meant, raises an objection. Toward the end of Yājñavalkya's speech the following statement occurs:

> As a lump of salt dropped into water dissolves and becomes water and there is nothing of it that one might draw out, but from wherever one might draw water it is salty, so, my dear, is this great endless unbounded being a mass of intelligence. Having arisen from out of these elements [the self] vanishes with them. Afterward there is no consciousness.[14]

This statement appears to indicate the destruction of the self; therefore the whole passage should be taken as referring to the individual soul, which might conceivably be subject to destruction.

Śaṅkara gets around this objection by the sort of deviousness that typifies this portion of his commentary. The self mentioned is the highest self after all, he says, because the "vanishing" mentioned is merely the vanishing of the limiting conditions falsely superimposed on the self by ignorance, which disappear when knowledge of its real (attributeless) nature is attained:

> Since the self is absolutely eternal, a mass of consciousness, its destruction does not follow; but by means of true knowledge there is effected its dissociation from the *mātrās*—that is, the elements and the sense organs created by ignorance. When that connection is gone then, because of the absence of specific cognition which depended on it [Yājñavalkya can say], "afterward there is no consciousness."[15]

And in support of this interpretation he cites Yājñavalkya's reassurance to Maitreyī (*BĀU* IV.5.14): "Certainly, my dear, I am not saying anything confusing. This self indeed does not vanish, my dear, not being susceptible to destruction."[16]

The opponent comes forth with a final argument. Since the Upaniṣad speaks of the self as an agent, that is, an agent of knowledge, in the concluding passage of the discourse (II.4.14/IV.5.15),[17] it therefore would seem to be referring to an individual:

> When there is duality, as it were, then one smells another, one sees another, one hears another, one speaks something else, one thinks something else, one knows something else. But when everything has become one's self, then what might one smell and by means of what, what might one see and by means of what . . . ? By means of what might one know that by means of which one knows all this? How might one know the knower, my dear?[18]

But Śaṅkara replies that this passage, too, is merely meant to underline the absence of specific consciousness in the case of the true self and that the word "knower" indicates "the element of knowledge itself."[19] Thus he appears to have narrowed down the philosophical point made at *BrSūBh* I.1.5. The self is essentially conscious, but indeed conscious in such a way as not to require an object of which it is conscious. Its consciousness is *pure.* At *BrSūBh* II.3.18 we receive further clarification of the other cardinal point suggested at I.1.5 and reiterated here—that pure consciousness is *essential* to the self, not as a property but rather as its substance.

At II.3.18, after a long discussion of Brahman's causality and the elements (ether, air, fire, water) to which it gives rise, Śaṅkara directly addresses the question whether the individual soul *(jīva)* is in itself unconscious *(svato 'cetanaḥ)* and its consciousness merely adventitious as the Vaiśeṣikas think, or whether it has consciousness as its nature *(nityacaitanyasvarūpa)* as the Sāṃkhyas believe, having previously determined (II.3.17) that the *jīva,* unlike the elements, is not produced. Śaṅkara asserts that the soul is eternal consciousness:[20] "Simply because it does not originate [from Brahman but rather] it *is* the highest, unmodified Brahman which exists in the form of the individual soul due to the admixture of limiting conditions."[21] And we know from scripture that Brahman's nature is consciousness, Śaṅkara maintains, quoting various passages. Thus "if the soul is the highest Brahman, then we know that the soul, too, is of the nature of eternal consciousness, just as fire is of the nature of heat and light."[22]

The objection that the soul sometimes appears not to be conscious, namely during sleep, is also rejected as contrary to the Veda. This may strike one as an extraordinary thing to say even under the compulsion of religious dogma, for it contradicts daily experience. But one quickly recognizes it as a variation of the thesis that the self is always conscious in a pure rather than a specific way. The scriptural passage Śaṅkara cites in this regard is *BĀU* IV.3.23: "When [during sleep] one does not see, then seeing one does not see. For there is no loss of the seer's seeing, since it is indestructible. Rather, there is no second thing separate from oneself to see."[23] Śaṅkara explains that apparent unconsciousness during sleep results from the absence of any object to be seen rather than from the absence of consciousness (thus he does acknowledge the facts of experience but implies that they are an illusion), just as light shining through the atmosphere does not manifest itself due to the absence of any object to shine upon.

We thus obtain from Śaṅkara's *BrSūBh* a unique view of the self which can be stated quite simply: The self is pure *consciousness* without an object. Still needed to complete the exposition of Śaṅkara's theory of the self is his view of the relation of the self to the human organism, including the mind, senses, and the body, which indeed are commonly identified, either singly or collectively, as the self by philosophers and nonphilosophers. Śaṅkara discusses this matter systematically in his *Bṛhadāraṇyakạ Upaniṣad* commentary, in connection with *BĀU* IV.3. Since Hacker has treated this discussion in several articles, we shall rely on his analysis.[24]

BĀU IV.3 begins as a dialogue between the sage Yājñavalkya and King Janaka that progressively determines the essence of man by increasingly specific responses to the question, "What does man have for his light?,"[25] that is, by what principle is man guided in his activity? Yājñavalkya first answers (IV.3.2): the sun. But when the sun sets, what reveals to man his working and his moving about? The moon. And when the moon sets, fire; and when fire is extinguished, speech; and when speech stops—that is, Śaṅkara explains, during dreaming—the self. The self is "the light which is different from one's body and organs and illumines them like such external lights as the sun, but is itself not illumined by anything else."[26] And it is *within* the body. Śaṅkara then proceeds to argue that this light is not a material one, like the sun, but immaterial and therefore unable to be perceived by the eye. In the course of this argument he attempts to establish on logical grounds why the body cannot be the self.

At IV.3.7 the Upaniṣad identifies the self as "the being comprised of consciousness among the *prāṇas*, the light within the heart."[27] Śaṅkara emphasizes that the self cannot be identified with body, senses, or mind by interpreting "among the *prāṇas*" (organs?) to mean *different* from them.[28] "Comprised of consciousness," on the other hand, does not mean "having consciousness for its essence," as our analysis of Śaṅkara's theory up to this point would lead one to believe, but rather "resembling or identified with the *consciousness* [of the intellect] due to the failure to distinguish the self's admixture with that as its limiting condition."[29] With regard to this last point Śaṅkara expounds the full relation of the self to the intellect and other faculties of knowledge, which may be considered his theory of knowledge, but which Hacker more appropriately calls a "metaphysics of knowledge" because it depends not so much on reasoning as on Śaṅkara's own transcendental insight.

The self is indeed pure consciousness, Śaṅkara says, but it exists in conjunction with the body and organs and tends to become confused with them. Because the intellect lies within the heart, it too may be located there, as it is by the Upaniṣad, which in this case adopts the mundane perspective. In conjunction with the other organs, the self illumines them and unifies them, as an emerald dropped into milk imparts to it its luster. This happens in a step-by-step manner according to the fineness of the organs.[30] The intellect *(buddhi)*, which is most fine—indeed, transparent *(svaccha)*—and "closest," is illumined first. It then imparts its luster to the mind *(manas)*, next fine and next proximate, which imparts it to the senses which impart it to the body. Thus, due to the reflection of the self's consciousness throughout the whole organism, one identifies oneself with either the body, senses, mind, or intellect according to one's capacity for discrimination. Without the light of consciousness, the body and so forth cannot function. Even when the organs are aided by external sources of light, such as the sun, they still require the light of the self since they are themselves insentient. Yet the self does not exist entirely to serve the body. It is "for itself" *(svārtha)* in contrast to other forms of light which are "for another" *(parārtha)*.[31]

Although the identification of the self with one of the various aspects of the body or psyche is an error, it is the basis of all practical life. Believing oneself to be an agent of thought or action by means of the mind or body, one incurs merit or demerit. This mistake happens because the light of the self tends to be assimilated to that which it illumines, just as physical light assumes the likeness of the objects it reveals. Illumining the intellect, the self resembles it. And through the intellect, which is "the organ for all" *(sarvārthakaraṇa)*, that is, which mediates the other organs,[32] it takes on the aspect of the other faculties. The light of the self is especially difficult to distinguish when those faculties are in operation. It cannot simply be drawn out from them like a straw from its sheath, Śaṅkara says. But during dreaming when only the intellect is functioning, the separate light of the self is easier to recognize.[33]

Summarizing the features of Śaṅkara's theory of the self presented here, one can only say that he envisions a transcendent self distinct from mind and body, which is itself pure consciousness only *contingently* aware of objects that the instruments of perception present. In this regard one may well contrast Śaṅkara's theory of consciousness to the theory that Kant presents in his section on the paralogisms of rational psychology in the *Critique of Pure Reason.* There Kant identifies the self as "the conscious thinking subject" which serves only to introduce all thought as belonging to consciousness.[34] It is a mere concept, a logical function which unites the manifold of intuition. It itself is devoid of empirical content. For that reason Kant says one cannot *know* the self, because one requires for knowledge, in addition to a concept, an intuition given in sense.[35] Those who would attempt to claim anything to be objectively true about the self merely on the basis of its character as the subjective unity of apperception (for example, that it is a substance, simple and identical throughout time) are guilty of a fallacy—specifically, a paralogism.

Now, as if arguing against precisely this view, Śaṅkara asserts that the self indeed has empirical content and can be experienced, though not by the senses;[36] yet it is not the logical thinking subject "I think" Kant believes it to be. For the self is separate from the faculties of understanding and sense perception and is identified with them only because of an error.[37] Śaṅkara, moreover, although he would seem to be prepared to deny that it can be known *as an object of experience*—that is, analogous to how we know tables and chairs—would insist that the self can nevertheless be known in the sense that it *is* knowledge itself or pure consciousness,[38] for the purpose of his entire philosophy is to provide knowledge of it. In short, it would seem that Śaṅkara is talking about a dimension of the self that Kant simply does not consider.[39] Precisely what this knowledge is, or indeed whether we can ever hope to achieve an understanding of it, is the problem we have set before us in this chapter.

2. *Self-Consciousness as a Self-Contradiction*

Having outlined the principal features of Śaṅkara's theory of the self, I turn now to evaluation. In the present investigation I shall be concerned only with the minimum requirement a theory must satisfy—namely, that its fundamental postulates be intelligible. Obviously intelligibility is even more basic than consistency; that is, before one can determine whether or not the postulates of a theory and their consequences conflict with each other, one must know what those postulates *mean*. If they are themselves paradoxical or otherwise incomprehensible, questions regarding the theory's completeness, explanatory power, simplicity, and so on cannot even be raised.

In this section I shall attempt to show that when one takes the word "consciousness" in its usual meaning, Śaṅkara's notion of pure consciousness is unintelligible and his theory of the self as pure consciousness is therefore inadequate. I shall first define the usual notion of "consciousness," taking into account some recent attempts to define it, and demonstrate that pure consciousness is by that standard a self-contradiction. I shall then show the extent of allegiance among philosophers to the usual standard, especially those who have directly considered the idea of a pure consciousness and rejected it. It will then be seen in the following section that pure consciousness ceases to be self-contradictory when one understands Śaṅkara to be using the word "consciousness" in an entirely new sense. The notion of pure consciousness nevertheless remains unintelligible, I shall argue, insofar as Śaṅkara is unable to explicate completely his own sense of the word. By forsaking the usual meaning of "consciousness," although not opposing it, Śaṅkara gives up the only viable mode of discourse about consciousness available.

Writers on Śaṅkara's Advaita Vedānta have already noticed the prima facie incoherence of his notion of consciousness. Deussen thus refers to "the monstrosity of an absolute perception (subject without object)."[40] Hacker, acknowledging the issue Deussen raises, achieves the more subtle view that pure consciousness, although problematic, at least is not absurd in the sense of being a reflexive awareness.[41] That is the beginning of a correct understanding of Śaṅkara's idea which will be taken up and developed in the course of this chapter.

The word "consciousness" (or one of its verbal or adjectival relatives) is most commonly used as a generic term. Animals "have consciousness" as opposed to plants because they have the capacity to feel, perceive, experience pain, sometimes even to think and talk, and so on. A person who is awake "is conscious" or "is possessed of consciousness" in contrast to one who is asleep or in a state of swoon, because he is actively thinking, talking, experiencing pain, and so forth. In either of these cases "consciousness" or an allied expression is applied to something that possesses either actively or potentially not one particular property but any one of several properties—which nonetheless may upon investigation turn out to have something in common. In this respect the word "consciousness" may be compared to a word like "fruit," which we use to refer to any number of specific fruits—a mango, a pear, an apple, an orange, all of which, of course, share certain features—but not to *the* fruit or fruit, pure and simple. It would be a mistake to look for a fruit in the world that is not the fruit of some particular plant or tree, but just plain fruit. On the basis of general linguistic intuition, therefore, we conclude that it would be a mistake to search for consciousness that is not some particular *kind* of consciousness.

Modern investigators in the philosophy of mind generally agree that "consciousness" is a generic term. Thus C. O. Evans defines "to be conscious" as "*inter alia*, to perceive, to feel emotions and sensations, to have images and recollections, and to have desires, intentions and thoughts."[42] In formulating his definition Evans appeals to James Mill, who writes:

> It is easy to see what is the nature of the terms Conscious and Consciousness, and what is the marking function which they are destined to perform. It was of great importance for the purpose of naming that we should not only have names to distinguish the different classes of our feelings, but also a name applicable equally to all those classes. This purpose is answered by the concrete term Conscious; and the abstract of it, Consciousness. Thus, if we are in any way sentient, that is, have any of the feelings whatsoever of a living creature, the word Conscious is applica-

> ble to the feeler, and Consciousness to the feeling: that is to say, the words are Generical marks, under which all the names of the subordinate classes of the feelings of a sentient creature are included.[43]

Evans astutely points out that the sort of merely verbal definition of "consciousness" he offers, which Mill also appears to be getting at, is the only possible one in this case. A "real" definition—a definition, that is, which would make clear the *definiendum* to one who had never encountered it—would be without point for "consciousness," as there is necessarily no one who has not encountered it (necessarily, obviously, because to be a person is to be conscious). Evans also suggests that his is a definition of "consciousness" in its *most basic* sense, thus taking issue with Gilbert Ryle who claims that "consciousness" is indefinable because there are many different senses of the word.[44] Evans argues that "consciousness" as defined is entailed by other senses of "consciousness," but they are not entailed by it,[45] and is thus a well-chosen representative of "what philosophers [or for that matter nonphilosophers] have in mind when they use the word."[46] In distinguishing a basic sense of "consciousness" Evans follows John Wisdom, who takes the term to mean basically "either feels or is aware."

To say that consciousness is a generic term is to say that consciousness is not a name; it does not single out one entity from all others. That is, consciousness is not an individual. Another consequence of its being a generic term is that "consciousness" is not, fundamentally, a so-called mass noun like "air" or "water" or, indeed, "light," each of which denotes a uniform, ubiquitous substance of some kind. One should not be misled into thinking that consciousness is that sort of thing by the fact that the word "consciousness," like other mass terms, sometimes occurs without an article.[47] Some Western philosophers, perhaps for this reason, have in fact misconstrued consciousness to be a substance. One of these thinkers, G. E. Moore, is discussed below.

A further important point to be made about "consciousness" as a generic term concerns the principle by which it serves as a generic term—that is to say, the principle according to which the various things that are collectively referred to by "consciousness" are grouped together in one class. To say that "consciousness" represents a genus immediately gives rise to the question: what characteristic do the members of the genus have in common that makes them constitute a genus? Since Wittgenstein, philosophers have stressed that this question does not always admit of an answer: members of a class may not have some one thing in common; they may constitute a class by virtue of an indefinite "family resemblance" among themselves. Yet I believe that this question can be given a reasonably precise answer in this case: states of consciousness seem to have in common that they are relations—specifically, two-term relations. One term, the subject, is that which is conscious of something; the other term, the object, is that of which something is conscious. I believe, moreover, that the notion of "consciousness" implies that this relation is not reflexive. The subject of consciousness is that which is conscious of *something else*; the object of consciousness is that of which *something else* is conscious. Finally, this relation does not seem to be commutative; it goes only one way. If an object of consciousness itself happens to be conscious of something, then the act of consciousness in which it serves as the subject of consciousness is distinct from the act of consciousness in which it plays the role of an object.[48] To say that consciousness is this sort of relation is to say that consciousness is *intentional*, a point often made by phenomenologists.[49] To be conscious is to be conscious *of* something.

Granted this definition of consciousness, which I shall refer to as our standard notion of it—namely, that the word "consciousness" is a generic term that denotes not an individual but a class, specifically a class of relations—Śaṅkara's idea of consciousness appears to be completely absurd. The word "consciousness" (Sanskrit: *cit*, *caitanya*),[50] as Śaṅkara uses it in relation to the self, is first of all a grammatical monstrosity. He suggests in various places that consciousness is that which constitutes the self as its essence (*ātman = caitanyasvarūpa*, especially at *BrSūBh* II.3.18), as gold might constitute a ring or wood a house or, to cite Śaṅkara's favorite example, as heat and light constitute fire—that is, he employs "consciousness" as a mass term rather than a generic term. Certainly expressions like "a mass of consciousness" *(vijñānaghana)* or "the element of consciousness [itself]" *(vijñānadhātu)*, which he uses with reference to the self, lead one to this conclusion. He also violates the function of "consciousness" as a generic term by suggesting that one can be conscious *simpliciter*—that is, one can still be conscious when "specific cognition" *(viśeṣajñāna)* has ceased.

Of course, it is possible that the grammatical function of Sanskrit words for consciousness is not the same as that of English expressions for consciousness—that *cit*, *caitanya*, and similar Sanskrit words are generally accepted and used as mass terms, not generic terms. But that possibility appears unlikely when one analyzes discussions about the nature of the self such as *BrSūBh* II.3.18. There Śaṅkara's opponent suggests that the self's consciousness *(caitanya)* is merely accidental, because one appears to be unconscious in states of deep sleep or swoon.[51] It is precisely this sense of "consciousness"—awake or sentient as opposed to insentient—that Evans and Wisdom attempt to distinguish as the "basic sense of the word" and construe as representing a class.

By claiming that one can be conscious without being conscious *of* something (thus in *BrSūBh* I.1.5 he claims that, just as the sun shines, Brahman can be said to "think" without an object of thought), Śaṅkara repudiates the one feature that philosophers have considered essential to all conscious states: intentionality.

In short, one can say that Śaṅkara's notion of consciousness is *self-contradictory*. For consciousness is, according to him, indeterminate and without an object. But the very word "consciousness"—in Sanskrit, apparently, as in English—implies that there be present an object of consciousness, which makes it determinate, one of a class of *specific* states of consciousness.

It is not surprising, then, that philosophers who have weighed the possibility of a pure consciousness have almost unanimously rejected it. Within the Anglo-Saxon tradition the classic denial of consciousness as such is that of William James in "Does Consciousness Exist?" He writes:

> To deny plumply that consciousness exists seems so absurd on the face of it—for undeniably "thoughts" do exist—that I fear some readers will follow me no farther. Let me then immediately explain that I only mean to deny that that word stands for an entity, but to insist most emphatically that it does stand for a function. There is no aboriginal stuff or quality of being, contrasted with that of which material objects are made, out of which our thoughts of them are made; but there is a function in experience which thoughts perform, and for the performance of which this quality of being is invoked. That function is *knowing*.[52]

That James's denial of consciousness has to do with taking "consciousness" to be a generic term is obvious: consciousness as an individual substance does not exist but undeniably thoughts, that is, particular *states* of consciousness, do. Consciousness is a *function*, which, one assumes, defines a class. Moreover, consciousness is emphatically not a kind of substance-mass. That James means to exclude this possibility is made particularly clear by the following account he gives of the analysis of consciousness he means to oppose:

> This view supposes that the consciousness is one element, moment, factor —call it what you like [compare Śaṅkara's term *vijñānadhātu*]—of an experience of essentially dualistic inner constitution, from which, if you abstract the content, the consciousness will remain revealed to its own eye. Experience, at this rate, would be much like a paint of which the world pictures were made. Paint has a dual constitution, involving, as it does, a menstruum (oil, size or what not) and a mass of content in the form of pigment suspended therein. We can get the pure menstruum by letting the pigment settle, and the pure pigment by pouring off the size or oil. We operate here by physical subtraction; and the usual view is that by mental subtraction we can separate the two factors of experience in an analogous way—not isolating them entirely, but distinguishing them enough to know that they are two.[53]

But, James asserts, "experience has no such inner duplicity, and the separation of it into consciousness and content comes, not by way of subtraction, but by way of [unwarranted] addition."[54] The term "consciousness," rather, refers to a particular ordering of experience (which James regards as in itself neither conscious nor unconscious) so as to represent thoughts, sensations, and so on in contrast to the ordering of the same data so as to represent objective things. Without going into the details of James's alternative, it is clear that it is completely opposed to what Śaṅkara has in mind.

Yet it is significant that the specific idea of consciousness James is criticizing—actually put forward by G. E. Moore in his famous paper "The Refutation of Idealism"—falls short of the kind of pure consciousness Śaṅkara envisions. "What is a sensation or idea?" Moore asks.

> We all know that the sensation of blue differs from that of green. But it is plain that if both are sensations they also have some point in common. What is it that they have in common? And how is this common element related to the points in which they differ?
>
> I will call the common element "consciousness" without yet attempt-

> ing to say what the thing I so call *is*. We have then in every sensation two distinct terms, (1) "consciousness," in respect of which all sensations are alike; and (2) something else, in respect of which one sensation differs from another. It will be convenient if I may be allowed to call this second term the "object" of the sensation. . . .[55]

Notice that Moore's effort to explain why different sensations can be grouped together as "sensations" must be judged unsuccessful—by appealing to the term "consciousness" he attempts to explain one generic term by means of another *more general* generic term which includes the former and is not included by it. Nevertheless, Moore's intention that "consciousness" is not a generic term—that consciousness is not a class but a substance which several other things might share—is plain. Thus the way seems open for *separating* in experience consciousness from objects—one imagines, in accordance with James's analogy, pouring off the pigment to get the size—yet Moore does not take that step. Rather, he goes on to say that when the sensation of blue exists, then neither the blue exists alone nor does the consciousness exist by itself: both must (or in fact always do) exist together.[56] Although he sometimes talks about distinguishing or abstracting the blue from the sensation of blue to arrive at consciousness,[57] he certainly has in mind only an analytical procedure of thought; he does not think we can ever *experience* consciousness by itself.[58] Moore, then, fails to arrive at the idea of an actual, experienced consciousness completely devoid of sense or thought content, while that is the central feature of pure consciousness for Śaṅkara.

Is an absolutely pure consciousness that is *lived* such an abomination that no philosopher besides Śaṅkara is able to conceive of such a thing, even if only to reject it? Indeed, one must look beyond Western philosophy to Śaṅkara's own tradition to encounter a specific refutation of his proposal. Rāmānuja, an eleventh-century Indian philosopher who wrote a commentary on the *Brahmasūtra* from a Viṣṇuite point of view, flatly denies that there can be a consciousness without an object;[59] for, he says simply, it is not perceived.[60] Nor is it revealed in states of deep sleep or swoon, as is suggested at various places in Śaṅkara's writings.[61] "If in those states [pure] consciousness *(anubhūti)* were experienced, then upon awakening there would be a memory of it. But that is not the case."[62] In fact, argues Rāmānuja, we remember upon awakening from sleep, "I was not conscious of anything"—that is to say, I was not conscious *at all.* As if in direct contradiction of Śaṅkara's interpretation of *BĀU* IV.3.23, to wit, that the apparent loss of consciousness during deep sleep or swoon is due to the absence of a separate perceived object and an individual perceiving subject, Rāmānuja says: "Neither the experience of a thing nor the absence of a thing can be the cause of the nonremembrance of some entirely different thing."[63] This is to say, in essence, if pure consciousness were in fact experienced during deep sleep, it would impress itself upon us regardless of how different it might be from ordinary states of consciousness. Thus Rāmānuja adopts a refreshingly prosaic stance on this quite abstruse issue.

Rāmānuja goes on in his polemic against a pure consciousness to show that consciousness must have a substrate, that is, a subject of consciousness, and therefore cannot exist as an independent substance out of which things (such as the self) are made:

> The permanence of the agent [the conscious subject], on the one hand, and the origin, duration, and cessation of the attribute of the agent known as consciousness *(saṃvedanā)*—like that of pleasure and pain—on the other, is clearly perceived. The permanence of the agent is established by the identification by memory: "I experienced this very same thing before." The origin, and so on, of consciousness are evident when one says, "I know"; "I used to know—the knowledge that I, who am the knower, had is now gone." Therefore, how can one assert the identity [of the knower and consciousness]? Thus if consciousness *(saṃvid)*, which changes every moment, were assumed to be the self, the recognition, "I saw today what I saw before," would not occur; for the remembrance by one moment of consciousness of what was experienced by another is impossible. Moreover, if [pure] consciousness *(anubhūti)* were assumed to be the self and were permanent, the impossibility of recollection would ensue on that basis. For recollection establishes an *agent* of experience existing at prior and later times, not just experience. . . . In the absence of a connection with a self, consciousness *(jñapti)* does not manifest itself—just as, when there is not a cutter, nor an object to be cut, there is no act of cutting. Thus it is established that this thing, the I, which is the knowing subject, is the inner self [and not pure consciousness].[64]

In summary, then, Śaṅkara's idea of consciousness has been denied by most philosophers who have ever considered the matter. Their rejection of this notion most certainly has to do with the fact that by the standard of ordinary language pure consciousness is an unintelligible paradox—specifically, a self-contradiction.

3. *Mysticism and Paradox*

Is the analysis of the preceding section correct? Is Śaṅkara's notion of consciousness really self-contradictory? In this section I shall argue that it is not, but that insofar as it is not, it is unintelligible in another way that is equally damaging to his theory.

The framework for understanding how Śaṅkara's notion of pure consciousness is *not* necessarily self-contradictory is provided in a recent article by G. K. Pletcher,[65] which itself is part of a larger discussion of the status of paradox in mystical writing. Many investigators of mysticism have observed that paradox is a central feature of mysticism, but they have disagreed on how it should be dealt with.[66] Should one attempt to explain it away with recourse to theories of ambiguity (a predicate is being applied to a subject in two different senses), "double location" (the subject of the paradoxical statement is ambiguous), rhetorical utterance (the paradox is not a description of a state of affairs but only a rhetorical device), and so on? Or should one accept it as literally true and indicative of another dimension of reality in which the laws of logic do not hold?

A major proponent of the latter view is W. T. Stace, who believes that baldly paradoxical statements are expressions of the unadulterated, unrationalized truth of mystical experience.[67] "All expedients of the commonsensical mind [to explain away mystical paradox] are in vain and . . . in the end the undisguised and naked paradoxicality and contradiction of all manifestations of mystical consciousness has to be met head on," he maintains.[68] The mystic, he believes, experiences a reality that is *really* self-contradictory. If he is confident of his experience, he will admit that it is self-contradictory; if he is intimidated by the conventions of philosophy, religion, and society, he will try to hide the fact or qualify it. Stace argues that openly self-contradictory statements are more apt to be found in Eastern than in Western mystical writings, for "the mysticism of Europe is an amateur affair compared with the mysticism of Asia."[69] The belief that the mystic encounters a state of affairs that is truly paradoxical, by the way, leads Stace to make some rather extraordinary claims about the validity of logic—

that it extends to only one sphere of existence; that the laws of logic are not "true in all possible worlds" as philosophers have thought; that they apply only to a particular sort of world, the space-time world, where things are uniquely distinct from each other, not to a world such as the mystic knows where everything is One.[70]

Pletcher, by contrast, while rejecting the usual stratagems for dealing with paradox in mystical writing (the theory of ambiguity and so on), proposes more modestly that what the mystic experiences is not really paradoxical, although it may not be expressible in a nonparadoxical form within our everyday conceptual scheme. In Pletcher's view logic is probably *not* a dispensable element of conceptual schemes. All systems of concepts must incorporate and conform to the usual logical laws, including the law of noncontradiction. But the concepts themselves have a certain range within which certain objects fall, and are therefore expressible, but beyond which certain other objects may fall and are therefore inexpressible (ineffable)—in that particular system.

Pletcher clarifies the notion of a conceptual system by means of an example originally devised by Paul Henle.[71] Henle describes a system of mathematical symbolism in which the noncommutativity of subtraction for the natural numbers (the fact that A − B never equals B − A when A ≠ B) cannot be expressed. In that system subtraction is represented only by an operation called "superimposition," by which one symbol is superimposed over another. (The symbols for numbers in the system are geometric figures rather than the usual arabic signs). Since the superimposition of A over B (for A − B) will look the same as the superimposition of B over A (for B − A), the inequality of the two operations cannot be symbolized; were one to attempt to symbolize it, one would come up with what looks like a manifest contradiction (something like $\bigcirc\!\!\!\!\!\triangle \neq \bigcirc\!\!\!\!\!\triangle$, where A = △ and B = ○).

Pletcher suggests with reference to this example that someone—in this case not a mystic but a mathematical genius—might conceive of a state of affairs that is perfectly reasonable, nonparadoxical, and true—the noncommutativity of subtraction for natural numbers—but expressible only as a paradox. The paradox in this case has to do with the unsuitability of the particular conceptual scheme used to express the state of affairs. Summarizing the importance of this illustration for the study of mysticism, Pletcher says it shows

> that *our apprehension of things is not totally limited to what is logically consistent within our own conceptual system.* It may be that the conceptual system of mankind is limited in the sense that not everything which is knowable about reality is sayable within that system. Now most of us, it seems reasonable to suppose, would fail to be aware of, or would simply ignore, what we could not conceptualize. But to a few individuals the reality of such things might be brought home in such a vivid way that they could not ignore it. They would have to express themselves using concepts which were not suitable, and contradictions would very likely result.[72]

It should be emphasized that Pletcher, unlike Stace, is not recommending that the law of noncontradiction be thrown overboard when contradictions arise.[73] For, obviously, the law of noncommutativity for subtraction is not a real contradiction, although it appears so in Henle's symbolism. In short, an apparent contradiction in mystical revelation or even scientific discovery does not necessarily mean that the law of contradiction is being violated. It may only mean that one is challenging or altogether renouncing the conceptual system in which the contradiction appears.

In light of Pletcher's suggestions one is called upon to ask whether Śaṅkara's notion of self-consciousness or pure consciousness, which I have depicted as a self-contradiction, actually represents the rejection of a particular conceptual framework—namely, the "standard notion of consciousness" I detailed in Section 2—and is, therefore, only incidentally, not in itself, self-contradictory. Is the idea of pure consciousness a paradox uttered in good faith, so to speak, in the awareness that it is indeed a manifest paradox in the terms in which it is expressed but there are no universally accepted terms available for expressing it? I believe there is evidence in Śaṅkara's writings that this is the case.

An important item of evidence is Śaṅkara's insistence that pure consciousness is not a reflexive self-consciousness involving a division of subject and object. In his *TUBh*, for example, he argues that the phrase, "Brahman is truth, knowledge, infinite" *(satyaṃ jñānam anantaṃ brahma)*, applies the term "knowledge" to Brahman in the sense of the eternal knowing expressed by the verbal root *jñā* (from which *jñāna* is derived), not in the sense of the agent of knowing.[74] For there is the *Chāndogya Upaniṣad* verse, "That is great when one does not know anything else; and when one knows something else, that is little."[75] The greatness of knowledge is clearly associated in the *Chāndogya Upaniṣad* verse with an absence of division, which, however, is implied by being an agent (an agent is separate from the knowing and the thing to be known); and apparently the same thing is being referred to by the *TU* as "knowledge" which is "infinite." Śaṅkara, however, allows someone to object that when it is said in the *Chāndogya Upaniṣad* that "one does not know anything else" it is meant that one knows *oneself.* In other words, *jñāna* is still a specifically active knowing, but a knowing directed at an object not different from the subject, a self-reflexive act. The opponent asserts flatly: "One self exists both as object and subject."[76] But Śaṅkara denies this, "because the self is without parts" *(anaṃśatvāt).* "What is without members cannot be known and knower at the same time."[77] He makes the same point many times in other works.[78]

Thus Śaṅkara is seen to deny consciously and explicitly the main principle of our standard way of thinking about consciousness—that it involves a separate subject and object (that it is *of* something). I take this to indicate that he is deliberately rejecting that way of thinking altogether. On the other hand: if he were to be found promoting self-consciousness as a sort of reflexive consciousness in which subject and object are identical, then I believe one would have grounds to doubt whether he had in fact succeeded in transcending our usual way of thinking about consciousness, since his proposal would be couched in those very terms. One has evidence here, at least, that in using the word "consciousness" (in this case *jñāna*) Śaṅkara is using it *knowingly* in a sense different from the standard one.

This interpretation is confirmed by the rest of his comment on *TU* II.1, where he discusses the meaning of the word "knowledge" *(jñāna)* at length. It will be well to review that discussion in detail here.[79] Since Śaṅkara is, ostensibly, engaged in the exegesis of a text, his investigation takes the form of a determination of the modifiers "knowledge," "truth," and "infinite" in the sentence "Brahman is truth, knowledge, infinite." He proposes, first, that they serve as modifiers insofar as they distinguish Brahman from other describable objects. "A thing is known," he says, "when it is separated from other things."[80] But it is immediately objected that a thing is described not insofar as it is shown to differ from all other things, but only from other things in its class. An adjective has meaning only with respect to a class of more than one object for which other adjectives are also suited;[81] and a thing is described when it is indicated as "deviating" from other predicates which might apply to it and which in fact do apply to other objects of its class. But Śaṅkara answers that the ascription of the words "knowledge," "truth," and "infinite" uniquely to one thing is acceptable in this case (Brahman is not a member of any class; it is *sui generis*) because those words are being used primarily to define and not to describe.[82] Descriptive words distinguish an object from others in its class; a definition distinguishes it from other objects *simpliciter.*

Śaṅkara goes on to say that the words "truth," "knowledge," and "infinite" are not related syntactically to each other. As adjectives they are syntactically dependent on the word they modify: Brahman. But in explaining their individual meaning he does take into account the fact that they stand in apposition to each other, for they are all equally true of one thing. Thus, as we saw, he argues that "knowledge" expresses an eternal, unchanging state of knowing *(bhāvasādhano jñānaśabdaḥ)* and not an agent; otherwise it could not at the same time be unchanging—that is, "true" (for the agent is modified by the actions he performs)—and without parts (not divided into subject and object)—that is, "infinite."

It is then suggested that the sentence "Brahman is truth, knowledge, infinite," taken as a whole, is devoid of meaning,[83] since the individual modifying words "truth" and so forth appear to function only negatively to *eliminate* such ideas as falseness and Brahman is not an already familiar entity *(prasiddha).* The point seems to be this: once the inapplicable ideas are denied, nothing is given in their place. But Śaṅkara replies that this suggestion, too, rests on the assumption that adjectives have meaning only by distinguishing items that belong to a class—by saying what is *not,* they say what is. In fact, Śaṅkara maintains, the truth is the other way around: even when used descriptively words separate a thing from what it is not by saying what it *is.*[84] For the sentence under consideration, only the word "infinite," *ananta,* can be said to have a primarily negative sense. The others—"truth," *satya,* and "knowledge," *jñāna*—express their own (positive) meaning.

Śaṅkara then explains the sentence "Brahman is truth, knowledge, infinite" as defining the essence or "self" of "the knower" *(veditur ātmā)*; for, he reminds us, in the Upaniṣads the word "self" is often used in reference to Brahman, and Brahman is said to enter into things in the form of the living soul after having created them. The most serious objection to Śaṅkara's argument about the meaning of the word "knowledge" in this passage is then brought forward: if it is indeed the self that is being defined here, then surely the "knowledge" that is talked about is nothing other than the agent of knowing; for the self is commonly thought to be just that. Moreover—and this is a somewhat obscure point—if this "knowledge" were the eternal, unchanging state of knowing expressed by the verbal root, as Śaṅkara wishes to maintain, it would still be related to concepts of agency. For the meanings of verbal roots depend ultimately on syntactic notions such as the subject, the object, and the instrument. It is in response to this objection that Śaṅkara clarifies the true status of "knowledge" as only *figuratively* true of Brahman.

To that end he explains that the individual acts of knowledge belonging to the intellect are in fact mere reflections of the self and are falsely assumed to be qualities of the self itself by undiscriminating people—an important part of his theory of the self which he develops at *BĀUBh* IV.3 (see Section 1). Those reflections of the self's consciousness—acts of cognition—are what is properly expressed by the word "consciousness" and are the real meaning of the verbal root "to know" or "to be conscious."[85] The consciousness of the self that they reflect, being completely different, is actually not the meaning of the verbal root. Here Śaṅkara gives a precise summary of what makes that sort of consciousness unique: it is not separate from Brahman itself; it forms its essence; it does not depend on other factors *(na kāraṇāntarasavyapekṣam)*; it is eternal; it is extremely refined *(niratiśayasūkṣma)*; not even the subtlest matter is concealed from it; it is all-knowing *(sarvajña)*.

Thus Brahman cannot be properly expressed by the word "knowledge" *(na jñānaśabdavācyaṃ)*; for it does not belong to any class, which is the usual basis for the employment of a word. Nevertheless, it can be "indicated by that word insofar as it refers to the qualities of the intellect, expressing its reflections."[86] Much the same goes for the word *satya*, "truth." "Thus," Śaṅkara concludes, " 'truth' and the other words, in proximity to each other [in the sentence "Brahman is truth, knowledge, infinite"] and delimiting each other, indicate Brahman [figuratively] while they set it off from what is [properly] expressed by the words 'truth' and so on." Here he quotes *TU* II.4.1,

"Not reaching it, words and the mind turn back from it,"[87] which suggests that Brahman is not *directly* expressible.[88]

This passage reveals that Śaṅkara was well aware that his use of the terms "knowledge," "consciousness," and so forth was not standard—and he intended it that way. Śaṅkara is obviously attempting to introduce a new meaning for the word *jñāna*, different from what is usually denoted by that word, although related to it—related not syntactically or semantically but *metaphysically*, as indicating the cause of that which we ordinarily refer to as "knowledge" or "consciousness." He is thus proposing in effect a new conceptual scheme for talking about Brahman to replace the one in which "consciousness" stands for an activity that is object-directed—an activity which (filling in aspects of the standard notion of consciousness Śaṅkara does not explicitly consider) always takes the form of a specific act of consciousness depending on the nature of its object (and thus defines a *class* of conscious acts). He is throwing out the old notion of consciousness, which is inadequate to express what he believes he experiences.

Thus the perspective according to which the notion of pure consciousness is to be seen as a self-contradiction is not really applicable to Śaṅkara. That is to say, Śaṅkara does not rely on it when he talks about the type of consciousness he considers to be the essence of the self. It was argued in Section 2 that pure consciousness is a self-contradiction because the very word "consciousness" suggests determinateness (hence it cannot be without an object) and specificity—the denoted consciousness is one of many possible states of consciousness: it cannot be a substance, a "mass," as Śaṅkara refers to it. Now it is evident that in talking about pure consciousness Śaṅkara is not in fact using that word at all. He has in mind a different word which has a different meaning although it happens to have the same phonetic shape. Suppose we consider the matter in the light of Pletcher's model: the contradictions that appear in Śaṅkara's discussions of consciousness have to do with the unsuitability of ordinary language for talking about what he has in mind. Śaṅkara's paradoxical statements are not the expression of an encounter with something truly paradoxical.[89] Nor are they careless mistakes or misdescriptions. They are, rather, the result of deliberate attempts to describe or, as Śaṅkara would prefer to say, "indicate" an actual, nonparadoxical state of affairs that is not directly expressible by means of the linguistic tools at hand. With no other tools at his disposal, Śaṅkara chooses to indicate it paradoxically rather than not at all. His statements only appear as contradictions when one interprets them rigidly in terms of the ordinary human conceptual system which he is, ultimately, discarding, and when one ignores his warnings that his statements are to be taken loosely or figuratively.[90]

At the same time that this becomes clear, however, it is also clear that the problem of unintelligibility for Śaṅkara's theory of consciousness is far from solved. For although the notion of pure consciousness no longer appears to be self-contradictory, it is nevertheless seriously problematic in that it refers to something with which hardly anyone besides Śaṅkara, it would seem, is familiar. This issue is touched on in the passage that has just been discussed. There, as we saw, the opponent suggests that the predication of "knowledge" and so forth to Brahman is altogether meaningless, because words serve only to set aside ideas that do *not* apply to what is being described. To say that something is "red," for example, is to say that it is *not* blue, *not* green, *not* yellow, and so forth. Nevertheless, in the case of "red," knowledge is conveyed, because after the false ideas have been removed, the *perception* of red remains—isolated, in effect, by the utterance. But for Brahman, the opponent assumes, we have no analogous perception. Śaṅkara is able to get around this objection for the moment by appealing to a theory according to which words do have positive meaning in themselves. Yet a version of it would seem seriously to threaten his final position that the predicates "knowledge" and so forth are true of Brahman only figuratively. For if that means—as Śaṅkara says—that Brahman is indicated by those words only insofar as it is set off from what they properly denote, and if Brahman is otherwise unknown or unfamiliar (Śaṅkara does not deny this assumption here), then there is nothing left for those words to isolate. No knowledge is conveyed.

In other words, it only makes sense to say that Brahman is knowledge (but not knowledge in the ordinary sense of the word) and truth (but not truth in the ordinary sense of the word) when one really knows what kind of thing Brahman is, so that one knows in what *other* sense those words are being applied to it.[91] Thus the problem of unintelligibility for Śaṅkara's philosophy seems to be: How are we to understand something new that is presented in a way that deviates from the only mode of understanding that we know—namely, the employment of language in accordance with established usage? This question poses a serious problem for Śaṅkara's system as a whole, because that system is meant to provide a vision, a direct intuition of Brahman or the self on the basis of correct understanding about it from scripture.

In the next section of this chapter I shall deal with this issue, which I consider to be the real problem of unintelligibility for Śaṅkara's philosophy. I shall attempt to show that it is resolvable only when one correctly interprets his philosophy as transformative.

Before turning to that question, it ought to be briefly mentioned that the offense which Śaṅkara avoids by announcing that his words are to be taken figuratively—that is, real contradiction as opposed to mere uncertainty of meaning—is precisely what Fichte is guilty of in certain passages in the earliest exposition of his philosophy, *The Foundation of the Entire Theory of Science (Die Grundlage der gesammten Wissenschaftslehre)*. In that work Fichte places at the basis of his system a principle of self-consciousness that is meant to be a perfect self-reflexive act—a "subject-object," as he calls it.[92] It is a consciousness that exists at the basis of ordinary (empirical) consciousness and, according to the theory Fichte develops, gives rise to it by a dialectical process. The trouble with such a principle as Fichte presents it, however, is that it is often understood in terms of the type of empirical consciousness it is supposed to transcend. There is a reason for this—self-consciousness is in Fichte's view motivated to evolve into a structured, manifest form of consciousness precisely because it is inadequate as a consciousness, and the description of it as a failed attempt at empirical consciousness highlights this fact.

But critics have balked at the postulation of a first principle of reality which is introduced in flatly self-contradictory terms. The very expression "subject-object," for example, makes use of categories of *experience*, but at the same time it denies those categories because, as far as experience goes, subject and object cannot be the same. One encounters other phrases and illustrations relating to the principle of self-consciousness in the *Grundlage* which imply that it exists only insofar as something can be both affirmed and denied at the same time. At one place Fichte likens it to a state in which a centrifugal force directed outward (the positive activity that establishes the self as a "real quantum") and a centripetal force directed inward (the self-reflexive activity of the self) both "fall together and comprise one and the same direction"—a self-contradictory and truly unimaginable state of affairs![93] In general, it can be said that in these passages of the *Wissenschaftslehre* Fichte is less successful than Śaṅkara in avoiding paradox when talking about something for which there are no accepted guidelines for discussion—primarily because he does not take the precaution of expressly disavowing the rules of thought and language by which it must appear paradoxical. Apparently still dependent on the ordinary human conceptual framework, Fichte tries to say something that is not sayable within it.[94]

4. *The Mechanics of Transformation*

Let us review what has been established thus far: I have argued that Śaṅkara's theory of consciousness is unintelligible when evaluated from the perspective of our usual way of thinking about consciousness. Initially I demonstrated that the notion of pure consciousness can be regarded as self-contradictory, a contradiction in terms. We have seen, however, that Śaṅkara does not accept the standard meaning of the term "consciousness" in this case; pure consciousness, therefore, is not necessarily a self-contradiction. Since we do not know any other meaning of the term "consciousness" than its standard one, however, pure consciousness remains unintelligible—*problematic*, I would say, as opposed to blatantly absurd.[95]

With regard to the final point, it is to be stressed that Śaṅkara's theory as a whole is jeopardized by its being problematic, because it is intended to convey an intuition, an experience, of pure consciousness *by understanding it.* This notion, perhaps, requires amplification. If Śaṅkara's system were offered merely as a set of statements that are supposed to be theoretically true about the world, then a certain degree of problematicity would be acceptable. For then, given that the reality it treats is not commensurate with the human mind, that it transcends the senses on which the human intellect is dependent in reasoning, an approximate or analogical knowledge of it may be the most one can hope to achieve.[96] But we saw in the first chapter that Śaṅkara's system is not intended to be purely theoretical. It is also practical; it is meant to effect a concrete, irrevocable change in the life of the student, an actual union with the Absolute it depicts. Therefore —since that change is to be brought about by means of a right understanding of the Absolute derived from the Veda—the failure of the system to provide such understanding is crucial. In short, the problematic character of the notion of pure consciousness is a difficulty for Śaṅkara's philosophy not as a dogma but as soteriology. It seems to *presuppose* the sublime revolution of awareness it is supposed to cause.[97]

When the problem is stated in this way, however, its solution becomes evident as soon as we recall other points brought out in Chapter 1. We saw there that Śaṅkara presupposes a certain state of purification as a prerequisite of the inquiry into Brahman. This purity is marked by certain qualities which it seems proper to label "spiritual"—dispassion, tranquility, control, and so forth. It is to be cultivated by the regular observance of religious and social ritual, by moral goodness, and by spiritual disciplines such as celibacy, austerity, meditation, and restraint of the senses. It is referred to variously as purity of the self, of the mind, of the intellect, but it is also closely associated with the concept "knowledge" *(vidyā)*—for Śaṅkara says that karma, while it is not the cause of liberation, is the cause of knowledge. In this section I shall argue that this purity in fact represents an unnoticed assimilation to the state of consciousness that is ultimately to be cognized as liberation. It is not knowledge in the fullest sense; therefore its presupposition is justified. Rather, it is precognitive knowledge—knowledge analogous to the possession of an object which, while I am seeking it, I already hold in my hand. (I know, but I do not know that I know.) Having, so to speak, already achieved union with Brahman on a precognitive level, the explicit statement that one *is* Brahman is all that is needed to precipitate a clear consciousness of that union and bring it into being as such for the first time.

In what follows I shall, first, attempt to clarify the notion of preconceptual knowledge. Here I shall again draw on the current philosophical discussion of mystical experience, especially insofar as it deals with the informing function of mystical language. I shall then apply this notion to Śaṅkara's system.

The contemporary discussion of the function of mystical language centers on the attempt by some to view all mystical experience as essentially the same. The main advocate of that position, W. T. Stace,[98] argues that the diversity of forms of mystical expression—from cabalistic Judaism to Sufism, from Vedānta and Zen Buddhism to medieval Christianity—is to be accounted for by different circumstances in which mystics have lived: by different social, political, religious, and philosophical influences to which they have been subjected, by different cultures and value systems into which they have been indoctrinated. The diversity is not, however, to be accounted for by a difference in the object of mystical experience. Stace maintains that when one compares the writings of diverse mystical traditions, one notices, despite superficial differences, striking similarities. On the basis of a rather cursory survey he assembles several features under the heading "the universal core of mystical experience" as representing an identical experience shared by mystics throughout the world.

To reduce the significance of discrepancies between mystical reports, Stace introduces a distinction between experience per se and one's interpretation of it. One experience, Stace says, can be viewed in different ways. He relates the anecdote of an American visitor to London who tried to shake hands with a waxwork policeman in front of Madame Tussaud's: "If such an incident ever occurred," Stace argues, "it must have been because the visitor had a sense of experience which he first wrongly interpreted as a live policeman and later interpreted correctly as a wax figure . . . which proves that an interpretation is distinguishable from an experience; for there could not otherwise have been two interpretations of one experience [as in this case]."[99] Applied to mysticism this principle accounts for various ways of talking about God or the Absolute without sacrificing the possibility that they ultimately refer to one thing. A Christian can speak of it as a personal being, a Hindu can say it is the impersonal Absolute, a Buddhist can deny that it is either personal or impersonal, because each is trained in advance to think of it as such.[100] As before, Stace is motivated by the desire to make a larger philosophical point—namely, if all accounts of mystical experience can be taken as indicating a single entity, then taken together they amount to compelling evidence in favor of its reality.

Resistance to Stace's proposals has issued from various quarters. Historians of religion in particular, following the lead of Zaehner and Otto, have argued that discrepancies between mystical traditions are often deeper and more significant than Stace allows.[101] Philosophers, on the other hand, have argued that there is probably a closer relationship between mystical experience and the mode in which it is expressed or conceptualized than Stace realizes.[102] Some philosophers have gone so far as to suggest that this relationship is a causal one. Perhaps the most sophisticated to have done so is Bruce Garside, to whose ideas I now turn.

Garside presents his ideas in conjunction with a general model of experience which is significant to our discussion and which will therefore be presented here at some length. (Garside himself regards his discussion of these matters as brief and summary, presupposing answers to questions of philosophy and psychology that have been debated for hundreds of years.) The main premise of his model is that "experience is a product of the interaction of the organism and the environment, involving both external stimuli and interpretive structures of the perceiver."[103] He follows the conventions of current psychological literature in referring to these two factors as the setting and the set. He notes that, philosophically, the model derives from Kant insofar as it views experience as the product of the synthesis of percepts and certain given structures of the understanding.

Garside points out that although this model has wide acceptance, there is disagreement about the possible variations of interpretive structures available to the perceiver and the extent to which they determine perception. He mentions Whorf on the one hand, who believed that experience can be ordered in a way that does not involve physical objects, and P. F. Strawson, on the other, who insists that the notion of physical objects is essential to every conceptual scheme. Garside does not attempt to decide whether components of the world independent of the experiencer are necessary for experience to happen (the problem of an external world). He leaves open the possibility that we experience objects and processes in the world much as they are "in themselves" and that our conceptual set contributes very little. He does maintain, though, that when one experiences more abstract things the conceptual set plays a greater role: "The more we move away from gross perceptions of physical bodies to discriminations among types of physical bodies and their properties, to perceptions related to other people, to perceptions of moral and artistic value, to perceptions of our emotions and 'inner' states, the more important and determining the peculiarities of particular cultural and conceptual frameworks become."[104] Some perceptions, in other words, are more highly socialized than others; and mystical experience, it would seem, is of the most highly socialized sort.

Garside, with Wittgenstein, views *language* as embodying a conceptual framework or form of life. It is the palpable form of an interpretive structure; in it are codified the interpretive structure's rules. Language represents an ontology. Moreover—and this point is of special importance for us—"language plays a crucial role in our perception in that to a great extent a thing is objectified for us through the imposition of a word."[105] Elsewhere Garside makes the same point when he says, "how the child really sees the world before the development of interpretive structures [that is, before learning language] is a question that cannot be answered because in a sense he doesn't see it."[106] Language illumines reality for us by serving as the means for it to be brought to our attention. Garside thus sees the relationship between language and experience as intrinsic rather than extrinsic or accidental and, noting that some philosophers (such as Stace) have tended to separate the two, recommends caution when asserting that an experience can be "interpreted" in different ways. He also suggests that any experience one might have should be able to be articulated or conceptualized in *some* way, at least to the extent that one can distinguish it from other experiences and relate some characteristics of it.

With this model in hand Garside turns to the issues of the philosophical discussion of mysticism. With regard to the alleged ineffability of mystical experience he argues that a completely ineffable mystical experience is impossible; for if that were the case, it would be impossible to single it out from other experiences as unique. But in fact this is done and, Garside suggests, mystical experiences are never completely ineffable. The *via negativa* of mystical theology is usually complemented by the *via positiva*; purely negative discourse about the Ultimate in mystical writings rarely stands alone.[107] He eventually proposes a view of the ineffability of mystical experience close to that of Pletcher: mystical experiences have a logic of their own. They are not truly illogical; but they require a unique language to be expressed and, Garside adds significantly, to be made possible.

Garside turns finally to the issue of the fundamental unity of mystical experience. Noting that the main premise of that view—namely, that divergent reports of mystical experiences are divergent *interpretations* of an identical experience—is in conflict with his model, he challenges the use of the word "interpretation" for the structures that originally order experience into an intelligible whole. With special reference to Stace's example of the American in front of Madame Tussaud's, he remarks that no interpreting whatsoever went on in that case. There was no application of a theory to evidence, no weighing of various accounts. The American simply *saw* the wax figure as a live policeman. This fact is prior to any interpretation. In short, says Garside, Stace fails "to realize that what he calls an interpretive framework and what I have referred to as a 'set' enters into the experience itself as a *constitutive* factor. *If experience is the product of stimuli and conceptual framework as suggested . . . then people of different cultures and religious traditions would necessarily have different religious experiences.*"[108] Furthermore, the attempt to arrive at a "pure" description of mystical experience "undistorted" by an interpretive framework is absurd. (Stace believes himself to have presented such a description under the rubric of "the universal core of mystical experience.")

Garside concludes that mystical experiences may belong to the same general class in that they have the same role within their respective religious traditions and cultures. But they are not all the same experience, he argues, nor do they relate to the same object. In reference to the philosophical motives at the basis of Stace's analysis, Garside astutely observes:

> The fact that such a claim cannot be made on behalf of mystical experiences weakens their usefulness as quasi-empirical evidence on behalf of the verity of some religious consciousness. Fortunately for those who value mystical experiences, the attempt to utilize them in such a manner does not reflect the functions they normally have within their respective traditions, and is of dubious relevance to the verity of religious life in general.[109]

Garside's observations indicate how the application of an interpretive scheme to a certain state of mind can be *revelatory* of an experience, for it will structure unordered data for the first time into a whole.[110] This is a consequence of the intrinsic relationship of experience and conceptualization. A conceptual scheme not only defines an experience but also makes it possible for one to have it, insofar as any experience, to be an experience, must be defined and determined. Perhaps this point can best be seen with reference to the situation of a child learning language. Certainly the child's perceptual faculties are functioning before it begins to speak or understand what is spoken to it. Without language it sees, hears, tastes, smells, in some way senses the world around it. Yet not until it has words for things does it *experience* a world that is concrete in terms of objects and processes—indeed, even in terms of its own thoughts and feelings. Until the child knows what tables, chairs, dogs, and cats are, it does not experience tables, chairs, dogs, or cats. If the child does not know what anything is, it does not *experience* anything. The addition of language thus brings into being for the child, for the first time, a world of concrete experience: a world of things that can be described, identified, remembered, forgotten, reflected on, accepted, rejected, although such a world was *in some sense* present before.[111]

Now, I believe that Garside's model can be applied to the process that underlies Śaṅkara's philosophy—as he himself must conceive it. The observance of religious ritual and spiritual techniques effects an overall change in consciousness—not by introducing new objects to consciousness but by adjusting the basic relation of the perceiver to what he already perceives. But this change remains unordered and unconceptualized and, therefore, ultimately unrealized. Putting the matter in epistemologically objective terms: the "new" reality one confronts—which, Śaṅkara reminds us, one has always confronted, for it is nothing other than oneself—is confronted unknowingly, because one does not *recognize* it as reality—that is, as oneself. The presentation of the new conceptual scheme of the Vedānta texts *reveals* the reality of the self to the Vedāntin as if for the first time, making it harmonious and acceptable and structuring it as a concrete experience.

That this interpretation is generally correct appears from Śaṅkara's frequent use of the rope-seen-as-a-snake metaphor to describe the condition of ignorance. Just as one mistakes a rope coiled in the corner of a dark room for a snake, one mistakes the self, which is partless, pure, and immortal, for an agent afflicted by pain, suffering, and death. And, as the mere statement that what one sees is not a snake but actually a rope removes the false image of the snake, so the mere knowledge that I am partless, pure, and immortal removes the delusion that I act, suffer, and die. Clearly implied by this metaphor is that the student of Vedānta is already in possession of a self-intuition which needs only to be articulated in order to become evident. In fact, Śaṅkara explicitly declares in a passage at the beginning of the *BrSūBh* that Brahman, the topic of *brahmajijñāsā*, is already "familiar" *(prasiddha)*.[112] Because this passage comes shortly after the listing of the prerequisites of *brahmajijñāsā*, one is inclined to think that purity and familiarity with Brahman are somehow related.

We may note, incidentally, that the "familiarity" of Brahman is precisely what is needed to get around the sort of objection brought forward in the *TUBh* against the application of terms to Brahman in unconventional ways. In extending the reasoning of Śaṅkara's commentary I suggested that "knowledge," "truth," and the like cannot be used of Brahman figuratively because we have no intuition to appeal to in assigning those words as a new sense. But now we see that Śaṅkara can assume that because Brahman is already known—although in an inexplicit way—the figurative meaning of those words will be filled in.

Yet our interpretation must be considered only tentative; for there is much about the process of transformation that Śaṅkara leaves undelineated. He does not specify what kind of condition "purity" is supposed to be—is it a certain unique inner experience, a disposition to think and behave in certain ways, a condition of the nervous system, or all of these? He does not clarify *how* such diverse activities as religious ceremonies and breathing exercises are capable of giving rise to it—nor, indeed, more generally how moral qualities, which are usually thought to apply to persons, could be relevant to the condition of one's *mind*. The last point is of concern in that Śaṅkara claims that austerity, celibacy, and so forth remove accumulated sins *(pāpa)* or unrighteousness *(adharma)* whereas the observance of obligatory ritual prevents the further accumulation thereof. In short, we are able fairly easily to comprehend how Advaita concepts may *inform* an emerging shift in awareness—if that is even a proper description of it—for we can resort here to modern psychology which has a theory ready for us. But the mechanics of the latter phenomenon—the emergence of a readiness to achieve an extraordinary self-cognition, which takes place as soon as it is edified—remain obscure. Psychology, which has only begun to investigate empirically the effects of spiritual practices and religious forms of awareness, cannot help us here.

Nevertheless, I believe that we are not left completely without guidelines. Śaṅkara may be mute when it comes to explaining the transformation of awareness through spiritual disciplines, but we can assume that he was familiar with the widely accepted explanation of the process of spiritual purification of yoga philosophy.

Yoga develops that explanation in the context of a general theory of experience. According to the *Yogasūtra* and its principal commentary, "impressions" *(saṃskāras, vāsanās)* of past experience stored in the mind influence the character of present experience. New experience arises when the residue of karma left in the mind from past karma (here taken in the most general sense as any action) bears fruit. The condition for the fruition of this residual karma is the copresence of memory impressions which color it as a pleasant or unpleasant experience according to whether the past karma was good or bad. In particular, karma depends on the existence of "afflictions" *(kleśas)*—that is, ignorance and the passions—which, like a husk around the seed of karma, nourish it and enable it to grow and bear fruit in the form of new experience.

Since liberation means freedom from transmigration, which is caused by karma perpetuating itself in a vicious circle, the first objective of yoga is to weaken or attenuate the *saṃskāras* of the *kleśas*. This is done by means of *kriyāyoga*, "the yoga of action," and *dhyāna*, meditation. *Kriyāyoga* includes asceticism, Vedic study, and devotion to God. These three items are also included under the "observances" *(niyamas)*, which collectively constitute one of the eight limbs of the "eight-limbed yoga" *(aṣṭāṅgayoga)*, among which *dhyāna* is also included. It is stated in the *YS* that the observance of the eight limbs is the cause of the removal of impurity leading to an expansion of consciousness which culminates in the discriminating cognition of the self,[113] which in turn, in the yoga system as in Śaṅkara's Vedānta, is the direct cause of liberation. The more the *kleśas* are attenuated, the brighter consciousness becomes.[114] It is evident, therefore, that the yoga theory of mental purification could well serve as the basis of Śaṅkara's notion of spiritual preparation. Indeed, a sensitive reading of the *Yogasūtra* yields the impression that the yoga and Śaṅkara's system are complementary. Both represent, in the final analysis, the path of knowledge to self-realization—yoga emphasizing the preparation for knowledge, Śaṅkara stressing knowledge itself.[115] In mentioning the process of purification Śaṅkara may have simply meant to refer his reader to the yoga theory.

Śaṅkara's successors too make a connection between Advaita and yoga. Although Sureśvara (eighth century), the immediate disciple of Śaṅkara who is thought to have followed the master's teaching closest of all his followers, rails against the acceptance of ritual karma as a real cause of liberation, he too finds a place for it among the preliminaries. According to him karma wipes away the impurities of activity *(rajas)* and sloth *(tamas)*—both fundamental yoga concepts—from the mind, making it bright and undisturbed "like a polished crystal."[116] Among a list of various factors of liberation he includes *yogābhyāsa* ("yoga practice").[117] Yet his analysis does not go very deep. He simply says that somehow dispassion arises in the heart of one whose mind, through constant application to righteousness, has been cleansed by regular ritual acts. Although yoga practice is mentioned, it is nowhere treated in detail; in one version of the path to liberation it is in fact left out.[118]

We find a more direct link with yoga psychology in Vācaspatimiśra (tenth century)—something one would expect from the author of commentaries on both the *Yogasūtra* and Śaṅkara's *BrSūBh.* In Vācaspati's *Bhāmatī* we encounter the expression "one whose mind is pure" *(viśuddhasattva)* qualified in its first occurrence as "whose inner impurities have undergone attrition *(tanūkṛta)* by means of sacrifices, giving, austerity, and fasting."[119] "Attrition" is the characteristic yoga expression for the weakening of the wrong tendencies or afflictions of the mind—ignorance, egoism *(asmitā)*, passion, aversion, and tenacity or the will to live *(abhiniveśa)*—which nourish the fruition of past karma and hinder concentration. Elsewhere Vācaspati refers to the uprooting of the "impressions" *(vāsanās)* of ignorance—another instance of yoga terminology.[120] From these and other remarks it is evident that Vācaspati considers yoga a suitable framework for dealing with the psychological mechanisms of transformation. And so it is for other Advaita thinkers.[121]

Let us summarize the tentative theory of the mechanics of liberation presented here and see whether it solves the problem of intelligibility for Śaṅkara's philosophy. That is: How can Śaṅkara's teaching be valid as a way to total transformation—liberation, enlightenment, salvation, call it what you will—when it seems already to presuppose a radically different perspective on human existence in the form of an understanding of one's self as pure consciousness, a concept falling outside all normal existential and epistemological categories? This transformation, we have seen, takes place on two levels. First is the precognitive level which entails the elimination of "impurity"—the psychophysiological sources *(saṃskāras)* of the behavior and beliefs which disrupt the wholeness of life and reinforce the sense of oneself as a separate individual distinct from an Other. This purification is accompanied by an expansion or clarification of consciousness. Second, it takes place on a level of explicit (propositional) knowledge of one's true nature, which informs the naive confrontation with pure consciousness achieved on the first level and culminates in a direct *experience* of it.[122] Thus the transformation which must be presupposed for the intelligibility of Śaṅkara's system is to be taken, in the first instance, as a precognitive attitude. A second, "philosophical" transformation—or a second, philosophical moment of the same transformation—simply converts this attitude into a more vivid knowledge.[123]

This interpretation constitutes only a partial solution of the problem of intelligibility for Śaṅkara's philosophy. For it does not make the central notion of his system, pure consciousness, intelligible for *us*. Nor does it even allow us to conceive of an experience of pure consciousness for others, since for the notion "the experience of X" to be intelligible the constituent term X must be so. But it does allow us to see how Śaṅkara's system can work. That is: given that we cannot determine a priori that intentional states of consciousness involving a dichotomy between subject and object are the only possible mode of human experience—an uncontroversial point, it would seem—given this, our solution at least helps us understand how Śaṅkara's teaching qua soteriology can appear intelligible to someone who believes in the *possibility* of such an experience. In fact, one who aspires to salvation via the Advaita Vedānta path will simply begin at the beginning, taking up the requisite purifying disciplines, assuming on faith that a worthwhile state will eventually be attained. One may not comprehend that state at the outset—or one may understand it only in negative terms, as a release from suffering and rebirth. But one can still reasonably hope eventually to be able to comprehend it—presumably, once one's mind is no longer bound by the shackles of karma to the mundane. All that is necessary for Śaṅkara's Vedānta to serve as a viable means to salvation, in other words, is that the problematic idea of pure consciousness be entertained as a *possibility*. Those who can do so are able to conceive approaching that awareness, in some sense, in advance of fully understanding it. Although Śaṅkara's system remains unintelligible on the theoretical level—that is, for us—on the practical level, once faith enters in, the question of its unintelligibility will never arise.

5. *Transformative Philosophy as a Type*

In this and the preceding chapter I have argued that Śaṅkara presents us with a philosophy that does not stand on its own as a theoretical edifice but requires a certain transformation in the student to be intelligible, which transformation it in turn finalizes. I refer to this type of philosophy as transformative, but it is known by other names. The Buddhologist Edward Conze, who finds it at the heart of Buddhism, calls it "wisdom" and contrasts it to the dominant mode of philosophizing in the West:

> In Europe, we have become accustomed to an almost complete gap between the theory of philosophers and their practice, between their views on the nature of the universe and their mode of life. Schopenhauer and Herbert Spencer, for instance, at once come to mind as particularly striking examples. If a philosopher here has proved that there is no ego [as Buddhists believe to have done], he is apt to leave it at that, and to behave very much as if there were one. His greed, hate and attachment remain practically untouched by his philosophical arguments. He is judged by the consistency of his views, not with his life, but with themselves, by his style, his erudition—in short, by purely intellectual standards. It just would not do to "refute" a philosopher by pointing out that he is insufferably rude to his wife, envies his more fortunate colleagues, and gets flustered when contradicted. In Buddhism, on the contrary, the entire stress lies on the mode of living, on the saintliness of life, on the removal of attachment to this world. A merely theoretical proposition, such as "there is no ego," would be regarded as utterly sterile, as useless. Thought is no more than a tool and its justification lies in its products.[124]

Conze goes on to say that the importance of Buddhist philosophy "lies in the methods it worked out to impress the truth of the not-self on our reluctant minds; it lies in the discipline which the Buddhists imposed upon themselves in order to make this truth into a part of their own being."[125] Hence virtually all systems of Buddhism presuppose some spiritual conditioning which prepares one to receive the truth. On the other hand, it is the comprehension of the truth which confers ultimate salvation.[126] This pattern has been observed for the Sāṃkhya system of Hindu philosophy as well,[127] so that we may plausibly maintain that it is a dominant feature of Indian metaphysics in general.

Some will indeed wonder why I have chosen Śaṅkara's Vedānta to illustrate transformative philosophy when more clear-cut examples from Oriental philosophy are available. But one of my purposes here has been to correct the standard interpretation of Śaṅkara as pure thinker. Scholarship has largely failed to recognize the transformative aspect of his "philosophy." In fact, it can be said in general that scholarship tends to ignore or even obscure the transformative elements of philosophical traditions unless they are so pronounced that it is impossible to do so. The reason should be clear: transformative philosophy radically calls into question the methods of academic scholarship. It presents itself as a humanistic phenomenon which cannot be understood by the uncommitted, theoretical mind. We shall have opportunity to return to this matter later. For now, let it suffice to say that my efforts to bring out the transformative elements in Śaṅkara's system will serve as a sort of preparatory exercise for dealing with European philosophy, where the phenomenon of transformative philosophy exists almost totally concealed.

I shall argue in the remainder of this study that while the transformative pattern may not be a dominant element, it is nevertheless an *important* feature of European philosophy. Conze's statement makes clear that this is by no means the accepted view. Rather, Western philosophy, although it may have its roots in the wisdom traditions of ancient Greece, is usually viewed as being concerned typically with *knowledge*, for which science and mathematics serve as paradigms. In modern times philosophy has turned "critical." It seeks not to establish new metaphysical truths to rival the ancient ones—for the possibility of any kind of metaphysics is doubted—but only to determine the nature of the subjective faculties of knowledge themselves or that of language. A Western philosopher cannot be challenged by an inconsistency between his thought and his life, as Conze rightly observes, because Western philosophy has by and large turned away from life. It believes that questions about the purpose and fulfillment of life, or about some greater reality behind appearances, are not its affair—or that in any case answers can be provided purely by thinking.

Although this is how European philosophy is regarded and regards itself—for, indeed, such has been the dominant trend for most of the modern period—I shall suggest that transformative philosophy is nevertheless a vital factor in the European tradition, as an occasional source of impetus and inspiration. And insofar as transformative philosophy emerges unscathed from the self-destructive struggle philosophy has waged with itself in recent times, it is a viable candidate for the philosophy of the future. The scope of the present work does not allow me to demonstrate this argument completely. I only hope to make a beginning by showing, at least, that there are in fact modern European philosophers who must be considered transformative thinkers. In the next chapter I shall take the nineteenth-century German philosopher J. G. Fichte as a prime example.

3

Fichte as Transformative Philosopher

JOHANN GOTTLIEB FICHTE occupies a peculiar position in Western philosophy. As the link between two great philosophical movements—Kant's "critical philosophy" and Hegel's "absolute idealism"—he is of crucial historical importance. But, overshadowed by those same two thinkers, he has been largely neglected as a philosopher worth studying in his own right. Fichte receives little more than a paragraph of attention in most histories of philosophy. Yet he was a powerful and original thinker. Although Fichte borrowed some of his ideas from Kant, he went far beyond him. And although he served as a stimulus for Hegel, it is hardly true that Hegel said everything Fichte had to say, only better. Absolute idealism takes off from the *Wissenschaftslehre*, but it by no means comprehends it. We can best appreciate Fichte's contribution to Western philosophy by considering two ideas of his which have endured far beyond his immediate historical situation. One is the principle of the dialectic; the other is the notion of striving.

The dialectic, to be sure, was made famous by Hegel as the motor which drives the *Weltgeist* and generates the stages of evolution of experience. It was put to a similar use by Marx in the construction of his system of materialism. But the importance of the dialectic extends far beyond its employment in system building. It has been adapted as a general principle of thinking and discovery and as such is central to all modern philosophy. Dialectical thinking recognizes that the content of a concept depends, to some extent at least, on the concepts to which it is opposed. It thus lies at the heart of all philosophical analysis, whether structuralist, phenomenological, or linguistic. To illustrate this familiar technique I offer a famous passage from Heidegger in which he analyzes, after Nietzsche, the will as a function of revenge. As I shall return to it in another context, I quote it here at some length:

> Since long ago, that which is present has been regarded as what is. But what representational ideas can we form of what in a way is no longer, and yet still is? What ideas can we form of that which was? At this "it was," idea and its willing take offense. Faced with what "was," willing

> no longer has anything to say. Faced with every "it was," willing no longer has anything to propose. . . . Thus the "it was" is revolting and contrary to the will. This is why revulsion against the "it was" arises in the will itself when it is faced with this contrary "it was." But by way of this revulsion, the contrary takes root within willing itself. Willing endures the contrary within itself as a heavy burden; it suffers from it—that is, the will suffers from itself. Willing appears to itself as this suffering from the "it was," as the suffering from the bygone, the past. But what is past stems from the passing. The will—in suffering from this passing, yet being what it is precisely by virtue of this suffering—remains in its willing captive to the passing. Thus will itself wills passing. It wills the passing of its suffering, and thus wills its own passing. The will's revulsion against every "it was" appears as the will to pass away, which wills that everything be worthy of passing away. . . . Hence the will is the sphere of representational ideas which basically pursue and set upon everything that comes and goes and exists, in order to depose, reduce it in its stature, and ultimately decompose it. This revulsion within the will itself . . . is the essential nature of revenge.[1]

This style of thinking, while not exactly Fichte's, would not have been possible without him.

The concept of striving, given its treatment by existential philosophers, does not need to be justified as a central concern in modern philosophy. But some may not be aware that it was Fichte who, perhaps inspired by Lessing's famous declaration, first systematically showed striving to be an essential feature of human existence. This idea is worked out in the original exposition of his philosophy in *The Foundation of the Entire Theory of Science.* There the striving of the self (the Absolute) to find itself fully embodied in life—an ultimately unattainable ideal—serves as the mainspring of all cognitive and moral activity.

Thus Fichte was a thinker to whom we owe more than we perhaps realized. Although an obscure philosopher—in more ways than one—let it be said that he was one of the greatest obscure philosophers we have had. I shall try to show in this chapter that Fichte's originality and greatness—perhaps, also, his obscurity—lie precisely in his view of philosophy as a process of transformation.

1. *The Intellectual Intuition and the Emergence of Self-Consciousness*

It seems most appropriate to approach Fichte's "science of knowledge" or *Wissenschaftslehre* through those works which he himself intended as introductions to it. Of these we shall consider here especially the well-known *First* and *Second Introductions to the Science of Knowledge* of 1797–1798 and the lesser-known *Introductory Lectures to the Science of Knowledge* of 1813.[2] The first two treatises were published three years after the appearance of *The Foundation of the Entire Theory of Science (Die Grundlage der gesammten Wissenschaftslehre* of 1794, henceforth *GWL)*, in which Fichte's system was worked out in complete form for the first time, and they represent an attempt to respond to the mixed reception it was given.[3] Significantly, though, Fichte does not attempt to deal with specific objections, except in the *Second Introduction*, which is defined in its title as being "for readers who already have a philosophical system"; instead, he for the most part undertakes to explain matters completely anew. For he was convinced that the opposition to his theory was due chiefly to lack of understanding. In the last *Introduction*, composed a year before his death, Fichte, now with a sense of futility and frustration over whether his philosophy will ever gain general acceptance, tries to reformulate in the simplest and most direct language possible the theory that he had repeatedly revised over two decades.

The *First Introduction* begins with these words: "Attend to yourself: turn your attention away from everything that surrounds you and toward your inner life—this is the first demand that philosophy makes of its disciple."[4] Thus Fichte's philosophy begins, uniquely, with a prescription: the command to think one's self. This does not mean that one must think *about* oneself; rather, one must withdraw from the consciousness of the world while focusing on one's inner consciousness and thus make a fundamental adjustment in one's mode of awareness. The science of knowledge is practical at its inception, insofar as it starts out not with a statement but with something to *do.* The enterprise of the science of knowledge cannot be undertaken if one does not perform the act in question.

At first it appears that this act is one that all of us are naturally able to perform. It is simply becoming aware that we are conscious and attending to our own conscious states as such. But as Fichte proceeds it becomes clear that for him the manner in which one interprets one's inner states of consciousness is vitally tied up with the clarity of one's vision and, therefore, in a sense, one's ability to carry out this act of introspection.

Upon looking within ourselves, Fichte suggests, we discover two basic types of mental representation: those that appear as products of our own free activity and those that appear to impinge on us from outside and are accompanied with a feeling of having to think them. Now the chief task of philosophy, Fichte maintains, is to provide an explanation for the system of representations of the latter sort, known as "experience," and this can be done in only two ways. One can attempt to explain experience as deriving from things outside of consciousness, "things-in-themselves," in which case one adopts the position which Fichte refers to as "dogmatism," but which, of course, is better known as realism. Or one can attempt to explain them in terms of the first type of mental representation—that is, as in some sense products of our own free activity of representation, arising within us, in which case one takes up "idealism." Fichte calls the source of the free activity of representation "intelligence." Intelligence is independent of all consciousness of outer things, and it manifests itself most evidently in the feeling of spontaneity one has in the exercise of imagination.

Although dogmatism and idealism are diametrically opposed philosophical positions, they lack any common ground on which their dispute can be resolved. Dogmatism cannot be refuted by idealism because the principle to which the idealist wishes to appeal in his argument—the inner consciousness of independence—is converted by the dogmatist into a mere illusion, an epiphenomenon of the interaction of unconscious things. The idealist, on the other hand, cannot be refuted by the dogmatist; for the idealist considers the thing-in-itself, to which none of our senses provides access, a pure invention. Thus, Fichte believes, from the speculative point of view the arguments of the two schools which have dominated the history of Western philosophy—for he claims that all true philosophy, because it must provide an explanation of experience, boils down to one or the other of these two views—are equal in force. Neither philosophy can refute the other.

How, then, can the conflict between dogmatism and idealism be resolved? Fichte gives the rather surprising answer that it is to be resolved on the basis of *interest*—that is, individual bias! But he does not mean that the theoretical dispute between them can be settled in this way. He only means that one in fact opts for either idealism or realism due to one's natural inclination rather than rational conviction. And this choice always provides a practical resolution of the conflict. Now, one's inclination depends on the way in which one experiences inner consciousness. If the principle of intelligence is dominant and one experiences oneself as distinctly independent of perceived objects, then out of the natural psychological instinct to affirm one's identity one advocates idealism, according to which experience arises as a consequence of free acts of intelligence. If one's awareness is lost in representations of external objects and one cannot separate oneself from them, then one asserts oneself as a dogmatist, for one's sense of self derives primarily from *things*.

> There are two levels of humanity . . . two major types of man. Some, who have not yet raised themselves to full consciousness of their freedom and absolute independence, find themselves only in the presentation of things. They have only that dispersed self-consciousness which attaches to objects and has to be gleaned from their multiplicity. Their image is reflected back at them by things, as by a mirror. If these were taken from them, their self would be lost as well. . . . The man who becomes conscious of his self-sufficiency and independence of everything that is outside himself, however—and this can only be achieved by making oneself into something independently of everything else—does not need things for the support of himself, and cannot use them, because they destroy that self-sufficiency and convert it into mere appearance. . . . His belief in himself is direct.[5]

Fichte's philosophy thus begins with a command to raise oneself to this higher level. The intelligibility of the whole enterprise of the science of knowledge as a system of idealism depends on it.

The science of knowledge does not, then, proceed by means of philosophical argument to establish idealism over realism. For this cannot be done. We are already, by virtue of the way we experience ourselves, committed to idealism or realism, and there is no standpoint outside the two systems from which they can be objectively viewed. Fichte, therefore, is not out to convert his readers to idealism. He merely seeks to confirm the idealism of those who have already in effect adopted it. The sort of philosophy one chooses depends on what sort of person one is:

> For a philosophical system is not a dead piece of furniture that we can reject or accept as we wish. It is rather a thing animated by the soul of

> the person who holds it. A person indolent by nature or dulled and distorted by mental servitude, learned luxury, and vanity will never raise himself to the level of idealism.[6]

Let us, then, look more closely at the insight which inclines one toward idealism and which we can say qualifies one to undertake the science of knowledge. Fichte refers to it as the intellectual intuition of the self. He formulated the intellectual intuition differently throughout the development of his philosophy. In the *First* and *Second Introductions* and the *GWL* he characteristically speaks of it as a unity of being and awareness. The intellectual intuition, that is, is an act of awareness which brings its own object into existence. It is moreover, paradoxically, a self-creative act; for that of which I am conscious in this act, the thing that I introduce into being, is nothing other than myself:

> The *self posits itself*, and by virtue of this mere self-assertion it *exists*; and conversely, the self *exists* and *posits* its own existence by virtue of merely existing. It is at once the agent and the product of action, what is active and what the activity brings about. Action and deed are one and the same. . . .[7]

The self has no existence apart from this self-reflexive awareness. It constitutes its essence, without which it may well have been a sensate organism but could not have been a *self*. For Fichte, the question "*What* was I before I came to self-consciousness?" has a definite answer: "*I* did not exist at all, for I was not a self."[8] The self does not predate self-consciousness. It does not exist as an individual being capable of self-consciousness which subsequently raises itself to self-consciousness. The self, the I, performs the act of self-reflection and originates at one blow. "*To posit oneself* and *to be* are, as applied to the self, completely identical."[9]

This line of reasoning underlines the independence of the self. Fichte refers to the self viewed from the standpoint of the intellectual intuition as the Absolute Ego. It does not derive from anything. Nothing logically precedes it. It has no conditions. Nothing determines its nature as a self-consciousness.[10] It creates itself freely and, it would seem, arbitrarily. "*I am absolutely, because I am.*"[11] Only for myself, because I must witness myself—that is, because the self cannot in principle exist unobserved, like a thing, but must be always present to a consciousness, namely, myself—does it in any way exist necessarily.

Because the intellectual intuition provides its own content, so to speak, it equals a full moment of consciousness. It counts as an act of *knowledge*, indeed, a moment of absolutely certain knowledge. We shall see that some of Fichte's remarks militate against this interpretation.[12] But the point is so strongly expressed at the beginning of the *GWL* that the burden of interpretation has to be shifted to explaining any apparent counterstatements. At the outset of that work Fichte attempts to locate his philosophy in the context of tradition by proclaiming that the purpose of the science of knowledge is to reveal the absolutely unconditioned first principle of all human knowledge. This concern clearly harks back to Descartes, who sought a perfectly certain and indubitable basis for what he knew.

One sees another parallel to the Cartesian enterprise in that for Fichte the first principle of human knowledge turns out to be nothing other than the Absolute Ego. Fichte argues that self-consciousness is a principle of truth higher than logical or mathematical truth. For, he suggests, logical truth, such as the law of identity A = A, is merely formal. It does not tell us anything about a real entity, but only what must be true of something *if* it is real. But the act of self-consciousness, which he formally expresses in the proposition "I = I," or "I am I," is valid purely formally—the subject and the object in the act of self-reflection are identical—as well as empirically—insofar as it constitutes the very thing it is about (myself) and thereby guarantees its existence. "I am I" therefore represents a necessarily true statement about a real entity. The transcendental apperception, which for Kant was to be presupposed as a necessary condition for experience but could not become an object of knowledge, becomes for Fichte the act of knowledge *par excellence*. For this reason he feels justified in calling it an intellectual intuition. It is "undoubtedly immediate." But it is not sensory, because it refers to a pure act, not an "existence"—meaning, here, a thing *(ein Sein)*. It was the immediate consciousness of the *thing*-in-itself that Kant denied under the heading of an intellectual intuition.[13]

Yet because it is the supreme condition of all experience, the intellectual intuition occurs within every experience: "I cannot take a step, move hand or foot, without an intellectual intuition of my self-consciousness in these acts."[14] "Without self-consciousness there is no consciousness whatever."[15] It is this mundane aspect of self-consciousness which has led Fichte scholars to deny that the intellectual intuition can be in any way a mystical experience to which only a privileged few have access.[16] Because this is a widely held notion, I shall now consider it with a view to clarifying further the idea of the intellectual intuition.

Fichte's statements concerning the intellectual intuition are by no means consistent at first. To be sure, it is not a state of trance or a kind of yogic *samādhi.* Fichte makes it clear that it does not occur in isolation from the consciousness of objects—"It is possible only in conjunction with a sensory intuition"[17]—and that the philosopher arrives at it only by a certain method of "abstracting" it from the rest of consciousness. Yet in the *Introductions* Fichte sometimes describes this process in a way which gives one the impression that self-consciousness is not a component that can be readily sorted out from other items in consciousness. It must be *postulated.*

> I can freely determine myself to think this or that. . . . If I now abstract from what is thought and observe only myself, I become to myself . . . the content of a specific presentation. That I appear to myself to be determined precisely so and not otherwise, as thinking [this particular thought], depends on my self-determination. . . . But I have not made myself as I am in myself; on the contrary, I am compelled to presuppose myself as that which is to be determined by self-determination. I myself, however, am an object for myself whose condition depends . . . on intelligence alone, but whose existence must always be presupposed.[18]

The last sentences of this passage suggest that the self in fact does not reveal itself within consciousness but hides behind it, as it were, as an entity to be inferred. But this suggestion contradicts Fichte's idea, expounded in the *GWL,* of the intellectual intuition as a moment of complete certainty on which the laws of logic and inference themselves depend. In the continuation of this passage we find Fichte shifting keys again to talk of the object of idealism as something which "actually occurs as something real in consciousness, not as a *thing-in-itself* . . . but as a *self-in-itself.*"[19] Thus it would seem that the intellectual intuition is some sort of direct experience after all. Yet emphatically, in the *Second Introduction,* "it is . . . no consciousness, not even a consciousness of self. . . . By the act described the self is merely endowed with the possibility of self-consciousness and therewith of all other consciousness; but no true consciousness comes into being as yet."[20] And Fichte's account of the process of abstraction there suggests even more strongly that it is to be arrived at by indirect thinking.[21]

Emerging out of these conflicting types of statements, instances of which could easily be multiplied, are three possible positions: (1) the intellectual intuition is a positive item in consciousness manifest to everyone ("I cannot take a step, move hand or foot, without an intellectual intuition of my self-consciousness in these acts"); (2) it is a necessary but *unmanifest* function of consciousness which can only be discovered by discursive means, that is, by reflecting philosophically on experience; (3) it is a combination of positions (1) and (2), that is, a necessary function of consciousness which is always presupposed as a condition of experience (Kant's transcendental apperception) but which *can* become directly manifest through a certain clarification of consciousness—and then necessarily in its true form, as a moment of certain truth. I wish to argue for the third position, but first I must show why Fichte sometimes talks as if he holds the first or the second.

The ingredients for the required explanation are already available. We have seen that Fichte claims to have discovered the intellectual intuition of the self at the basis of all experience, the ground of explanation of experience. Now he notes that the ground of experience must necessarily fall outside experience. "The task of seeking the ground of something contingent means: to exhibit some other thing whose properties reveal why, of all the manifold determinations that the explicandum might have had, it actually has just those that it does. By virtue of its mere notion, the ground falls outside what it grounds."[22] Therefore, the self "occurs as something real in consciousness . . . not as an object of experience . . . but as something that is raised above all experience."[23] As the *source* of experience it shares its substance but not its structure—just as the source of a stream shares its nature as water but does not flow. The intellectual intuition is a kind of consciousness but is not yet a full-fledged, expressed consciousness.

Fichte puts this point more accurately when he says in the *GWL* that self-consciousness does not rise to *empirical consciousness:* "The principle of life and consciousness, the ground of its possibility, is admittedly contained in the self; but this gives rise to no genuine life, no empirical existence in time."[24] If we identify consciousness with the processes that transpire in *experience*, then self-consciousness does not amount to a consciousness. Rather, it is a "mere intuition."[25] But this does not negate its nature as a moment of absolute certainty. On the contrary, certainty is not a feature of experience, of knowledge a posteriori. And we have seen that Fichte argues that *absolute* certainty is not a feature of analytic truth either, which is true only vacuously and not of any existing thing in particular. Thus we are able to explain Fichte's reluctance (when he adopts the spirit of caution) to declare the intellectual intuition an immediate experience. For he, in fact, finds himself in much the same position as Śaṅkara—the intellectual intuition of the self falls in between available categories. It is neither a consciousness nor is it not a consciousness.

On the other hand, Fichte speaks sometimes as if the intellectual intuition is accessible only through reasoning, because he must address those who have not yet awakened themselves—that is, natural dogmatists—as well as idealists. It is no accident that the passages in which the intellectual intuition seems particularly remote from experience and in which Fichte introduces the idea of the intellectual intuition with special rigor as an entity to be postulated are to be found in the *Second Introduction*. For in that work he attempts to go as far as reasoned argument will allow to bring "the enemies of the intellectual intuition" over to his side. There is no guarantee of success in this enterprise, however, a point driven home in other statements of the *Second Introduction:*

> We cannot prove from concepts that this power of intellectual intuition exists, nor evoke from [those who would deny it] what it may be. Everyone must discover it immediately in himself, or he will never make its acquaintance.[26]

And again in the *First Introduction:*

> One could deny the claim that there is immediate self-consciousness involved in a free action of the spirit. We would only have to remind such a person once more of the condition of self-consciousness we have detailed. This self-consciousness does not force itself into being and does not come of its own. One must really act freely and then abstract from objects and concentrate on oneself. No one can be compelled to do this, and even if he pretends to, one can never know if he proceeds correctly and in the requisite way. In a word, this consciousness cannot be demonstrated to anyone; each person must freely create it himself.[27]

Thus we are brought back to the first step of the science of knowledge: the command to enact the intellectual intuition of one's self—to shake off the lethargy that inclines us toward dogmatism and awaken ourselves to a full sense of our inner freedom.

Toward the end of the *Second Introduction*, as a kind of afterthought—perhaps having recognized that the point may have been lost in the technical discussions of previous sections—Fichte returns to state this idea in unmistakable terms. It would seem that those who claim that Fichte thought the intellectual intuition to be an ordinary consciousness evident to everyone simply could not have read very carefully the final sections of the *Second Introduction*. There, for example, we find Fichte considering the skeptical objection that the concept of self-consciousness is self-contradictory. For it is not the concept of a "real being" *(reelles Sein)*—that is, a permanent entity in time and space—and "all thought is directed necessarily toward a being."[28] But Fichte derides his opponent for overgeneralizing about consciousness from his own rather limited perspective. If one has not yet risen to consciousness of the Absolute Ego, then it certainly will be the case that *for him* all his concepts, which can have arisen only from sense perception, will be determined by the categories of real existence in time and space. But that in no way affects the objective validity of the concept of self-consciousness.[29]

Again, most philosophers are caught up in their own individuality. They cannot conceive of anything under the concept of the self save their own identity as persons in contrast to others. For them, if one abstracts from the individual self in order to postulate an Absolute Self, one is left with nothing. But such is precisely what Fichte calls upon us to do: "This self . . . is selfhood in general."[30] Later he will say, "It is not the individual but the one immediate spiritual Life which is the creator of all phenomena, including phenomenal individuals."[31] Fichte responds to the inability to conceive of this notion by pointing out that the distinction of oneself as an individual from other things rests on an original feeling of *selfhood*. For one does not distinguish oneself as a thing among other things but as a *self* or person among other persons, opposed to things. And this concept of self is absolute; we do not get it anywhere but from within. One's identity as an individual person therefore points to a unique quality of our existence which is communicated to us by an inner intuition. Fichte continues:

> But [our critics] stand firm on their inability to frame the concept [of an intellectual intuition], and we must take their word for this. Not that they have been wholly deprived of the concept of the pure self through mere ratiocination, for then they would have had to abstain from objecting to us, just as a block of wood is obliged to.[32] But it is *the concept of this concept* that they lack and cannot rise to. They certainly have it within them, and are merely unaware of possessing it. The ground of this inability of theirs does not reside in any special weakness of intellect, but rather in a weakness of their whole character. . . . In declaring their inability, these latter are, for their own part, perfectly correct; only they should not give out as objective truth what is only valid for themselves.[33]

Again:

> Reason is common to all, and in all rational beings is exactly the same. A capacity inherent in one such being is present in every one. . . . The pure *self*, which our critics profess to find unthinkable, is basic to all their thinking and is present throughout it, in that all thinking comes about only with its aid. So far, everything proceeds mechanically. But insight into the necessity just claimed, the thinking upon this thinking, is not a mechanical affair; it requires an elevation by freedom to an entirely different sphere, into mastery of which we are not thrust immediately by the mere fact of our existence. If this capacity for freedom is not already present and employed, the science of knowledge can make no headway with a person.[34]

If the critic should complain that Fichte ought to be able to present all the premises of his philosophy systematically at the outset in a manner that everyone can understand, he will reply:

> The very reason why these prior notions do not lend themselves to systematic presentation, do not arise of themselves and cannot be made to do so, is, in a word, that they are intimations which we can only generate from within ourselves, thanks to a readiness previously attained. Everything depends upon having become really intimately aware of one's freedom, through constant exercise thereof *with clear consciousness*, so that it has come to be dear to us beyond all else.[35]

Fichte goes on to say that this capacity can be cultivated through a proper system of education, a point to which we shall later return.

Thus most objections raised against the science of knowledge are, in Fichte's opinion, simply expressions of the inability to *see*. And so it should be evident that he insists, as does Śaṅkara, on the active cultivation of a higher state of consciousness as a prerequisite of his philosophy. Indeed, Fichte is more emphatic than Śaṅkara about this. We may presume the explanation of this difference to lie in differences in the social and intellectual contexts in which they philosophized. As I have suggested, Śaṅkara's reticence about this matter can be attributed on the one hand to a need to distance himself from philosophical opponents who sought to reduce wisdom to ritual and, on the other hand, to the widespread familiarity—within his tradition—of the notion of higher states of consciousness. But Fichte propounds this idea in a context in which it seems strange and unsuitable—post-Enlightenment Europe—even though he did not get it from any foreign source. (In contrast to Schelling and Hegel, Fichte shows no evidence of having been acquainted with Oriental philosophy.) Realizing that his contemporaries are not ready to receive it, he must announce it with great emphasis and insist on its importance.

To remove any doubt about this point we turn now to Fichte's striking presentation of the matter in the late *Introductory Lectures to the Science of Knowledge* (1813). Fichte commences the work with a lament. The science of knowledge, he declares, has been understood by hardly anyone over a period of twenty years. To be sure, some have been able to draw certain consequences from its darkly apprehended premises or show a certain cleverness in juggling its principal theses. But there has by no means emerged a "comprehension, possession, and mastery of the *basic principle*."[36] He expresses despair over whether the science of knowledge will ever be understood in its totality. In any case, positive misunderstanding must be done away with, and to this end he feels that the distinct and unambiguous pronouncement of its main point is called for: "*This teaching presupposes a completely new inner organ of perception (Sinnenwerkzeug) by means of which a new world is given which is not at all present for the ordinary person.*"[37] Fichte elaborates:

> This teaching is thoroughly incomprehensible for men as they are by virtue of their birth and their usual education *(Bildung)*. For the objects of which it speaks do not at all exist for them, because they do not have the [perceptual] faculty *(Sinn)* by means of and for which these objects . . . are present. For such men it is just talk about nothing, about what for them is not there. This teaching cannot, therefore, be transmitted to men as they are. They cannot understand it; they must misunderstand it. The

> first condition is therefore that the faculty for which these objects are present should be cultivated. . . .[38]

He compares those who lack this faculty to blind people listening to a discourse on colors. If the blind person admits that he does not have the perceptions to understand what is being said, that is better than his pretending to understand it but only creating an absurd caricature of it in his imagination.

The science of knowledge, Fichte goes on to say, is the unification in thought of what is immanent in experience. Therefore it rests on experience. This point, of course, relates directly to the analysis of the mechanics of transformation I have offered for Śaṅkara's Vedānta. Fichte provides basically the same explanation of his own system. In general, he observes, all theory is the ordering of what is presupposed as known and acknowledged. However, it is immediately known prior to all doctrine only by means of the *faculty* appropriate for it and its immediate perception. His science of knowledge, likewise, is the ordering and unified comprehension *(Erfassung in Einheit)* of something that is given by means of a perceptual faculty—not the usual one, but one which must be developed anew.[39] The first task of the science of knowledge is therefore to awaken this new sense in the student. The science of knowledge thus constitutes not just theory or doctrine but a total recreation of the person: "transformation and regeneration, the expansion of his entire existence from a restricted to a wider circumference."[40]

We have now considered the first component of Fichte's system qua transformative philosophy—the precognitive experiential state which is to be informed by theory and, as we shall see, elevated to supreme knowledge. Before taking up the theoretical doctrines of the science of knowledge themselves and the final vision their comprehension will cause, we must consider a question which naturally arises at this point: Are Fichte's intellectual intuition and Śaṅkara's self-experience the same?

There are some indications that they are. In his philosophy of religion, put forth in *The Way to the Blessed Life* (*Die Anweisung zum seligen Leben*, 1805–1806), Fichte calls what there serves the function of an intellectual intuition "concentration" *(Sammlung)*, a term which resonates with the Sanskrit concept *samādhi*, one of the four essential prerequisites of Vedānta. In the same passage he asserts—very much like Śaṅkara—that the way to salvation (the blessed life) does not consist in acquiring or producing it but simply doing away with its opposite—suffering. Blessedness, which is our eternal possession, will then emerge spontaneously:

> Suffering is the state of being strewn over the manifold and diversity of experience. Hence, the state of becoming blessed is the turning of our love (or interest) away from the manifold toward the One. . . . This dispersion is our actual nature, and in it we are born. For this reason the withdrawal of the mind *(Gemüt)* toward the One, which never comes of its own to the natural mind but must be brought about with effort, appears as a concentration of the mind and an introspection *(Einkehr)* into itself; and as thoughtfulness *(Ernst)* in contrast to the frivolous game which the manifold of life plays with us; and as profundity *(Tiefsinn)* in contrast to the superficiality which, because it has much to apprehend, apprehends nothing securely. This profound thoughtfulness, this rigid collecting of the mind and introspection into itself, is the sole condition under which the blessed life can approach us. Under this condition, however, it approaches us certainly and unerringly.[41]

Perhaps more significant are Fichte's descriptions of the self as the witness of conscious activity (compare Śaṅkara's *sākṣin*):

> At the basis of all consciousness lies the immediate Consciousness [of self]. The latter we have postulated because it never presents itself to consciousness as an object but constitutes the Subjective *(das Subjektive)*, that which is conscious *(das Bewusstseiende)* in all consciousness. . . . All that of which we are conscious is not the immediate Consciousness itself but only occurs within the latter, has it as its ground and is merely the individual subject *(das subjektive)*, the idea. . . . The eye witnesses the *seeing*, that is, the eye is the immediate Consciousness, the *seeing* all other consciousness. Empirical consciousness is no more the immediate Consciousness itself than the *seeing* is the eye itself. [The latter] is the mere inner intellectual intuition or the intuition of the I acting within itself.[42]

Although these parallels are suggestive, they are by no means sufficient to establish an identity. That can be done—if, indeed, the phenomenological identity of two experiences can ever be established—only by means of a much more extensive and detailed analysis than the scope of this work allows. Such an analysis would have to account for certain discrepancies. Fichte's *Sammlung*, for example, is not a total exclusion of intentional consciousness; for, as we have noted, he states that the intellectual intuition does not occur in isolation. But the *samādhi* of the yoga tradition, upon which Śaṅkara presumably draws when he refers to that concept, is a "stilling of the fluctuations of the mind," a state in which the self is left completely alone with itself.[43] We shall content ourselves, therefore, with simply noting that both Fichte and Śaṅkara believe that adequate knowledge of the self is based necessarily on a certain maturing of self-consciousness, without which any talk about the self is empty.

2. *The Transformation Wrought by Knowledge*

It is hoped that the reader now appreciates that what Fichte calls the *Wissenschaftslehre* is by no means a mere collection of postulates and theses. It is rather a program to transform life—a program which is intended to be practiced and which has true significance only insofar as it is realized. Nevertheless, a conceptual structure does play a central role in this program and determines the nature of the transformation to be achieved. We now turn to this theoretical component of the science of knowledge, which has been hitherto erroneously equated with it by almost all students of Fichte.[44]

We have seen that Fichte characterizes his philosophy as idealism. For him this means that our awareness of external reality, or nature, depends *entirely* on our consciousness. Thus Fichte takes idealism beyond Kant's "transcendental idealism," even though he insists on calling it that, too. For Kant was concerned with explaining, not the original existence of objects, but only our ways of knowing them, especially our knowledge a priori. This approach leaves a certain unexplained residue—the What apart from the How—which is to be subsumed under the limiting concept of the thing-in-itself. But Fichte wishes to consider objects of experience as *emerging* out of consciousness in every respect.[45] Things are not first given independently of consciousness and then encountered by the knowing subject. They do not affect the subject of consciousness in a process of perception in which it plays an initially passive role. Rather, things are *originally* posited by the self. The thing-in-itself is an abomination.[46]

We rely again on Fichte's *Introductions* for the most straightforward presentation of this idea. Although the positing of the self by itself, the act of intellectual intuition, is preeminently free and undetermined, Fichte maintains that it nevertheless takes place according to certain rules, that it is *determinate*, and that its determinacy is grounded in the very nature of the self. "The [absolute] intellect acts, but owing to its nature it can only act in a certain fashion."[47] In bringing itself into being through the act of self-awareness, the self commits itself necessarily to a certain unfolding of consciousness, and that means a certain division and opposition within consciousness. This structured consciousness is contained as a seed within self-consciousness and is also its immediate consequence. Fichte refers to it somewhat misleadingly as its "condition."

> Idealism proceeds in the following way. It shows that what is first set up as a fundamental principle and directly demonstrated in consciousness [that is, the Absolute Self] is not possible unless at the same time something else occurs, and this other is not possible unless at the same time a third occurs until the conditions of what was first exhibited are completely exhausted. . . . If the presupposition of idealism is correct and one has correctly proceeded in the deduction, then the system of all necessary representations or the totality of experience must emerge as the last result, the essence of all the conditions of what was first asserted.[48]

By calling the structured impulses of consciousness the conditions of self-consciousness Fichte does not jeopardize the unconditioned, absolute status of the latter. For the Absolute Self freely generates these limitations of itself in completing its own self-manifestation. Absolute self-consciousness evolves naturally by becoming fragmented and entering into an interplay with itself.

It would not be appropriate for us to attempt to chart all the twists and turns of this process here. That has been the principal concern of other commentators on Fichte, to whom the reader is referred.[49] We shall restrict ourselves to considering only the first stage.

We have noted that Fichte does not regard the act of self-consciousness as a true consciousness. In its original condition of self-positing the I is completely uniform and whole. There is no difference between that which posits and that which is posited. Thus it is inadequate as a consciousness in the usual sense which, as we saw in the previous chapter, necessarily involves two poles. In the *GWL* Fichte makes this point by attempting to picture the act of self-consciousness as a tension between two forces. One force, a centrifugal force directed outward, establishes the self as a "real quantum," a positive entity. Another force, a centripetal force directed inward, represents the reflective, self-intuiting activity of the self. But for the Absolute I both directions, centrifugal and centripetal, must "fall together and comprise one and the same direction."[50] In other words, as a conscious relation the Absolute I is inconceivable.

It is because of this inadequacy, this inability to constitute a "real," expressed consciousness all by itself, Fichte maintains, that the self is forced to evolve beyond its absolute state and posit a world of individual subjects and objects of experience so that consciousness, in the true sense of that word, can arise.

> The Absolute I is completely identical with itself; everything in it is one and the same I and belongs . . . to one and the same I. There is nothing there to differentiate, no manifold. The I is Everything and Nothing, because it is nothing *for itself*, because it cannot distinguish in itself a positing and posited. It *strives*, . . . by virtue of its essence, to assert itself in this condition. There arises in it an inequality and therefore something foreign to it.[51]

Fichte refers to this foreign principle as the Not-I. He emphasizes that when the Not-I gets posited, it is the I that posits it. The Not-I is not an independent reality that presents itself to the I. Rather, the I divides up its own domain, as it were, and designates a portion of it as the Not-I. In positing the nonself, however, it reduces itself to a limited intelligence and is no longer able to comprehend its initial causality. At first the I was everything—infinite—because nothing besides itself was present to consciousness, that is, to itself. Now the Not-I infringes on it.[52]

The process of self-revelation of consciousness continues by means of the further specification of the opposition between the self and the other. Consciousness requires not just an indeterminate nonego but definite and distinct objects. Therefore the self creates a sphere in which objects delimit one another—space—and another realm in which mental representations, that is, the passive determinations of the self which are now regarded as being caused by things outside itself, can be ordered—time. In this capacity it is known in Kantian philosophy as the productive imagination. Since also according to

Kant's critical philosophy a manifold of representations does not constitute an object unless it is brought under a concept, the categories of experience are called into being and so on. Each of these steps is necessitated by the fundamental urge of the self to display itself and contemplate itself directly as a thing standing opposite itself. They are the inevitable outcome of the give and take between the two basic passive and assertive sides of the I. Although they are presented as succeeding each other by a kind of logic, they are not blindly inferred from the nature of the Absolute I as the first principle of all experience. Rather, Fichte suggests that the transcendental philosopher simply *observes* this process within himself, having cognized the intellectual intuition.

> System makers . . . proceed from some concept or other. Without caring in the least where they got it from or whence they have concocted it, they analyze it, combine it with others to whose origin they are equally indifferent, and in reasonings such as these their philosophy itself is composed. It consists in consequence of their own thoughts. The science of knowledge is a very different matter. Its chosen topic of consideration is not a lifeless concept, passively exposed to its inquiry merely, of which it makes something only by its own thought, but a living and active thing which engenders insights from and through itself, and which the philosopher merely contemplates. His role in the affair goes no further than to translate this living force into purposeful activity, to observe the activity in question, to apprehend it and grasp it as a unity. He conducts an experiment.[53]

But the transcendental philosopher—the true idealist—must be able to present a certificate vouching for his firm apprehension of the process in question. He must be able to demonstrate it by showing how it takes place according to fixed laws which express the very essence of absolute self-consciousness.[54]

While this is the basic account of the science of knowledge one finds in the *GWL* and the *First* and *Second Introductions*, in later works Fichte identifies the creative activity which grounds consciousness as the moral will.[55] Here the moral will is not the consciousness of an individual moral agent; it is an infinite, universal Will. It is in order to have a field in which to exercise its mandate—the categorical imperative—that the universal Will reduces itself to the status of an individual agent by projecting a world of external objects and other persons separate from itself. In doing so it proceeds by the same laws which were found to bind the Absolute Self in the process of self-expression. Indeed, for Fichte the universal Will is simply the Absolute Self by another name. By identifying the Absolute Self with Will he achieves an economy in his philosophy which eluded Kant; for he is able to refer all aspects of experience, theoretical as well as practical, to one source.

Our primary concern with Fichte's theory of the self-manifestation of the absolute, however, is the profound change in life which results from fully comprehending it. The most vivid descriptions of this process are to be found in two works which Fichte presents as popularizations of his system: *The Vocation of Man* (1800) and *The Way to the Blessed Life* (1806). It is not to be wondered at that the matter is not discussed explicitly in his more rigorous "scientific" works. For, as will be seen, they are the instruments which are to effect the transformation in question and do not therefore address it as a *topic*.

In *The Way to the Blessed Life* Fichte presents his science of knowledge to the philosophically untrained reader as a "Doctrine of Religion." Thus the goal of philosophy becomes "the truly religious life," which is conceived as the perfect harmony of human consciousness with the universal, divine Will. This achievement entails relinquishing the idea of self-determinedness *(Selbständigkeit)*—emptying one's individuality into the "eternal outpouring of divine life" which is the deepest root of existence.[56] Although this act is a sort of self-denial, it constitutes the highest freedom. For the mode of being of the Absolute itself is absolute flexibility. It lifts itself above the inert solidity of absolute Being and in human consciousness pictures itself in an infinity of ways.[57]

Such perfect harmony with the divine Will is not achieved at once, however, but in stages. In the fifth lecture Fichte outlines five of them.[58] The first stage is the standpoint of common sense which regards what the senses show us as preeminently real. All else—freedom, consciousness—has only a secondary, derived reality. We recognize this stage as the dogmatism of the *Introductions*. It is merely the point of departure for spiritual evolution; it does not itself count as a stage of progress. Fichte says that the philosopher should simply ignore those who insist on this perspective.

The second stage is morality. Morality sees the ultimate truth in the categorical imperative. That which is most real is a *law* which orders the relations of free moral subjects—not material things. Fichte identifies this standpoint as that of Kant.

The third stage of spiritual evolution is a naive, subconscious identification with the divine Will as a principle of cosmic evolution. One innocently, spontaneously, takes up its universal purpose as one's own. Fichte refers to this attitude as a "higher morality," contrasting it to the strict observance of the categorical imperative as the mere avoidance of what is wrong. A higher righteousness is the will positively to *reform* the world to what is right and true. It does not consist simply in reacting ethically to situations at hand; it desires to change humanity into what it is ultimately meant to be—the image of the "inner divine essence." One who has reached this stage sees beyond the merely formal law of morality to the Real, the Holy, the Good, the True, and seeks to actualize it on earth. But it is *insight* into the actual nature of this ideal which brings about true religiousness, the fourth stage:

> [Religion] is the clear cognition that the Holy, the Good, the Beautiful is by no means our illusion or the illusory appearance of an essentially nonexistent spirit, light, or thought; but that it is the immediate appearance of the inner essence of God in us . . . His expression and His image, completely and simply and without any reduction. . . .[59]

Philosophical knowledge confers, beyond this preliminary insight, a more profound and precise level of understanding which leads to an even higher level of realization. This knowledge understands, in neutral and objective terms, *how* the reflections of the Absolute arise out of its own Being. This is the fifth stage.

> Knowledge [or science: *Wissenschaft*] goes beyond the insight that absolutely everything manifold is grounded in the One and refers back to it, which religion already reveals, to the insight into the How of this relationship. What is for religion only an absolute fact arises for it genetically. Religion without knowledge is somehow naked, nevertheless unshakable faith. Knowledge supersedes all faith and transforms it into vision.[60]

Fichte provides an extraordinary description of this vision in *The Vocation of Man*. In that work, written as a sort of spiritual diary, he first attempts to work out a metaphysics based on pantheism—à la Spinoza—and then on skeptical idealism, according to which the objective existence of the self as well as external things is called into question. Having pointed out the shortcomings of these systems, he expounds the doctrine of the universal Will as the only true philosophy. At the conclusion of his exposition he declares, through the seeker who delivers the discourse, that when one understands it, an entirely new existence begins. The passage deserves to be quoted at some length:

> I raise myself up to this standpoint [of the universal Will] and I am a new being. My whole relation to the present world is changed. The ties by which my mind was previously bound to this world and by whose mysterious pull it followed all the turmoil in it are forever severed, and I stand free, calm and unmoved, a world unto myself. No longer by means of the heart but only by means of the eye do I apprehend objects and relate to them; and this eye too becomes transfigured in this state of Freedom and looks through error and deformity to the True and the Beautiful [which reveal themselves] as shapes reflect themselves purely, in a soft light, upon a motionless surface of water.[61]

This vision brings peace and contentment. The mind is forever closed to confusion, uncertainty, and fear, the heart to sadness and desire. And it reaches a climax in a tangible feeling of the unity of all life:

> After my heart is closed to desire for the worldly, after I truly have no interest in the ephemeral, the universe appears to my eye in a transfigured form. The dead, burdensome mass which merely stuffed up space has disappeared and in its place flows and surges and rushes the eternal stream of the Life and the Power and the Deed—of the original Life—of Thy Life, O Endless One! For all life is Thy Life, and only the religious eye penetrates the realm of true Beauty.
>
> I am kindred to You, and what I see around me is kindred to me. All is enlivened and ensouled and regards me with shining spirit eyes and addresses my heart with spirit tones. I see myself again in all the shapes outside me, divided and portioned in the most manifold ways, and I radiate outside myself toward them, as the rising sun, broken into a thousand dewdrops, gleams back at itself.[62]

Fichte continues in this mood for several more pages, employing such vivid images that one can hardly doubt that he is reporting an actual experience. The divine Life "streams as a self-creating and self-forming matter throughout my veins and muscles and deposits its fullness in tree, plant, and blade of grass . . . unthinkable and incomprehensible but nevertheless plainly there for the spiritual eye to see."[63] It is a "stream of light" which weaves all things together. "There is no man but only Humanity, no individual thinking and loving and hating but only *one* Thinking and Loving and Hating—in and through each other."[64] Indeed, it is suggested, as in *The Way to the Blessed Life*, that this divine Will is the *substance* of Love.[65]

Those familiar with the literature of mysticism will be aware of the striking parallels between Fichte's account and the statements of certain mystics. A few brief quotes will suffice to bring out the coincidence. First Meister Eckhart:

> When the soul comes into the light of reasonableness it knows no contrasts. Say, Lord, when is a man in mere "understanding?" I say to you: "When a man sees one thing separated from another." And when is a man above mere understanding? That I can tell you: "When he sees all in all. . . ."[66]

With remarkable closeness to Fichte's language he says elsewhere:

> All that a man sees here externally in multiplicity is intrinsically One. Here all blades of grass, wood and stone, all things are One.[67]

Fichte's metaphor of the sun gleaming back at itself in a thousand dewdrops echoes the ubiquitous reflection imagery of Oriental mysticism. In his autobiography the modern guru Swami Muktananda quotes a Śaivite saint:

> This universe is a mansion containing the mirror of Shiva. Whoever looks in it, feeling one with Shiva, sees His own images and reflection, sees Shiva everywhere.[68]

Another Indian mystic, Ramakrishna, saw, as did Fichte, everything filled with life:

> The Divine Mother revealed to me that . . . it was she who had become everything . . . that everything was full of consciousness. The [temple] image was consciousness, the altar was consciousness . . . the door sills were consciousness. . . . I found everything in the room soaked as it were in bliss—the bliss of God.[69]

Whether Fichte should be classed a mystic rather than a philosopher in light of these parallels seems a moot issue, however.[70] Or if it is not merely a semantic quibble—if, that is, a real question of evaluation is involved and the application of the term "mystic" implies condemnation—then the issue is better dealt with in the context of a systematic discussion of the validity of transformative philosophy. And that we shall take up in the next chapter.

In any case, it should be clear that for Fichte as for Śaṅkara philosophy culminates in intuition and a complete and dramatic uplifting of life. This I consider the crux of transformative philosophy. Knowledge, when applied to the intellectual intuition, crystallizes in a direct experience:

> [The science of knowledge] must refer back to life again and again and cannot replace it with itself or vicariously represent it. What, then, does [the science of knowledge] do? It makes life clear and teaches one to distinguish the true from the apparent, the real from the form. Without it something remains quite hidden: the origin and root of existence. . . . But one who goes through life with his eye cultivated by the science of knowledge, for him this origin is clear always and everywhere.[71]

But, again, there is a difference between Śaṅkara and Fichte—this time, the reverse of the difference we noticed earlier. Śaṅkara often stresses the importance of philosophical knowledge as the crucial means of transformation whereas Fichte only infrequently—and casually—mentions it as such. But, as before, we find the explanation in their situations. In Fichte's day, amid the atmosphere of great expectation and enthusiasm for the prospects of philosophy brought about by Kant, it was taken for granted that human fulfillment would be achieved through philosophical thinking. But we have seen that this was not the case for Śaṅkara's milieu.[72]

3. *Fichte's Educational Program*

To complete this exposition of Fichte's philosophy as a transformative program it remains to be shown what specific practical measures he envisioned for cultivating the intellectual intuition—the faculty which enables one to comprehend and derive full benefit from the science of knowledge. We have seen that Śaṅkara, with certain qualifications, recommends a system of spiritual and moral discipline, or yoga, to supplement his philosophy. Is there anything analogous to that approach in Fichte's philosophy? Indeed, the system of education that Fichte outlines in the *Addresses to the German Nation* (*Reden an die deutsche Nation*, 1807–1808) would seem to serve that purpose.

In the second lecture of that series Fichte talks about the goal of education—once again, primarily in ethical terms—as the creation of a will in the student to do good that is so complete that an evil deed is utterly impossible. Fichte argues that the established manner of education of his day is, at best, able to provide only guidelines for distinguishing right from wrong but is unable to mold the will into one that will *always* do right—that is, compel one always to choose the former over the latter. The very fact that it depends so on the concept of duty, on admonishments and incentives, reveals that it has failed in its main purpose: to build a permanent disposition in students to pursue good automatically. "All education strives to bring about a particular stable and enduring state of being which no longer becomes but is, and cannot be other than the way it is. If it did not aim at such a state of being, then it would not be education but some kind of purposeless game. . . ."[73] Now, Fichte notes that the human being does naturally what he loves. The goal of the new education is, therefore, simply to instill in the student the positive love of what is good:

> Love for the good purely as such and not, perhaps, because of its usefulness to us, has . . . the form of delight in it—the type of inner delight such as one is moved to reveal in one's life. This inner delight, then, should be what the new education must produce as the stable and unalterable state of being of its pupil, whereupon this delight would, by means of itself, establish as necessary the pupil's unalterable will to do good.[74]

Pleasure in bringing about a certain state of affairs that is not actually but only ideally available presupposes the capacity to envision it; thus the new education, while engendering a positive love for doing good, enlivens the capacity to structure freely, spontaneously, images of what ought to be. Fichte emphasizes that this capacity is to be spontaneous—creative. If the student does not actively participate in framing his ideals, his heart is not drawn into the matter, his love is not aroused. The course of the education is thus to awaken the faculty that naturally gives rise to right thoughts, upon which right action directly follows. In Kantian terms, this is to make human interest conform perfectly with the categorical imperative, in which case the categorical imperative as an imperative loses its meaning—a circumstance which Kant himself considered impossible.

The goal of education for Fichte is indeed very close to what he characterizes elsewhere as "higher morality." It is simply the free and unhampered unfolding of natural intelligence, which is rooted in deeper levels of divine Being. Fichte argues that the growth of this intelligence is itself a pleasurable experience; it is therefore invariably associated with love of its object.[75] The mind naturally desires to break away from the shackles of sensibility, to speculate, to incorporate the values of unboundedness and order. It has only *not* to be prevented from doing so. Although Fichte conceives his educational program as *Nationalerziehung*, a system for developing the unique spirit of the German *Volk* and providing good citizens as the foundation of the state, it clearly relates to the *Wissenschaftslehre*; for the quality that sets Germans apart from members of other cultures is, for Fichte, the ability to integrate life with thought, to realize the life that is in the highest sense religious and philosophical. "Cultivation in true religion is thus the last enterprise of the new education."[76]

> Until now the world of sense was generally considered the perfectly actual, true, and really subsisting world; it was the first thing that was introduced to the pupil. He was led on to thinking only from it, and mostly to a thinking about it and subservient to it. The new education [or upbringing: *Erziehung*] reverses this order: as far as it is concerned, only the world which is grasped through thinking is the true and really subsisting world. It wants to introduce its pupil to this as soon as it begins with him. It wants to tie his entire love and his entire delight to this world, so that for him a life solely in this world of the spirit necessarily arises. . . . Until now in most people only the flesh, matter, nature were alive. By means of the new education only the spirit, the firm and certain spirit, should be alive in most, indeed, in everyone. . . .[77]

Fichte offers few details about the actual content of this education. He refers in general to the work of the Swiss philosopher Johann Heinrich Pestalozzi (1746–1827), who, he believes, recognized the same goals and had already worked out an effective program of instruction to achieve them. A few main points are mentioned, however. The student is from earliest childhood to be trained in certain exercises of "intuition and sensation" which, in Fichte's paraphrase, stimulate the free production of images and enliven the independent activity of the spirit.[78] He describes "the ABC of the sensations" thus:

> Just as the child begins to apprehend speech tones and make them crudely himself, he must be taught to make completely clear to himself:

> whether he is hungry or sleepy, whether he sees the sensation which is present to him and designated by this or that expression, or whether he hears it, and so forth, or whether he simply imagines something; how the various impressions of the same sense, designated by specific words, are different—such as the colors, the sounds of different objects—and in what degree. He should do all this in the right sequence, so as to develop steadily the faculty of sensation itself. By this means the child obtains for the first time an I which he sets apart in a free and reflective concept and is imbued with it. And immediately upon his awakening into life a spiritual eye is embedded in life which will certainly never leave it from now on.[79]

The point of such practices seems to be always this: Simply activate the intelligence and it will develop properly on its own if it is not artificially bound or hampered. Thus even when it later comes to learning objective relationships of time, number, and mass, the facts are secondary to the manner in which they are to be apprehended:

> Freely pursuing his imagination, the pupil attempts to enclose an area with straight lines—that is the mental activity of the pupil that is stimulated first [in the process of learning]. When he discovers in this attempt that he cannot enclose a space with fewer than three straight lines—that is the subsidiary cognition of a second, completely different activity of the faculty of knowledge, which restricts the originally stimulated free faculty [of imagination]. Accordingly, with this education a knowledge arises at the start which is truly elevated above all experience, supersensory, strictly necessary, and which includes within it all possible subsequent experience.[80]

Memorizing is discouraged as contrary to the creative instinct; a mere passive affection of the mind, it is not simultaneously exhilarating. Even reading and writing can distract one from the direct intuition of things, they can transform the clear consciousness—which knows it knows something when it grasps it on the spot—into one that depends on writing things down.[81] Reading and writing should not be introduced too early. In general, Fichte's method of education consists of exercises involving facts and skills to be learned not for their own sake but to stimulate the *Grundprinzip* of consciousness; it should ultimately lead the student away from the world of sense perception and desire:

> To come back to the pupil of the new education: it is evident that, driven by his love [of the spirit], he will learn much and—because he grasps everything in its context and practices what is grasped immediately in action—will learn it correctly and retain it. But this is only of secondary importance. More important is that his self is uplifted and, self-consciously and systematically, introduced to a whole new order of things in which until now only a few happened to arrive by chance, through God's grace. A love moves him which is by no means directed toward some sensual pleasure . . . but toward the activity of the spirit for its own sake, and toward the law of the spirit for its own sake.[82]

Thus we find that Fichte's philosophical system contains all the elements we identified in our study of Śaṅkara as constituents of transformative philosophy: (1) experience—a higher level of consciousness which is a precondition for the intelligibility of the system; (2) praxis—a method for cultivating this higher consciousness; (3) knowledge—a body of doctrine which constitutes the main topic of the system and articulates the experiential component; and finally (4) transformation—a dramatic and thorough rebirth resulting from this insight. I maintain that this is a general type of philosophy of which Śaṅkara and Fichte are complete examples. All the components of transformative philosophy are present in their systems. Other thinkers to be classed as transformative philosophers may exhibit only some of these traits.

The point of setting up a category in this way is not, of course, to provide a principle of philosophical taxonomy. It is rather to provide a principle of interpretation. I believe that other important figures in the history of philosophy will gain clarity if the notion of transformative philosophy is applied to them—that is, if we see them each attempting to articulate not just a system of ideas but a vision. I can only suggest the possibility of such an extended use of this idea in the present context. In the next section I shall show how transformative philosophy hangs together with the notion of necessary truth that is central to Western philosophical thought; then, in the next chapter, we shall consider a particular case—Heidegger—who stands firmly in the mainstream of philosophical tradition. I hope that these few observations will be sufficiently valid and provocative to justify further attempts along these lines.

One thing must be kept clearly in mind if transformative philosophy is to serve at all as an interpretive framework—namely, the term "transformative" is meant to characterize a certain relation between the statements of a philosophical system and experience. It has nothing essential to do with the specific content of those statements. To class together two philosophical systems as transformative philosophies is in no way to equate them as world views. Transformative philosophy is not the concept of a *philosophia perennis*, in other words, although some transformative philosophies may in fact turn out to be doctrinally very close.

The absence of a perfect ideological unity among transformative philosophies can be seen quite plainly from a comparison of the theoretical components of Advaita Vedānta and the *Wissenschaftslehre*. As has been noted, the doctrines of Śaṅkara and Fichte have been declared similar in the past, but nothing like an absolute identity can be established. Indeed, the differences are as remarkable as the parallels. To be sure, both Fichte and Śaṅkara consider the absolute to be in essence the self. Both call it Being and, in one way or another, bliss or blessedness. It is, according to each, a consciousness, and both held the unusual theory that the phenomena to which this absolute gives rise are mere illusion and have no independent reality apart from it. On the other hand, Fichte thinks of his absolute primarily in ethical terms—as the Good, the divine Will—whereas Śaṅkara's philosophy is notably without an ethics. (Ethics is preempted by the doctrine of salvation in Śaṅkara's system.) Fichte is a staunch idealist; all phenomena for him are to be viewed as stages of the self-representation of consciousness. But Śaṅkara is to be found defending the existence of an external world, and he develops a sort of natural philosophy, a cosmology. Further, Śaṅkara's Brahman is especially silent, inactive and unchanging, while Fichte describes his first principle as pure activity. Still other discrepancies could be listed.

It is not, then, an identity of their views of reality which justifies classifying these two thinkers as of one type but the fact that their views are meant to be incorporated into life in a unique way. Each philosopher propounds a philosophy which demands a commitment and must in some way be *lived*, and the statements of their systems are themselves instrumental in effecting this conversion from reflection to life. I suspect that the logical status of such systems, defined by the unique causal relation they have to their objects, that is, the visions of reality they formulate, is as much at the basis of the notion of a *philo-*

sophia perennis—and hence much of the current discussion of mysticism and philosophy—as any doctrine.[83] To conclude this study of Śaṅkara and Fichte we turn now to this relationship.

4. *The "Logic" of Transformative Philosophy*

In his book *Individuals* P. F. Strawson makes a distinction between "descriptive metaphysics" and "revisionary metaphysics." "Descriptive metaphysics," he says, "is content to describe the actual structure of our thought about the world; revisionary metaphysics is concerned to provide a better structure."[84] Descriptive metaphysics accepts things as they are. It operates on the belief that the proper way of thinking about things is already inherent in ordinary language or in the standards of science and merely seeks to expose it. It may proceed by a critical analysis of the human faculties of consciousness, or it may rely on the analysis of the patterns or "grammar" of ordinary discourse. The conclusions of descriptive metaphysics emerge not as statements about the world but as general observations about what has to be true about the conceptual apparatus of the knower if scientific knowledge is to take place or else as dispositions to resist statements that lead into "revisionary" metaphysical channels. Revisionary metaphysics, on the other hand, tells us that since our usual concepts are inadequate to grasp the essence of reality, we must create new concepts. It is directed toward the unknown and the unseen, toward underlying structures that account for surface appearances.

Descriptive metaphysics usually contains, implicitly or explicitly, a critique of revisionary metaphysics. The descriptive metaphysician generally believes that the revisionist has overstepped his bounds in attempting to apprehend things through the employment of reason beyond its proper scope, or else, in replacing ordinary concepts with novel ones, that he has disturbed the order and integrity of language and created artificial, unnecessary, and characteristically irresolvable puzzles. There is no question that Strawson, in choosing descriptive metaphysics (*Individuals* is subtitled "An Essay in Descriptive Metaphysics"), believes that he is following the safer course.

It is, I hope, clear that the metaphysics of transformative philosophy falls into neither of the categories "descriptive" or "revisionary" as Strawson defines them—even though it has features of each. Transformative metaphysics is not descriptive because it does not rest content with the categories of ordinary experience; the mode of experiencing that concerns it does not correspond to them. On the other hand it is not revisionary in Strawson's sense because it does not call for conceptual change that is not immediately justified by the present situation, in which the experience in question is already at hand. Even when it evokes an experience it only makes concrete an experience that is in a sense already there. Transformative philosophy, as we have seen, presupposes practical techniques for developing consciousness or more holistic modes of perception. It is clear, then, that it does not immediately succumb to the type of criticism usually leveled at revisionary philosophy—namely, that it extends thought precariously beyond verification. Indeed, I have tried to show that the conceptual aspect of transformative philosophy performs the function of merely bringing to notice objects already made available to perception—though, of course, in an extended meaning of that word.

Let us consider further the unique logical or grammatical status of the assertions of transformative philosophy. They cannot be *descriptions*—at least from the point of view of those for whom they are made—because there is not initially a conscious grasp of the reality they treat, on the basis of which they could be judged accurate or inaccurate. Only if circumstances are right does the object of those statements present itself at all—and then, of course, only as being in agreement with them. Since the possibility of a misdescription is precluded here, the notion of a description cannot apply.

On the other hand, the main theses of a transformative philosophy are not *prescriptions*. As Śaṅkara intends them, at least, they do not represent the world as it should be or as one hopes it to be. They do not attempt to depict the world wishfully, as something it actually is not. Rather, they represent matters of fact.[85] It might have been correct to say that they are descriptions from the point of view of the philosopher who makes them if they involved any elaboration of the states of affairs they depict. But they do not. Thus for lack of a better term we can, following Śaṅkara, call them *definitions*, in the sense of a definition that originally delineates an object. They are definitions for the one for whom they are intended, because he does not know their object to exist until it is defined for him. And they are properly definitions, not descriptions, for the one who propounds them, because they merely indicate an object (as Śaṅkara himself says) without providing any detail beyond what is necessary for it to be identified. After identification has been made and several interlocutors share in the recognition of an object, description is possible.

As I have suggested, the language of transformative philosophy defines objects much in the same way that the language of parents spoken to their children introduces new things. In teaching a child to use words an apple is held up; the parent calls it "apple"; he points at the stem and says "stem"; he holds it next to a tomato and says "red"; placing it together with peaches and bananas he calls out "fruit." The game of ostensive defining thus delimits an object so that it necessarily matches how it is characterized.[86] That is, indeed, the function of defining. The one who defines, moreover, is primarily engaged in *naming* rather than portraying, in establishing an original connection between words and things rather than relying on established connections. It is observed often enough in contemporary philosophy that in these circumstances the teacher is giving the learner a rudimentary framework for dealing with reality for the first time; he is structuring "logical space" for him. But it is important to keep in mind that no alternative framework is being offered. Thus the utterances of the language teacher can have no margin of error. There is a kind of perfection about this knowledge. The apple is "apple" for the learner because it has been so named; and the teacher in naming it merely reiterates what he himself once received in the capacity of a language learner.

Transformative philosophy, then, shows us new things with language. It would not be wrong to say that the transformative philosopher teaches us language for areas of experience that our parents neglected to teach us about when we were young. Although a version of this statement is sometimes crudely made with reference to learning the facts of sexual behavior and may therefore appear ludicrous, the parallel between transformative philosophy and the emergence of sexual awareness is quite significant. Expressions and jokes about sex acquire meaning with the growth of certain feelings and impulses. Likewise, transformative philosophy corresponds to the growth of a precognitive or subconscious impulse, a spontaneous tendency of correct thought and action for which the word "reason" has sometimes been used, as it was, for example, by Fichte. The transformative philosopher appropriates this area of experience and charts it for us so that we can live more consciously in accordance with it.[87] And his directions and assertions have the force of self-evident truth.

The language which the transformative philosopher uses may be a language he devises himself, or it may be handed down to him through a tradition. This is one of several ways in which transformative philosophers may differ. Śaṅkara, obviously, has recourse to a language that is already finished. The Veda, of which the Upaniṣads form a part, is in his view eternal and nonhuman in origin, and he sees himself as merely interpreting Vedic statements in the only consistent manner.[88] For Śaṅkara an established way of thinking about the self as pure consciousness is already available as a portion of language that is unknown or unused—a secret language inaccessible to the uninitiate. One gains access to it and the right to use it by satisfying certain criteria. Fichte, although he borrows much of his language from Kant, is clearly engaged in inventing to some extent his own language for originally conceived realities. This, I believe, accounts for some of the confusion and inconsistency to be found in his early philosophy. There he is still searching for an adequate mode of expressing his insight. Śaṅkara, on the other hand, more or less keeps to the same style and terminology throughout his development.

The source of the transformative philosopher's concepts, whether it is institutionalized or not, determines to a great extent the intention with which he employs them. The philosopher thinking within an established tradition is primarily engaged in transmitting knowledge from one generation to the next. One who thinks outside a tradition, on the other hand, can also be seen to be transmitting or communicating a truth, to be sure, but he is in addition concerned with securing that truth for himself. The unorthodox transformative philosopher is conceptualizing experience for himself *and* his students; in talking about it he is getting a firm grip on it himself.

Regardless of the source of the transformative philosopher's language, his employment of it cannot be labeled speculative. This is, perhaps, the most important point to be made about transformative philosophy with regard to its significance relative to other types of philosophizing. In the present context it seems appropriate to put the matter in Kantian terms: transformative philosophy does not involve an (illegitimate) transcendent use of concepts of the understanding; nor does it even involve their (legitimate) regulative use. Rather, it introduces new concepts of understanding for immanent or empirical use. The transformative philosopher does not endeavor to apprehend through mere reasoning objects that lie beyond the field of possible experience; he activates regions of experience hitherto unappreciated by supplying concepts pertaining to them.

That transformative philosophers are not engaged in speculation is evident from the attitudes they have toward the independent use of rational argument. (If we were to develop a typology of transformative philosophy, this might be a criterion for identifying a transformative philosopher.) For Śaṅkara, the employment of reason is admissible only in support of scripture, "as an aid to intuition."[89] Otherwise, the self is to be known through holy tradition; thus he quotes *Kaṭha Upaniṣad* I.2.9: "This wisdom is not to be attained by logic, but when it is spoken by another person [who knows], it is easy to know, my dear. . . ."[90] Śaṅkara is less confident in the ability of humans to secure absolute knowledge through their own efforts—he notes the seemingly endless disputes of dialecticians[91]—than in the power of tradition to confer it definitely and finally. Nevertheless, other transformative philosophers (among them Fichte) may rely on reason as a means for expressing truths. But that is not to say that they rely on reason for *discovering* them. The arguments of certain thinkers in the history of Western philosophy give the impression of being, not attempts to get at the unseen by use of an instrument mistaken to be more powerful than perception, but attempts at formulating what is seen but somehow more dynamic than can be expressed in simple categorical terms.[92]

The claims of transformative philosophy, then, are not made on behalf of the possibilities of reason but on behalf of the possibilities of experience and consciousness. The transformative philosopher tells us, in effect, not simply that experience potentially extends beyond what is known in daily life but that there are other *modes* of experience.[93] In this way the transformative philosopher differs from the scientist who discovers new phenomena but still approaches them from the point of view of sensory consciousness. Although I have concentrated on a unique possibility for *self*-experience—that the subject-object dichotomy can be transcended—there are other extraordinary possibilities that philosophers seem to have entertained. Thus some philosophers have considered value to be an *intrinsic* component of things: that the essence of certain entities is best expressed in terms of modality (necessity is *de re*), or, for that matter, that things have essences.[94] I propose that such ideas be placed hypothetically in a transformative context and be seen as relating to modes of observation rather than dialectical reasoning (in the Kantian sense) or dogmatism.

No doubt modern philosophers will strongly resist the suggestion that there are extraordinary modes of experience or consciousness. I have carefully tried to avoid this assumption in my explanation of Śaṅkara's and Fichte's theories of the self. To see that each theory is intelligible we do not have to accept this claim; we need only see that Śaṅkara or Fichte accepts it. Nevertheless, it should be made clear that, from a given perspective, there are no *formal* reasons for judging other modes of experience or consciousness impossible. That means, there are no formal reasons for judging that consciousness must be intentional, potentially directed toward various kinds of objects, and continually changing—in a word, sensory. That is our *habitual* mode of consciousness. But surely it is wrong to make claims about what must be the case on the basis of what is ordinarily or habitually the case. That consciousness is dual—that the objects of consciousness or experience are of a particular sort (namely, sensory)—is obviously not something we know a priori. The testimony of the transformative philosopher that there are other modes of consciousness cannot, therefore, be dismissed out of hand. Whether such testimony itself constitutes sufficient evidence for such modes is of course an entirely different matter.

To summarize from a slightly different point of view what has been said here regarding the general nature of transformative philosophy: A transformative philosophy does not represent a view of reality but a view which *transforms* reality. If it is revisionary, then it is so in that it revises not just our thinking but our perceiving as well. A transformative philosophy does not amount to a *Weltanschauung* that one can casually entertain as a matter of experiment or amusement, as one tries on a hat. Nor is it meant for our cultural edification. But it really alters what we perceive as facts—concrete states of affairs. As descriptive statements, the theses of transformative philosophy are self-verifying. To state this is not to explain how it is possible—only preliminary suggestions have been offered here—but simply to interpret transformative philosophy as it demands to be interpreted. Indeed, the logic of transformative philosophy raises major philosophical issues—relativism and transcendental idealism not the least among them. Although we may not yet be prepared to come to grips with these issues, it is at least necessary to recognize them and see that the holistic interpretations of certain figures in the history of philosophy forces them upon us.

4

Ramifications of Transformative Philosophy

In his *Second Introduction to the Science of Knowledge* Fichte makes the rather incredible assertion that the science of knowledge "is perfectly in accordance with the teaching of Kant and is nothing other than Kantianism properly understood."[1] Given the exposition of Fichte's philosophy in the previous chapter, I am sure that most will agree that this statement simply cannot be true.[2] But it seems that Fichte himself does not wish to stake too much on this assertion. He declares that he makes it only to reject credit for someone else's discovery, not to compel the reader to accept the science of knowledge by appealing to another authority.[3] In fact, it would seem that the real reason for his claiming the science of knowledge to be just Kant's critical philosophy in another guise is to suggest that it is, if not in harmony with, at least *relevant* to the established philosophy of the day. Therefore, it cannot be cast aside as simply the maunderings of a mystic; it must be reckoned with. It must be seen in relation to tradition.

This issue will occupy us in the present chapter in a more general way. How is the phenomenon of transformative philosophy to be located within Western philosophy? Is it, for example, a mere aberration that crops up from time to time—a mutation, so to speak, which is usually selected out because it does not embody responses to real philosophical concerns? Or is it, perhaps, in fact a general trait, albeit a hidden one, which has dominated the development of philosophy but has hitherto seemed unimportant because we had yet to identify its function?

To answer such questions requires, obviously, a view of the development of the entire Western philosophical tradition. I do not presume to offer any such view of my own. Less confident than Fichte, I appeal instead to others. In this chapter, then, I shall first take up Martin Heidegger as an important modern thinker whose philosophy is permeated by the concern to rediscover and renovate the original point of view of European thought. By considering Heidegger we shall see the possibility of extending the concept of transformative philosophy to thinkers besides those already dealt with and, at the same time, discover how transformative philosophy can be related to some of the underlying themes of Western metaphysics. I then turn to Richard Rorty, who has recently considered the evolution of European philosophy from an engaging new angle. Rorty proposes a new type of philosophy—"edifying philosophy"—to replace traditional philosophy, which he believes has exhausted its potentialities. In determining whether transformative philosophy falls into this category we shall have an opportunity to elucidate more fully its general character. Finally, as a consequence of the discussion of Rorty, the question of the validity of transformative philosophy will arise—is transformative philosophy, irrespective of whether it has in fact exerted an important influence on Western thought, a method of philosophizing that *ought* to be pursued? Does it have any philosophically—as opposed to historically—significant contribution to make?

1. *Heidegger and the Task of Thinking*

In the preceding chapter we saw how Fichte characterizes the "transcendental philosopher" as one who possesses an expanded inner faculty of intelligence—explicit consciousness of the intellectual intuition. Sometimes he also speaks of this capacity as the fully developed faculty of *thought.* Ordinary thought, according to Fichte, is mere opinion. It is able to grasp things only externally, sorting out what must be closest to the truth among various possibilities. Fully developed, genuine thought, on the other hand, carries within itself its own object, inseparable from it, which it apprehends directly. "The true, higher thought is that which, without any assistance from external sense or any reference to it, creates its purely spiritual *(rein geistiges)* object simply out of itself." It is, therefore, absolutely certain.

> This true thought does not reflect or think things out, but there comes to it of itself, not that which exists next to and among other things, but that which alone is possible, real, necessary. And this confirms itself not through any sort of proof which lies outside it, but it carries its confirmation immediately within itself. As soon as it is thought, it occurs to the thinker with unshakable certainty and evidence—destroying any possibility of doubt—as the only thing possible, the completely and absolutely true.[4]

In Heidegger we have another philosopher who believed that true philosophy depends on the cultivation of genuine thinking. The question of the meaning of Being around which his philosophy revolves cannot be answered before we truly learn to think. It would seem that for Heidegger these two matters are closely connected indeed—the attainment of authentic thought itself constitutes part of the answer to the question of the meaning of Being. For the latter is not a query posed from the outside, as it were, but it arises naturally as an expression of the very one who, as a being that thinks, reflects on it and attempts to answer it. With the apprehension of the essence of thinking one gains important insight into the root of this concern and hence into Being itself. Moreover, Being is that which is in and of itself deserving of thought, that which exists as the most appropriate thing to be thought about. When true thinking is reached, the meaning of Being is ipso facto disclosed.

In an important series of lectures, which taken together with his *Letter on Humanism* defines the orientation of his entire later philosophy, Heidegger takes up the crucial inquiry: *What is thinking?*[5] Although this essay is ostensibly a study *of* thinking, Heidegger immediately points out that thinking is something we come to know insofar as we *do* it. Thus his task in these lectures is actually to guide us in thinking. Although the human being is commonly defined as the animal endowed with the capacity of thought *(animal rationale)*, thinking is not in fact something we all automatically engage in. It is a possibility that all humans share, but not one that they all realize. In order to know what thinking, in the proper sense of the word, is we must therefore first *learn* to think. Heidegger's study is, in fact, not a scientific investigation of an object—thinking—but an exercise in thinking. Similar to Fichte, he begins his philosophy not with a statement but with an act we must perform.

With this Heidegger has already shifted into the mode of transformative philosophy. For the later Heidegger, philosophy does not consist in a description of the nature of things. Nor is it an investigation of the mind or the apparatus of knowledge. In fact, it is not an attempt to account for anything. True philosophy, rather, is essentially a process of engendering full awareness—of awakening and unfolding the neglected potential of human consciousness. We have identified this trait at the heart of transformative philosophy, although, to be sure, the systems of transformative philosophy we have dealt with thus far have each had a theoretical component. But we have seen that the theoretical constructs of a transformative philosophy serve primarily to consolidate an expanded state of consciousness; they are not meant to stand on their own as scientific statements. Heidegger as a transformative philosopher is completely absorbed in the task of cultivating in us a higher consciousness—that is to say, in coaxing, urging, and cajoling us into performing the "genuine act of thought"—to the almost complete neglect of theory. And yet we shall see that he is the least mystical of all.

I maintain, in other words, that Heidegger's later works—to which I limit myself here—are primarily intended as *practice in thinking.* The reader who follows the discussion of *What Is Called Thinking?*, for example, does not at the end have a summary definition of the essence of thought. Rather, he has—ideally—improved his ability to think. This is why it can be so exciting to read Heidegger. One feels that one has at last entered a new precinct of experience and that the process of freeing and developing awareness has really begun, if only on a modest scale—that is to say, one feels that one is actually being led to think *differently.* What corresponds in Heidegger's "system" to the state of consciousness set up by Fichte as the unconditioned first principle of all knowledge (and sometimes mistakenly assumed by him to be evident in everyone's life) is something which Heidegger works actually to arouse in us by a method which, we shall see, is indeed a kind of purification. The careful and sympathetic reader of his writings cannot help but notice the effects of this exercise.

Given Heidegger's purpose in "philosophizing," so to speak—for that is not really what he is doing—it is difficult to summarize his ideas. Many works of his later period do not yield statable conclusions; as meditations, they simply come to an end.[6] Nonetheless, certain observations serve as guideposts in Heidegger's discourses—themes to meditate on, as it were.[7] In *What Is Called Thinking?* the first of these regards the proper object of thought: "The most thought-provoking matter in our thought-provoking time is that we are still not thinking." Heidegger's interpretation of this peculiar self-referential statement is fairly straightforward: the thing most deserving and suitable for thought has withdrawn, and continually withdraws, from man. That is, we are not not thinking for reasons that have to do just with our own stupidity, our lack of motivation or effort, but because that which can truly be thought is elusive, even concealed—although concealed perhaps in that it is most obvious.[8] In short, what most calls for thinking is exceedingly difficult to contemplate. But what is that? Clearly, if it eludes easy contemplation it cannot be captured in a mere name. Nevertheless, one can confidently say that it is the same as what Heidegger sought for in *Being and Time* under the rubric "the Being of beings":

> . . . Withdrawing is not nothing. Withdrawal is an event. In fact, what withdraws may even concern and claim man more essentially than anything present that strikes and touches him. Being struck by actuality is what we like to regard as constitutive of the actuality of the actual. However, in being struck by what is actual, man may be debarred precisely from what concerns and touches him—touches him in the mysterious way of escaping him by its withdrawal. The event of withdrawal could be what is most present in all our present, and so infinitely exceed the actuality of everything actual.[9]

What most concerns us, what will satisfy our minds most of all, what, therefore, is most real, is what also escapes our attention as we respond and relate to the immediate, "actual" world. Thus that which withdraws—call it Being or even Nonbeing, so long as you acknowledge its primacy—can only be apprehended through a style of thinking which empties itself into this withdrawal and does not rely on the fixed categories of actuality.[10] Heidegger points out that the human being qua being that thinks—therefore, qua being that strives to think in the fullest sense—is essentially oriented toward this phenomenon. Man is a "sign" that refers to this withdrawing or, more cryptically, "His essential nature lies in being . . . a pointer."[11]

What has thus far been said, although it may not tell us much about what thinking *is*, implies certain things about what thinking is not. When it comes to the negative demarcation of thinking, Heidegger is especially lucid and expansive. First of all, thinking is not calculating.[12] It is not the mere manipulation of ideas. Therefore science, precisely because it is more successful than any other method at generating knowledge with the established categories of experience—making observations, applying models, inventing and testing theories—never attains thinking in Heidegger's sense. Nor does traditional philosophy

—metaphysics—which originally devises these categories. Heidegger declares a great war on metaphysics in his later works and attacks such notions as matter, form, subjectivity, cause, substance, time, and truth as contrivances which have led to the false stereotyping of the Being of beings. Finally, genuine thinking is not common sense. Common sense ascertains facts and appeals to particulars in a self-assured way. It is "always trimmed to fit a certain conception of what is and ought to be and may be" and thus fails to leave itself open.[13]

In the essay under consideration, as elsewhere, Heidegger identifies the essence of these three principal modes of traditional thinking as *the forming of representational ideas (Vorstellen).* This is, in turn, the essence of reason, *ratio,* which is often conceived as man's nature. Man, the *animal rationale,* is *animal representans.* Heidegger develops this thought in typical fashion with recourse to the Greek and Latin terms:

> *Homo est animal rationale. . . .* Man is the beast endowed with reason. Reason is the perception of what is, which always means also what can and ought to be. To perceive implies, in ascending order: to welcome and take in; to accept and take in the encounter; to take up face to face; to undertake and see through—and this means to talk through. The Latin for talking through is *reor*; the Greek *rheo* (as in rhetoric) is the ability to take up something and see it through; *reri* is *ratio*; *animal rationale* is the animal which lives by perceiving what is, in the manner described. The perception that prevails within reason produces and adduces purposes, establishes rules, provides means and ways, and attunes reason to the modes of action. Reason's perception unfolds as this manifold providing, which is first of all and always a confrontation, a face-to-face presentation. Thus one might say: *homo est animal rationale*—man is the animal that confronts face-to-face.[14]

Man, in other words, usually thinks in terms of ideas which he sees standing opposite himself, on the one hand, and the reality they reflect, on the other, as things to be worked on and manipulated. Recent Heidegger commentators have particularly emphasized how subjectivism arises from this attitude:[15] ideas are postulated as mental entities which mirror what goes on in the world. But equally important for Heidegger is that the *animal rationale* fundamentally *reckons* with ideas. He moves from one idea to the next, using available ones to get at remote ones, replaces bad ideas with good ones, and constantly rearranges those he has settled on. Heidegger says, "[The nature of] the *animal rationale* . . . consists in the way he sets up everything that is, as his objects and subjective states, confronts them, and adjusts to these objects and states as his environing circumstances."[16] Hence thinking as representation entails a certain idea of truth as adequacy or correspondence—the motivating ideal of all theory.

In *What Is Called Thinking?* Heidegger relates all this to Nietzsche. He sees Nietzsche as one who "with greater clarity than any man before him saw the necessity of a change in the realm of essential thinking," a man who had to rave and shout to awaken us to this need.[17] In *Thus Spake Zarathustra* Nietzsche condemns the habitual mode of thought—the forming of representational ideas—as blinking: "We have invented happiness, say the last men, and blink."[18] The last men, the men of this age, have gone to a peculiar extreme in their commitment to reason, science, and "common sense." They represent the final stage in a process which—Nietzsche was convinced—must eventually expend itself and make way for the emergence of a new type of man. The Superman *(Übermensch)* is, on Heidegger's interpretation, the man *(Mensch)* who passes over *(über)*, the man who overcomes his habitual nature as a representing animal.

In a brilliant analysis Heidegger shows how these matters are dramatized in Neitzsche's doctrine of will. As did the great German thinkers preceding him—Leibniz, Kant, Fichte, Schopenhauer—Nietzsche conceives of being, cognition, and will as fundamentally one. The character of thinking can therefore be identified as a particular feature of willing. In the case of representational thinking, this is "the spirit of revenge"; for this mode of forming ideas "at bottom opposes everything that is . . . as it is, . . . sets upon everything it sets before itself" in order to depose it.[19] That is to say, it reduces Being to beings (things) and then coerces beings to fit concepts, making them into alien objects of thought distinct from a subject who thinks them. This attitude of will—hence this frame of mind—can be overcome only by a sort of inversion of will—namely, the glad willing of what actually *eludes* the will, of what the will cannot change, of what therefore frustrates or even repels the will when it is governed by the spirit of revenge. This is simply the *past.* And so this new attitude of thought is expressed by Nietzsche most radically as the willing of the eternal recurrence of the past.[20]

But Nietzsche's Superman is perhaps more notorious as one who has transcended all values and passed beyond good and evil. This too, Heidegger emphasizes in his *Letter on Humanism*, is part and parcel of transcending traditional thinking, which makes possible genuine thought. It is not nihilism:

> To think against "values" is not to maintain that everything interpreted as a "value"—"culture," "art," "science," "human dignity," "world," and "God"—is valueless. Rather, it is important finally to realize that precisely through the characterization of something as "a value" what is so valued is robbed of its worth. That is to say, by the assessment of something as a value what is valued is admitted only as an object for man's estimation. But what a thing is in its Being is not exhausted by its being an object, particularly when its objectivity takes the form of value. Every valuing, even where it values positively, is a subjectivizing. It does not let beings: be. Rather, valuing lets beings: be valid—solely as the objects of its doing. . . . To think against values therefore does not mean to beat the drum for the valuelessness and nullity of beings. It means rather to bring the lighting of the truth of Being before thinking, as against subjectivizing beings into mere objects.[21]

In the first part of *What Is Called Thinking?* Heidegger delineates thinking as a process, chiefly in negative terms. In the second part he reads the question "*Was heisst Denken?*" slightly differently to mean "What calls *for* thinking or what calls upon us to think?" As such, it is a question concerning the topic of genuine thought; for what calls upon us to think is itself, as the source of thought, thought-provoking per se.[22] We have seen that Heidegger initially identified this as something which continually withdraws from us in our efforts to apprehend it, and we noted that this seems to be what he elsewhere calls Being. Indeed, in this part Heidegger will explicitly make that identification and go on to examine the function Being serves in motivating us—leading us on—to think. But here, too, one will be disappointed if one expects to receive a direct explanation of the matter—a doctrine of Being. As a withdrawing, Being is, if anything, an event (and not the common sort of event that relates things; for relating, too, takes it ground on Being); really to comprehend it is to *participate* in the event.

As Heidegger appealed to Nietzsche in the first part, he now appeals to Parmenides, centering his discussion on Fragment VI: *Chre to legein te noein t'eon emmenai*, "One should both say and think that

Being is." Since his remarks are intimately bound up with the complexities of translating this saying from the Greek, we shall do better to summarize the idea of Being independently.

In Heidegger's later writings, Being is the element in which thought lives and progresses. He refers to it frequently as an "openness" or "clearing" *(Lichtung)*. As the element for thought it is not a substance —as is water, the element in which fish live, or air, the element for birds—but a "free space" in which the matter of thinking, that is, ideas, can come to light. Thus Being is different from the light of intellect that Western philosophers have spoken of and different, too, from the light *(prakāśa)* of pure consciousness of Oriental philosophers. For light in the sense of brightness (the sense of the word which accords with such metaphors) *fills up* space and therefore presupposes Openness.[23] Being—Openness—is the most fundamental condition for anything, brightness as well as darkness, to appear.[24] As an event or process Heidegger calls it the presence, or presencing, of what is present:[25]

> All metaphysics, including its opponent, positivism, speaks the language of Plato. The basic word of its thinking, that is, of its presentation of the Being of beings, is *eidos, idea:* the outward appearance in which beings as such show themselves. Outward appearance, however, is a manner of presence. No outward appearance without light—Plato already knew this. But there is no light and no brightness without the opening. Even darkness needs it. How else could we happen into darkness and wander through it? Still, the opening as such as it prevails through Being, through presence, remains unthought in philosophy, although it is spoken about in philosophy's beginning.[26]

All thinking in the sense of representation is the illumining of things and thus requires a free area in which things can be illumined. This can only be Being (the condition of all appearance)—what is unthought in every act of representation, what withdraws in our trying to think it but nevertheless permeates each act of thought. Heidegger hints that it can perhaps be glimpsed in the interstices between thoughts. But as soon as we start moving from one thought to the next —as soon as we start philosophizing, that is—it falls out of the picture. When philosophy is complete, the task of thinking which remains is to experience the presencing as such, not simply what is presented.

But then, obviously, Heidegger is not going to tell us what Being is—that is, represent it to us. Closeness to Being does not consist in having the right view of it. His remarks, although they touch on many topics, do not yet add up to a theory.[27] They only point in the direction of Being in a vague way. They are primarily determined by the need to become explicitly aware of a matter that has yet to be thought; and for it really to be thought, thinking must evolve considerably:

> The matter of thinking is not achieved in the fact that talk about the "truth of Being" and the "history of Being" is set in motion. Everything depends on this alone, that the truth of Being come to language and that thinking attain to this language. Perhaps, then, language requires much less precipitous expression than proper silence. But who of us today would want to imagine that his attempts to think are at home on the path of silence? At best, thinking could perhaps point toward the truth of Being, and indeed toward it as what is to be thought.[28]

I believe that this fluidity of method is at the core of Heidegger's message and is to be emphasized beyond any substantive thing he has to say. We must still learn to think. Repeatedly Heidegger tells us that the path to Being is a way that persists in questioning. We have to overcome the urge to snatch at answers and be ready for what might present itself unexpectedly—something perhaps so wholly other than what we anticipated that it cannot at first be put into words. We must learn to think in an altogether new way. In his *Letter on Humanism* he says:

> If man is to find his way once again into the nearness of Being he must first learn to exist in the nameless. . . . Before he speaks man must first let himself be claimed again by Being, taking the risk that under this claim he will seldom have much to say.[29]

In *What Is Called Thinking?* he observes:

> The real nature of thought might show itself . . . at that very point where it once withdrew, if only we will pay heed to this withdrawal, if only we will not insist, confused by logic, that we already know perfectly well what thinking is [namely, the forming of ideas]. The real nature of thought might reveal itself to us if we remain under way.[30]

Again, at the beginning of his essay "The End of Philosophy and the Task of Thinking," he explains:

> The title designates the attempt at a reflection that persists in questioning. Questions are paths toward an answer. If the answer could be given

> it would consist in a transformation of thinking, not in a propositional statement about a matter at stake.[31]

Heidegger's later discourses, I suggest, are meant to involve us in this very process of transformation. As such they cannot really be summarized; they must be *gone through.* They are guided, irrespective of their substantive concerns (technology, thinking, metaphysics, science, humanism), by the purpose actually to reduce the noise of ideas and enhance receptivity, to allow us to release ourselves toward what withdraws and become "owned" by it again. Hence Heidegger's unique, if notorious, style—which is nothing other than a manner of dealing with ideas yieldingly, meditatively, not coercing them but seeing where they lead on their own. Often they lead to the very limit of discourse where they slip through all ready-made categories and merge into silence.[32]

At the same time, through trenchant and persistent criticism of the metaphysical way of looking at things, thinking is purified of the old notions which kept it bound. Yet this does not mean that all statement is to be abandoned in the end, although we may be called upon to abandon it for the time being. For Heidegger holds out the possibility that, once thinking has matured, its object can be accurately defined.[33] Some scholars see already in his framework of *Ereignis* and *Geviert* the beginnings of such a definition.[34] But for the most part, the meditative thinking which he takes up for now—which is in fact crucial at this stage—is only preliminary:

> Above all, the thinking in question remains unassuming because its task is only of a preparatory, not a founding, character. It is content with awakening a readiness in man for a possibility whose contour remains obscure, whose coming remains uncertain. Thinking must first learn what remains reserved and in store for thinking to get involved in. It prepares its own transformation in this learning.[35]

On the basis of this very brief and simplifying overview it would seem that Heidegger's program begs to be understood in the context of transformative philosophy—and not merely because he coincidentally employs the word "transformation." For the gist of his writings is that the philosopher must be made somehow to measure up to the matter of philosophy, to Truth, while the writings themselves are intended to effect this uplifting (if only partially). Although Heidegger's "system" is not a fully rounded transformative program—for it lacks the highly developed theoretical component which plays a crucial role in the other systems we have studied, that is, the assertions which inform a fully matured consciousness and thus precipitate a sudden enlightenment—he is nevertheless guided primarily by the concern to restructure not just thinking but life as a whole in a radical way.[36] How Heidegger explains this new attitude as a kind of "poetic dwelling" cannot be entered into here.[37]

Fichte gave us the results of his vision of reality in the form of a system—ideas relating to all areas of human experience arranged hierarchically in a whole. Only after he had worked this out did he give thought to how others might achieve this insight for themselves. He suggested vainly in the end a revamping of the traditional system of childrearing and education—a woefully unsatisfactory suggestion to those whom he hoped to inspire and convince (who, nevertheless, did not understand him) and who were supposed to carry out his reforms.

Heidegger, on the other hand, does not articulate results; he does not proclaim a vision. Rather, he sets to the work of reforming us now, as we are. He engages us in actually cultivating a higher consciousness through a kind of thinking which overcomes thinking. He provides transformative philosophy with immediate practical means.[38] Once again, historical circumstances help account for this difference. By Heidegger's time philosophy had lost all patience with dogmatism in the usual sense of that word—the sense in which Fichte was egregiously dogmatic. Philosophy had become absorbed again in the business of thrashing out solutions to ancient issues; in many areas, such as logic, it was starting anew. A philosopher standing aloof from all this, declaring his own absolutely certain insight, simply would not have been heard. Heidegger had to enter the fray, engaging in historical research and conceptual analysis himself, in order to transmute consciousness with consciousness. I suggest, nevertheless, that in the cases of Heidegger and Fichte we are dealing with basically the same process: the raising of consciousness.[39] This is the matter of transformative philosophy in its broadest sense.[40]

It remains only to be said that Heidegger believed genuine thinking to be at the heart of the Western philosophical tradition. That does not mean, of course, that it has dominated the evolution of Western thought. On the contrary, the history of European thought according to Heidegger has been largely determined by an estrangement from the true matter of thinking, by a "forgetfulness of Being." While the inquiries into logic, ethics, physics, metaphysics, and so on set in motion by Plato and Aristotle served originally only as substitutes for the direct encounter with Being that genuine thinking had achieved earlier (with Homer, Pindar, Parmenides, and Heraclitus), posterity mistook these investigations for the substance of philosophy and lost sight of its real concern. In fact, these disciplines only elaborate Being in a readily comprehensible, schematic way; fundamentally, they distort it. To say that true thinking lies at the heart of Western philosophy although it has not been its actual method is to say that a whole tradition can become sidetracked from its original purpose. In proliferating its footnotes to Plato the history of philosophy has overlooked the spirit and substance of the text.[41]

Interpreting the raising of consciousness—hence authentic thinking in Heidegger's sense—as the crux of transformative philosophy, we see that Heidegger in effect assigns transformative philosophy a crucial role as the forgotten source and inspiration of the entire Western philosophical tradition. Did Heidegger believe that true thought could ever emerge again and resume its rightful position of sovereignty? Indeed, he seems alternately hopeful and skeptical. In one of his last essays, "The End of Philosophy and the Task of Thinking," he singles out the Being of beings as what is left to be reflected on now that philosophical problems—rooted in the conception of Being as things and relations—are being taken up and solved by science. But this means that the need to meditate directly on the Being of beings confronts us plainly once again and cannot be ignored. On the other hand, Heidegger doubts that genuine thinking will ever have much impact on a public dominated—as it is in the present age—by the *Gestell* of an uncompromisingly technological world that is diametrically opposed to the spirit of thinking. Far greater is the abiding influence of traditional philosophy, which in fact originally gave rise to science and technology.

The question then remains: What is the future of transformative philosophy? Are we entering a phase where it could, or perhaps with Heidegger already has, come forth as an important trend; or is it likely to continue to appear only intermittently as a sort of philosophical sidelight if not an aberration? In order to evaluate its prospects thoroughly we consider next Richard Rorty's repainting of the history of philosophy and assessment of present tendencies.

2. *Is Transformative Philosophy Edifying Philosophy?*

In a recent work the American philosopher Richard Rorty has offered a new reading and critique of the history of Western philosophy. I devote considerable attention to his account in this and the following section for several reasons. First, Rorty stands firmly in the analytic tradition and therefore sees the essence and development of Western thought somewhat differently than Heidegger. By setting the notion of transformative philosophy in relation to his ideas we achieve another perspective on its position with respect to the tradition. And, as Rorty's story of philosophy includes Heidegger, we shall have an opportunity to carry our investigation of Heidegger further. More importantly, Rorty sets up a compelling metaphilosophical framework. He divides philosophies into two main categories. One type, "systematic philosophy," represents the mainstream of the Western philosophical tradition, which according to Rorty has lost its vitality. The other type, "edifying philosophy," is put forward as the rightful heir of the tradition—the philosophy of the future. Transformative philosophy bears a resemblance to both types. In determining which category it belongs to we shall have an opportunity to sharpen our knowledge of what transformative philosophy is—and is not.

Because an all-encompassing interpretation of the character and evolution of Western thought has not until now been offered by an analytic philosopher (John Dewey, the last American philosopher to have done so, cannot really be so classified), Rorty's work is bound to have a major impact—all the more so because he does not merely express his individual point of view but unfolds an attitude implicit in much of recent analytic philosophy. I therefore hope to connect the notion of transformative philosophy with what is anticipated to be a dominant trend in Western metaphilosophy for some time to come. Finally, the consideration of Rorty will set the stage for a proper discussion of the validity, or at least defensibility, of transformative philosophy as a philosophical enterprise, a theme to be taken up in the final section of this chapter.

In his book *Philosophy and the Mirror of Nature* Rorty, much like Heidegger,[42] challenges the notion of knowledge as accurate representation, which he believes to be at the heart of Western philosophy. This notion manifests itself in the form of the theory of knowledge as initiated by Descartes, developed by the British empiricists, brought to its culmination by Kant, and kept alive in new and unexpected forms by contemporary philosophers of language and cognitive scientists—in short, as practiced by the mainstream of modern philosophy.

The main purpose of a theory of knowledge, as Rorty views it, is to provide a secure foundation for knowledge. Although its roots go back to Plato, the theory of knowledge as an explicit discipline is a relatively recent development. It emerged when it became clear that the role of metaphysics and theology in discovering truths about the world would be taken over by the empirical, experimental sciences and that if philosophy was to retain any useful function at all it would have to be that of *justifying* the results of such sciences—that is, showing how they constitute what may be called knowledge. This task, of course, entails, among other things, giving a definition of knowledge as well as an account of the processes involved in it. By way of defining knowledge, the theory of knowledge has typically proclaimed one kind of knowledge to be the most trustworthy—namely, the direct acquaintance with particulars in consciousness. The latter have been known variously throughout the history of philosophy as "clear and distinct ideas," "intuitions," "sense impressions," "sense data," "raw feels," and the like. The job of justifying science then amounts to showing, first, that these particulars do accurately represent objects which exist in some sense outside the mind and, then, how scientific knowledge is built from them.

Rorty's critique of the Western philosophical tradition focuses on the notion of the reflection of ideas in the "glassy essence of the mind" —the mirror of his book's title—as the epitome of knowledge. He maintains that, far from being a paradigmatic form of knowledge, this is not knowledge at all. He does not attack the objectivity of mental representations, however. Rather, he argues that the model of mirroring simply does not fit what we call knowing. For to know, according to Rorty, is to have *justified belief*; it is to adopt a certain position within a matrix of reasons and evidence, arguments and observations. Knowledge is a stage in discourse. So it is hardly evoked by a metaphor which turns on a relation between *things*; instead, it is a relation between persons and propositions. Moreover, to attempt to justify scientific knowledge by appealing to the occurrence of ideas or representations in the inner arena of consciousness is to "confuse explanation with justification," Rorty says.[43] It may well be that the occurrence of representations in the mental arena, or something very much like it, is involved in the mechanism which produces states that can eventually be correlated, if not identified, with beliefs and knowledge claims.[44] In calling attention to such occurrences one goes part of the way toward explaining the *emergence* of knowledge. But to explain how something arises is not the same as to identify what it is. That is always done in advance of providing an explanation. In the case of knowledge it is accomplished by giving justification—that is, producing evidence, relating what we believe to what we already know, and so forth.[45]

Rorty points out that besides the desire to save a place for philosophy, the interpretation of knowledge as the possession of accurate representations is motivated by the quest for certainty—the urge to trace all knowledge back to something indubitable:

> It helps to think of the original dominating metaphor [of the theory of knowledge] as being that of having our beliefs determined by being brought face-to-face with the object of belief. . . . The next stage is to think that to understand how to know better is to understand how to improve the activity of the quasi-visual faculty, the Mirror of Nature, and thus to think of knowledge as an assemblage of accurate representations. Then comes the idea that the way to have accurate representations is to find, within the Mirror, a special privileged class of representations so compelling that their accuracy cannot be doubted. These privileged foundations will be the foundations of knowledge, and the discipline which directs us toward them—the theory of knowledge—will be the foundation of culture. The theory of knowledge will be the search for that which compels the mind to belief as soon as it is unveiled. Philosophy-as-epistemology will be the search for the immutable structures within which knowledge, life, and culture must be contained—structures set by the privileged representations which it studies.[46]

And yet it is precisely the notion that these are privileged representations, that we *know* them better than we know anything else, that has given birth to the great bugbear of modern philosophy which has, in turn, called the whole enterprise of philosophy into question—namely, skepticism regarding the external world. For the notion that the immediate confrontation of the mind with an object—the mind's being compelled to see it as it is—is the best of all knowledge carries with it the notion that where this confrontation is less than immediate—where inference and argument enter in—knowledge is second rate and ultimately doubtful. Hence the emergence of the point of view of epistemology is simultaneous with the rise of the conflict between realism and idealism.

Rorty wants to overcome this attitude, and so he declares that knowledge comes into being through "conversation, not confrontation." We verify our beliefs by determining that the evidence supports them, that others are unable to refute them, perhaps even that they lead us on to further discoveries. We do not do so by tracing them back introspectively to certain self-evident ideas in consciousness. The images, words, sensations, and so forth that the mind seems to "confront" are nothing more than neuropsychological events that invariably *accompany* thinking, saying, perceiving, believing, and knowing—all of which latter activities, however, really take place in the dimension of interhuman discourse, research, and discovery. Ultimately the character of mental events as inner seeings, utterings, feelings, and so forth is read back into them from this more public sphere, where the meanings of those concepts are originally established.[47] Rorty maintains that this more correct point of view has been practiced in this century in the discipline of hermeneutics. In general, he puts forward hermeneutics as the intellectual enterprise to replace philosophy-as-epistemology.

Hermeneutics was founded (principally by Schleiermacher) as a science of interpretation. It was not originally conceived as a response to philosophical developments, but only as a way to recover the meaning of ancient (specifically: biblical) texts. Nevertheless Rorty, following Dilthey, Heidegger, and Gadamer, discerns in the hermeneutic method a counterbalance to the epistemological attitude. For it proceeds on the assumption that there is not always to be found a common ground between the perspective of the interpreter and the text he has to interpret. That is to say, the interpretation of a poem, a scripture, a ritual, or a social practice cannot be constructed piece by piece out of simple, basic elements of meaning—say, in the case of a poem, words—which are initially available to the investigator by means of a fixed lexicon. Rather, all units of meaning, the simple along with the complex, have to be worked out at the same time. Interpretation always evolves holistically. The meaning of a particular kinship term within a culture, for example, is not understood before it is known where the person bearing that title is located within the kinship system at large. A kinship system, on the other hand, is not fully understood in isolation from the economic and political systems in which it is embedded.

Thus one cannot approach any single phenomenon of a culture—even a poem or a word in a poem—without in some way taking the whole culture into account. One cannot approach an item of an alien culture with a fixed dictionary of "things we do know about the culture" (except, of course, heuristically), because as one proceeds the meanings in the dictionary change. Thus many things are not going to be wholly translatable into the language of the interpreter. Perfect translation would require a perfect correspondence between entire cultures—which in no instance exists. Interpretation, according to the hermeneuticist, demands that one give up the attempt to translate from an outside (neutral) position and develop the ability to enter into the world view containing the phenomenon to be understood. Hermeneutic understanding (for which the German word *Verstehen* has been reserved as a technical term) calls for the capacity to adopt (temporarily, for the sake of understanding) the perspective of the culture of the phenomenon in question.

Rorty sees the hermeneutic method as diametrically opposed to the implication of the theory of knowledge which has determined the course of philosophy perhaps more than any other—namely, that there is a common ground for all knowledge upon which all human beings can come to agree about certain things. This assumption is implied by the image of a universal process of knowing based on elementary knowledge events having special authority, which ultimately justify what we know. Epistemology—or "systematic philosophy," as Rorty calls it in this aspect—suggests that the fact that we all share this process guarantees that, at least on the most fundamental level of experience, we all "know" the same things. Moreover, philosophy-as-epistemology typically suggests that there is ultimately one way to view the world—namely, the view that science, building on universal experience, will give us when it is complete.

Hermeneutics, however, submits that knowledge, which of course is dependent on *meaning*, is pursued in many different spheres of life which are incommensurable with each other—that is, which cannot be wholly translated into each other. Therefore, there is no common ground for all knowledge. Generally the hermeneutic perspective implies that knowledge belongs to the sphere of interhuman discourse and social practice—the realm of meaning. It is in no case to be justified by recourse to its physiological-neurological causes.

Rorty identifies certain figures of recent times who, he believes, have taken up the point of view of hermeneutics as philosophers: Dewey, Heidegger, Wittgenstein, Sellars, and Quine. He names them "edifying philosophers." They are not committed to standardizing knowledge—achieving a universal framework in which the truth can be stated once and for all—but to making us aware of new realms of discourse besides those to which we have become accustomed and which, only for that reason, have taken on the aspect of the normal. They are concerned "to take us out of our old selves . . . to aid us in becoming new beings."[48] As we explore Rorty's characterization of the edifying philosopher we shall ask ourselves whether transformative philosophy can be seen as edifying philosophy.

Despite the promise that the edifying philosopher will in some way change us, he appears in Rorty's description primarily as one who manages to refrain from getting involved in systematic philosophy. Heidegger, the later Wittgenstein, and the others Rorty mentions stand out in his analysis chiefly as negative thinkers. They tell us that there is no one way to go about knowing the world, no final picture of the way things are. Therefore man is not essentially a "knower of essences"; the purpose of his intellectual exertions is not to meet up with some objective truth forever etched in the fabric of the cosmos. Rather, man is a being who constantly shapes and reshapes himself in his living; knowing is only one kind of activity among many others.[49] But knowledge will change with praxis. Thus the "objective" kind of knowledge that has been the fascination of systematic philosophers is for edifying philosophers little more than the way of finding things out in conformity with the norms of the day: "[These writers] have kept alive the historicist sense that this century's 'superstition' was the last century's triumph of reason, as well as the relativist sense that the latest vocabulary, borrowed from the latest scientific achievement, may not express privileged representations of essences, but be just another of the potential infinity of vocabularies in which the world can be described."[50] And yet they themselves may choose not to introduce us to any of these new vocabularies; they may not have a new vision to offer. Perhaps the most significant thing about the edifying philosopher as Rorty presents him is that he avoids taking any view at all.[51]

Perhaps this evasiveness is due to the fact that the edifying philosopher of recent times has had a propaedeutic task. The notion that knowledge is a kind of accurate representation has held such a relentless grip on our minds that a special effort must be made at this juncture to break it. Nevertheless, Rorty does speculate about the form the philosophical impulse (not philosophy per se, for that will have been abolished) will take after the task of "deconstruction" has been completed. In essence, it seems, the philosopher will become a kind of virtuoso of life. He will be at home in a variety of vocabularies and world views. He will be able to shift easily from one perspective to another and see that each is grounded in its own dimension of discourse and holds no real sway over the other. When involved in a conflict of theories, he will be mainly interested in "keeping the discussion going," that is, preventing it from freezing into the fixed vocabulary of normal discourse; he will not be looking for the revelation of an underlying reality that the conflicting theories have in common but only for agreement among the disputants—or, if that cannot be reached, then at least interesting and intelligent disagreement. In short, he will embody—and in edifying us, encourage us ourselves to embody—the pragmatist conception of truth.

The edifying philosopher, Rorty says, is "interested not so much in what is out there in the world, or in what happened in history, as in what we can get out of nature and history for our own uses" in our lives and actions. "In this attitude, getting the facts right . . . is merely propaedeutic to finding new and more interesting ways of expressing ourselves, and thus coping with the world."[52] Rorty does not seem to have merely an intellectual coming to grips in mind here, but a complete adjustment of one's whole being. Thus some kind of transformation seems to be involved after all. Following Gadamer, he suggests that the development of a virtuosic ability to relate to many realms *(Bildung)* implies a "remaking of our natures."[53] In the following passage he plays down the essentialist overtones which this phrase carries —yet its holistic sense is preserved:

> To say that we become different people, that we "remake" ourselves as we read more, talk more, and write more, is simply a dramatic way of saying that the sentences which become true of us by virtue of such activities are often more important to us than the sentences which

> become true of us when we drink more, earn more, and so on. The events which make us able to say new and interesting things about ourselves are, in this nonmetaphysical sense, more "essential" to us (at least to us relatively leisured intellectuals, inhabiting a stable and prosperous part of the world) than the events which change our shapes and our standards of living ("remaking" us in less "spiritual" ways).[54]

Without attempting to decide whether this is true—for to do so, it would seem, would be to put ourselves quite at odds with the spirit of Rorty's thinking—let us see whether "edification" in this sense squares with the notion of transformation I have developed here.

Perhaps the best way to go about deciding this issue is to consider Heidegger again—a figure of interest to Rorty also. Rorty presents Heidegger as a mortal enemy of the epistemological program and the idea of knowledge as accurate representation. According to Rorty, "He is concerned to explore the way in which the West became obsessed with the notion of our primary relation to objects as analogous to visual perception, and thus to suggest that there could be other conceptions of our relations to things."[55] He further depicts Heidegger as an expert philosophical deconstructionist who knew how to dissolve the problems posed by his predecessors without offering new solutions to them or new problems to replace them:

> He does not, like Descartes and Hegel and Husserl and Carnap, say, "This is how philosophy has been; let philosophy henceforth be like this." Rather, like Nietzsche and Wittgenstein and Dewey, he asks, "Given that this is how philosophy has been, what, if anything, can philosophy now be?" Suggesting, as they did, that philosophy may have exhausted its potentialities, he asks whether the motives which led to philosophy's existence still exist and whether they should.[56]

While this passage does not exactly misrepresent Heidegger, it does not fully capture him either. For, as we have seen and as Rorty himself is aware, before dismantling the epistemological framework comes into question for him, Heidegger is intent on entering into a real relation with Being.[57] It turns out that a program of philosophical deconstruction is necessary because the type of schematic thinking that philosophy has set up and practically institutionalized obstructs our sense of nearness to Being; in presenting us with clever devices to express Being it necessarily stands between us and It. Thinking must therefore be purified. But this task involves much more than getting away from one particular philosophical perspective which has held us hypnotized and seeing the relativity of all perspectives. It involves, in some sense, a gaining of independence from conceptual thinking altogether. As Heidegger says:

> [Authentic] thinking is not grasping or prehending. In the high youth of its unfolding essence, thinking knows nothing of the grasping concept *(Begriff)*. The reason is not at all that thinking was then undeveloped. Rather, evolving thinking is not yet confined within limits. . . . All of the great thinking of the Greek thinkers, including Aristotle, thinks nonconceptually.[58]

Thus Heidegger's representational or ideational thinking is not exactly what Rorty calls "mirroring." It is not chiefly the confrontation of the mind with "essences"—though, to be sure, the notion of reality-as-presence (= idea) and the subject-object dichotomy are seen by Heidegger as pillars of the metaphysical framework which must be toppled.[59] Rather, it is thinking in terms of ideas: shuffling ideas around, depending on them to speak for things (instead of letting things speak for themselves), using them to make comparisons, draw inferences, and so forth. The opposite of authentic thinking for Heidegger is, as we have seen, calculating. He proposes to overcome the calculating frame of mind by cultivating an Openness which is, ultimately, a state of silence and "releasement" *(Gelassenheit)*—a state of simple dwelling without imposing ideas onto things. But this purpose would be defeated if, like Rorty, Heidegger were to encourage us, once we have cast off metaphysics and its ideal of a fixed, universal truth, to learn readily to switch perspectives and get the hang of other world views. That would just involve us in more thinking in the inauthentic sense of the word.[60]

Far from being a pragmatist, as Rorty makes him seem, Heidegger tells us that if we are to realize the ultimate meaning of our lives we must learn to live in harmony with the Being of beings. And although this coming to grips with Being does not mean representing it, asserting something about it, it does entail some kind of measuring up or opening up to it—a real (dare one say objective?) encounter. If we cannot speak of "truth" in this instance, because Heidegger takes pains to avoid any suggestion that this is a confrontation between a subject and an object, we can do so when it comes to the other, more definitive, transformative philosophers we have dealt with. Liberation is the result of perfect knowledge for Śaṅkara—simply calling a spade a spade (calling the self the Absolute); Fichte's intellectual intuition itself is the highest certainty. Thus far, then, it would seem hardly appropriate to call Heidegger, or any other transformative philosopher, an edifying philosopher.

It seems, rather, that we should ask this: Is the transformative philosopher a systematic philosopher in Rorty's sense of the term? Is he, with his standard of absolute truth, seeking a common ground on which to settle philosophical disputes once and for all; does he believe in the possibility of a universal, "normal" mode of discourse and the desirability of instituting one? The concept of transformative philosophy will gain in clarity as we consider this side of the matter.

The answer to this question too would appear to be no—although a guarded no. At first glance, it seems that the transformative philosopher is not one who assumes a context in which all parties can come to agreement. As we have seen in each case we have considered—Śaṅkara, Fichte, Heidegger—the transformative philosopher demands the fulfillment of spiritual prerequisites prior to inquiry. Such a demand destabilizes the realm of discourse and sets groups of discussants radically at odds with each other. On the one side stand those who are gifted with the knack of insight; on the other stand those without it. This polarization is most evident in the case of Fichte, who drives a sharp wedge between the "dogmatist," who has lost his identity amid impressions of sense and lives in a scattered consciousness, and the "idealist," who is able to single himself out from other things and enact the intellectual intuition. No amount of discussion can settle their dispute; they dwell in different worlds. When Fichte ascribes their inability to come to terms to a difference in *interest* and fundamental mode of experiencing, he sounds like a pragmatist indeed.[61] We can imagine how Śaṅkara's insistence on the attainment of peace of mind, concentration, dispassion, and so forth prior to the inquiry into Brahman would similarly polarize discussion. Thus the transformative philosopher recognizes a fundamental unevenness in the accessibility to the truth he espouses; in Rorty's language, he appreciates that his own discourse is radically incommensurable with others, that it is "abnormal." This recognition is, indeed, at the very heart of transformative philosophy.

Yet the transformative philosopher speaks of absolute truth. It would be quite wrong to suggest that a philosopher such as Śaṅkara or Fichte does not believe that he is offering a view which, if it does not settle matters once and for all, then finally ascertains every fact which has to be taken into account. For he claims to have opened up a wider vista and awakened a new faculty. He shows us an aspect of things we never saw before; he uncovers more of the world. This new perspective pertains to truth, simply because what we formerly took to be the sum total of reality stands, now a mere fraction of the whole, in relation to something else which obviously grounds it. We see how things *really* stand. Moreover, absolute truth can be spoken of here because, as I have maintained, the statements of the transformative philosopher not only focus the scene before us but also engender an experience of it. They therefore have special authority.

This does not mean, however, that a transformative philosopher arbitrarily invents a world. On the contrary, the philosophers we have studied speak in terms of coming to know things as they are in fact. But an encounter with fact cannot be realized—converted into experience—until it is adequately articulated. We have seen that because the framework of concepts of the transformative philosopher, being radically "abnormal," is usually the only one available for delineating a new side of reality made present to an expanded consciousness, it acquires a kind of apodictic self-verifying status. It is certain.

Still, this does not mean that the transformative philosopher is seeking a privileged class of representations upon which to base all knowledge. He may be systematic in some respects, but he is not bound to be an epistemologist. Fichte sometimes seems as if he were motivated by an epistemological concern. He hopes to discover "the primordial, absolutely unconditioned first principle of all human knowledge"; he endeavors to give us an "explanation of the entire system of experience." But here he really means that the philosopher should simply explain all there is. He should expose the entire gamut of being from the first cause to the last effect. For knowledge that one's existence is rooted in the Absolute Self is the key to freedom and blessedness. Only because Fichte thinks of reality strictly as something experienced by a subject of consciousness do his investigations sound epistemological. In fact, however, Fichte has generally not been considered relevant to the theory of knowledge—hence he has been removed from the mainstream of Western philosophy—precisely because he gives no thought to *justification.* He seems unaware of the problems raised by Kant concerning the validity of the synthetic a priori and its importance for science; and, as we have seen, he dismisses the problem of the objectivity of sense impressions as simply undecidable.

Śaṅkara as well is noted for having had little to say about the hotly debated epistemological issues of his day. In fact, transformative thinkers tend to focus exclusively on explanation and ignore justification. They aim to explain the whole of life; issues of knowledge and perception come in only to the degree that they are relevant. The great error of the theory of knowledge in the West may not have been, as Rorty believes, to think that by providing an explanation of knowledge relating to causes one could justify it (as if causes were reasons). Rather, the real error may have been to mistake for justifications the accounts of experience of transformative philosophers originally offered merely as *explanations.*[62] This is a slight difference, but it will make a great difference when it comes to telling the story of philosophy.[63]

Nor, finally, does the fact that the transformative philosopher espouses an absolute truth mean that he must ultimately seek to freeze philosophical conversation in terms of a standard vocabulary and, therefore, be condemned as a systematic philosopher in Rorty's sense. For the absoluteness of the absolute truth of the transformative philosopher has mainly to do with the revolution in awareness it causes, not its specific content. It is a function of form, of revelation and conviction, not of subject matter. Conceivably, even a transformative philosopher committed to *his* framework could see another description as able to bring about a similar effect. Thus, although debates among transformative thinkers have taken place in the history of philosophy, especially in Asian philosophy, nothing in principle prevents one from adopting a relativist perspective on the various conflicting views put forward. Nothing prevents one from seeing them as individually determined largely by historical, intellectual, cultural, and social forces while still acknowledging that each is successfully transformative and, therefore, defines its own absolute truth.[64] One who adopts such an attitude might well be called an "edified transformative" philosopher. The transformative philosopher, then, could be one who appreciates that, in the final analysis, philosophies differ from one another only aesthetically; yet at the same time he will seriously consider as philosophy only what has the power fully to transform us.[65]

We may sum up our discussion of whether the transformative philosopher is an edifying or a systematic philosopher—or, indeed, neither—by noting an interesting ambiguity in Rorty's definition of the edifying philosopher. It would seem that some edifying philosophers can turn out to be quite systematic:

> The attempt to edify (ourselves or others) may consist in the hermeneutic activity of making connections between our own culture and some exotic culture or historical period, or between our own discipline and another discipline which seems to pursue incommensurable aims in an incommensurable vocabulary. But it may instead consist in the "poetic" activity of thinking up such new aims, new words, or new disciplines, followed by, so to speak, the inverse of hermeneutics: the attempt to interpret our familiar surroundings in the unfamiliar terms or new inventions. In either case, the activity is . . . edifying without being constructive—at least if "constructive" means the sort of cooperation in the accomplishment of research programs which takes place in normal discourse. For edifying discourse is supposed to be abnormal, to take us out of our old selves by the power of strangeness, to aid us in becoming new beings.[66]

Transformative philosophy is very close to the "poetic" kind of edifying philosophy Rorty talks about here. I have drawn attention to the fact that transformative philosophy identifies itself as a mode of discourse which is incommensurable with other modes not embedded in the transformative philosopher's way of life. The transformative philosopher, moreover, sets up a vocabulary which defines new aims and thoroughly reinterprets our surroundings, much as Rorty describes. And he takes us out of our old selves and transforms us—as the edifying philosopher will do. But when it comes to the nature of this transformation there is an important difference between the transformative and the edifying philosopher: for the transformative philosopher the change is more extensive, more profound.

The transformative philosopher does not merely reorder our familiar experience; he introduces another dimension to experience. He does not merely redesign consciousness; he expands it. He does not merely rearrange the components of our familiar surroundings; he opens the heavens. The edifying philosopher, on the other hand, even when he waxes poetic, is still primarily a talker.[67] Although he may weave a spell with words, create new images and meanings, he still talks about what we knew already in another guise. Moreover, his words have little to do with what Heidegger calls the Being of beings; rather, they treat of the relations of beings to other beings—primarily, matters of science, art, society, and morality. The transformative philosopher does not wish to give us a perspective on these things; he wishes to supersede them. As students of transformative philosophy we are not redefined as we are when we read more and write more;[68] we are redefined as we are when we pass from sleeping to waking. Although the transformative philosopher is akin to the edifying philosopher in attempting to break down normal discourse and established ways of looking at things, he does this with the purpose of eliminating barriers to the unfoldment of consciousness. Being without a view is not an end in itself for him. (He is not simply out to show that philosophy is bankrupt.)[69] Rather, he wishes to release thought in order to promote its growth—to clear a space for consciousness to expand.

In the end, then, the issue of whether transformative philosophy belongs to edifying or systematic philosophy turns out to be moot: it falls between both categories or embraces them both. But our consideration of this issue has not been in vain, for it has brought out the character of transformative philosophy in sharper detail. We concluded the preceding section with a question regarding the future of transformative philosophy. We now return to this question, keeping in mind that transformative philosophy does resemble edifying philosophy in one important respect: it tends to be radically incommensurable with other discourse.

In speculating about the prospects of edifying philosophy Rorty notes that it is necessarily reactive.[70] The edifying philosopher, in order to convince us that a universal mode of discourse based on knowledge of "essences" is impossible, typically criticizes philosophies that have gained wider acceptance, and sometimes even pokes fun at them, without putting forward a constructive proposal of his own. He dreads nothing more than "the thought that [his] vocabulary should ever be institutionalized, or that [his] writing might be seen as commensurable with the tradition."[71] Thus the possibility of an edifying tradition is precluded. As long as there is systematic philosophy, the edifying philosopher has a role to play—as a detractor. But were systematic philosophy ever to be successfully annihilated, the edifying philosopher would cease being a philosopher in any professional sense and would have to be reclassified—perhaps simply as a poet or scholar or cultural anthropologist.[72]

Since transformative philosophy is not reactive or deconstructive in principle but only out of expediency—to free the mind from its metaphysical shackles—the possibility of becoming an established tradition remains for it. But it would hardly seem realizable. For as we have seen, transformative discourse is necessarily cut off from other modes of discourse. It can only be appreciated by those who share the interest of the transformative philosopher—his way of life, his state of consciousness. A tradition of transformative philosophy could only come about if a *community* of philosophers were to take up the way of transformative philosophy generation after generation—that is, become committed to a life of purity and the observance of spiritual practices. And we have no reason to believe that such a thing will ever happen.

On the other hand there is no reason to think that transformative philosophy will not continue to emerge sporadically and unpredictably as it has always done. The conditions for the appearance of a transformative philosopher are, indeed, inscrutable. In many cases—in the case of Fichte, for example—it seems quite unrelated to social and intellectual circumstances. Even though Kant was the spark that set him off, Fichte himself stresses that he philosophized on the basis of his particular way of experiencing life and his character. Given such imponderables, who can say when another such figure will appear?

In the meantime, the significance of Rorty's study is to remind us of the innumerable eddies and currents in the vast river of philosophy—a veritable Ganges. These cross each other, flow in and out, combine and cleave. The designation of one as the mainstream, others as tributaries and backwaters, is to a large extent arbitrary; and if it is done without noting the influence on the mainstream of lesser currents, it is perverse. While one may not be inclined to become a transformative philosopher in one's own case, as a scholar one still has his task cut out for him: to document truthfully the impact of that trend on major classical and modern traditions.[73]

3. *In Defense of Transformative Philosophy*

The question whether transformative philosophy will continue to manifest itself is, of course, quite different than the question whether it *ought* to. In the present study, while transformative philosophy has been presented as something to be taken seriously, no effort has been made to defend it. Since it will seem quite indefensible to some, a few concluding remarks are therefore in order regarding the various approaches a defense of transformative philosophy could take.

The severest criticism of transformative philosophy is already implicit in Rorty's criticism of systematic philosophy. The latter, he claims, stifles discussion. It seeks to present us, once and for all, with a fixed truth; to disclose "essences" and "objective" matters of fact which will practically impose themselves on us and compel universal agreement. Thus it precludes the creation of new realms of significance—hence knowledge—through moral and social action. It discourages one from accepting the responsibility of "choosing his own project"[74]—determining his own essence and building his own truth through living and experiencing, and then securing that truth by discursively setting it off from other perspectives. While transformative philosophy is not entirely guilty of this kind of bad faith—for, as we have seen, it insists on a more extensive commitment to praxis than Rorty himself imagines—it can still be seen as threatening the flow of conversation. For once the transformative philosopher has realized his absolute truth, he becomes isolated within his world of perfect certainty. No one can understand him unless one has converted to his sect. The communication of ideas, the endeavor to understand other world views which Rorty regards as essential to human rationality (when the conversation stops, we stop being human),[75] is thus jeopardized.

The most serious challenge to transformative philosophy, in other words, will question its right to call itself philosophy—instead of, say, mysticism. For although it cannot be reduced to it, philosophy is nevertheless thought at least to *involve* arriving at conclusions by way of arguments accessible to anyone, putting forward assertions with which anyone who has followed the course of inquiry ought to be able to agree, or else dispute, on commonly intelligible grounds.

Every transformative philosopher must in some way come to grips with this problem if he is to be worthy of the title "philosopher." Each of the figures we have studied has dealt with it in his own way. Śaṅkara embeds his mystical experience in an interpretation of scripture. Correct exegesis of the Upaniṣads, he argues, compels us to accept the anomaly of a self that is really at one with an Absolute that is consciousness in nature. Thus he articulates his system in a domain to which every Hindu lays claim and in which positions are negotiated according to established rules. Heidegger, as we have seen in this chapter, establishes a relation to philosophical tradition by criticizing it. As the object of his criticism is a common concern and his arguments themselves are intelligible, he remains within the province of philosophy. Fichte, who felt the charge of mysticism most acutely of the three, gives the most straightforward defense against it. Although his defense is determined by contemporary philosophical issues and attitudes, we can see in it features of a general argument. We shall therefore inspect it more closely.

There is a special historical circumstance which motivated Fichte's consideration of the restricted intelligibility of the *Wissenschaftslehre.* In 1796 Kant published a tract *Concerning a Recent Arrogant Tone in Philosophy (Von einem neuerdings erhobenen vornehmen Ton in der Philosophie)* in which he criticized the appeal to an extrasensory feeling, a *Wesensschau*, as the ultimate standard of philosophical truth.[76] Such had been advocated by the Jacobi school. Friedrich Heinrich Jacobi himself (1732–1819), in opposition to Kant, had declared the origin of perception by the affection of sensibility untenable.[77] He argued that Kant's critical philosophy, if worked out consistently, must become pure idealism—thus giving Fichte his cue. Jacobi, for his part, in rejecting idealism, opted for realism. There is an ultimate reality that is to be apprehended not by the senses, nor by the understanding, but directly in a consciousness of immediate certainty. This consciousness is the basis of all truth and experience. Jacobi gives it various names: *Empfindung, Erfahren, Erleben*, but most often *Glaube*, "faith."[78] Against such an intuition Kant complains that the philosopher who resorts to it does not *work* for knowledge; he simply consults his own private oracle. To the extent that he does not have to work he feels superior to those who do. Moreover, he removes himself from the arena of public scrutiny. He joins a private club whose members all share and support the same esoteric bias. Kant, importantly, does not deny the existence or possibility of such an intuition (he does that elsewhere); rather, he disputes its legitimacy as the basis of any real advance in philosophical understanding. His argument, it must be said, is mainly *ad hominem:* the so-called Intuitive Philosopher is arrogant, presumptuous, even lazy.

In his *Second Introduction to the WL* Fichte takes Kant's treatise very much into account. He considers it first in his defense of the intellectual intuition as distinct from a *Wesensschau*—namely, insofar as "it . . . is not at all directed toward a being but toward an action" and is therefore not in violation of the rule that the *thing*-in-itself is inaccessible.[79] But he considers it also in his defense of it as an objective sort of knowledge. I emphasize again that Fichte is not seeking here to justify all knowledge by grounding it on the intellectual intuition as a "privileged representation." (He is not proceeding as a classic epistemologist.) Rather, he is challenging the very idea that knowledge, in the proper sense of that word, necessarily depends on something external to the self. The crucial passage comes in his discussion of how the philosopher knows that the intellectual intuition he freely initiates exactly reproduces the act that gave birth to his consciousness in the first place:

> One can ask . . . , if this entire philosophy is built on something that is brought about merely by means of an act of the arbitrary will, does it not thereby become a chimera *(Hirngespinst)*, a mere invention? *How, indeed, does the philosopher intend to guarantee this merely subjective act its objectivity?* . . . I answer: this act [of the intellectual intuition] is *by nature objective.* I exist for me; this is a fact. Now I can only have come into existence for myself through an act—for I am free—and only through this particular act—for through this one I come into existence every moment for myself and through every other [act] something else comes into existence for me [that is, awareness of an *object* of consciousness—perception, experience]. The act is precisely the notion of the I and the notion of the I is precisely that act; both are quite the same. And under that notion nothing is or can be conceived except what has been indicated [that is, a self-reverting activity]. It [the I] *exists* thus because I *make* it thus. . . . The question concerning objectivity is based on the queer proposition that the I is something other than its own thought of itself and that there underlies this thought . . . yet something else outside of thought, about whose actual nature [the proponents of that view] are anxious.[80]

Specifically Fichte is challenging here the doctrine that knowledge depends on the affection of the knowing subject by an external thing-in-itself. But his statement applies as well to the doctrine, taken for granted by Kant in his criticism of the philosophers of the *Wesensschau*, that knowledge is secured, ultimately, only out in the open, so to speak—with recourse to the conventions of public debate and investigation. Clearly the intellectual intuition has no relation to the ways of discourse; it is a withdrawal, an inversion. Fichte's point is that this spontaneous act defines an authentic, concrete kind of knowledge nevertheless. For it is the nature of the self as self-reflection that stipulates that it can—indeed, must—be approached by a *subjective* act, an inward-turning of the mind. It is the nature of the self as free, on the other hand, which requires that I in some sense invent my own knowledge of myself. Fichte points out, moreover, that the act in question constitutes knowledge according to the standard Kantian definition; for both indispensable features, intuition and concept, are present:

> Does a consciousness arise for the philosopher herein? Without a doubt. For he not only intuits, he also *conceives*. He conceives of his act as an *acting in general*—of which he already has a concept from his previous experience—and, further, as this *particular, self-reverting* action such as he intuits within himself. He thus picks it out of the sphere of action in general by means of this characteristic difference.[81]

Fichte thus implicitly challenges Kant's dismissal of the transcendental apperception as a suitable basis for a science of the soul—for it is a *mere* consciousness, thought Kant, an attitude or assumption, but not *Erkenntnis.*

The teaching of the intellectual intuition as an objective act of knowledge is executed with greater rigor in the *Grundlage der gesammten Wissenschaftslehre*, where it is revealed as a sort of superknowledge.[82] There, in search of the first principle of all knowledge, Fichte considers logical truth, taking as his example the law of identity A = A. Does it, he asks, set the highest possible standard of conviction? He concludes that it does not. For necessary, logical truth, although perfectly certain, abstracts from the *existence* of the entities it treats. It seems, indeed, that for Fichte perfect knowledge must not only be formally true but must also reveal its object as *being*. It must, in other words, epitomize not only logical truth, which is certain but tautologous, but also empirical knowledge, which is immediate and actual; for empirical knowledge conforms to an independent state of affairs and is supplied with content. But the combination of both of these essential features of knowledge—certainty and immediacy—is achieved only in self-consciousness. Self-consciousness is necessarily formally adequate—there can be no possible discrepancy in this knowledge between knower and known—while it guarantees the existence of its object insofar as the latter, which is identical with the knower, is brought into being through the very act of knowing: "The I *posits itself* and it *is* by virtue of this mere self-positing. Conversely, the I *is* and it *posits* its being by virtue of its mere being."[83] Thus:

> The proposition "I am I" has a quite different meaning from the [mere logical truth], "A is A," namely, the latter has content only under a certain condition. *If* A is posited, then, of course, it is [posited] *as* A. . . . But that proposition ["A is A"] by no means establishes whether [A] is posited at all, hence, whether it is posited along with some predicate. But the proposition "I am I" is valid unconditionally and absolutely. . . . It is valid not only according to [its] form but also according to its content. In it the I is posited along with the predicate of being identical with itself, not on condition, but absolutely. Hence, it *is* posited, and the proposition can [also] be expressed: "I am."[84]

The identification of the intellectual intuition as "the supreme principle of human knowledge" and the development of a "science of knowledge" on that basis exhibits the cause of consciousness or experience and thus, like any other science, clarifies a particular state of affairs. Fichte believes to have ascertained that conviction is the mark of knowledge. This is what distinguishes it from opinion, sensation, emotion, and other varieties of consciousness; this is what all knowledge has to some degree. Fichte's "insight" is that all conviction issues from a single source and that all modes of knowledge derive their character as such from it. Experience, judgment, and inquiry are all but reflections of a higher, more introverted kind of knowing in which objectivity and certainty are perfectly combined. This is self-consciousness—pure knowledge. Of course, the relationship between pure knowledge and more public, social, and schematic ways of knowing turns out to be not rigorously logical but organic. Fichte's greatest achievement was to have worked out this relationship in terms of the dialectic.

Thus, in essence, Fichte answers the question—Is the *Wissenschaftslehre* (ergo transformative philosophy) philosophy?—by affirming that philosophy is essentially the apprehension of the source of all truth.[85] He turns the tables on those who would challenge the objectivity of his enterprise by insisting that the standards by which they would judge the matter—namely, the processes of perception and experience, or the ways of settling disputes among scientists—are themselves derived from the principle he has discovered, however little they may be aware of it. Although the requirement of a special ability is maintained in his system—thus it is still reserved for an elite—Fichte at least argues in a commonly intelligible, philosophically interesting way for the need for such a requirement. If his arguments sometimes take on an arrogant, *ad hominem* tone, that is not to be taken as a retreat into irrationality—a concession that the *Wissenschaftslehre* is, alas, a mystery that no one should attempt to defend philosophically—but as recognition that his arguments will naturally be appreciated most by those for whom such a need is already apparent.

This sort of defense of transformative philosophy—defense by direct counterassault, so to speak—is implied in the writings of the other transformative philosophers we have looked at. One sees it in Śaṅkara's doctrine of *jñāna*, detailed in Chapter 2.[86] It is hinted at by Heidegger when he suggests that "there is a kind of thought more rigorous than the conceptual."[87] And we see it expressed by many other figures in the history of philosophy, who have in effect said that one does not really know what it is to *know* something until one has experienced certain forms of knowledge altogether higher than the merely empirical or the merely logical.

But there are times when more subtle maneuvering is called for. This is especially the case when one is dealing with the Rortian relativist who puts no stock in "objectivity"—or even mutual intelligibility—to begin with and is, instead, apt to suspect the transformative philosopher of "systematic" tendencies. I believe, in fact, that a compelling defense of transformative philosophy can be made by skirting the intelligibility/objectivity issue altogether and appealing instead to a pragmatist notion of knowledge as power and progress.[88]

The transformative philosopher would do well to argue roughly as follows: Let us embrace the pragmatist idea of knowledge as an open-ended affair. That is, let us agree that knowledge does not consist merely in the possession of information but, rather, primarily in the discovery of new facts. It is not acquired through the observation of given states of affairs but through their exploration—acting on them to see how they respond, testing their potential. It does not aim at squaring with reality but at generating hypotheses which will carry investigation forward. But let us also recognize that this principle should be applied to the study of our own being, our inner experience, as well as the world around us. Let us recognize that the complete unfoldment of life may well depend on our submitting, even committing ourselves, to radically new ways of living—including those which have been recommended by prophets and wise men of the past and present—just as the nature of a microbe is revealed by placing it in new environments. Let us acknowledge that the basic character of experience can change as we adopt new attitudes and life-styles, and that our present acquaintance with its varieties may be far from exhaustive. Let us resolve to explore human consciousness as we have explored the natural world—by realizing its possibilities. The defense of transformative philosophy will then, perhaps, emerge out of the *practice* of transformative philosophy—as natural science validates itself in its usefulness—in the form of the exalted attainments held out to us by the thinkers called to our attention here: blessedness, fulfillment, feeling at last at home in the world.

Notes

Chapter 1

1. *BhGī* III.3. The following abbreviations will be used to refer to Śaṅkara's writings and other frequently cited Sanskrit works:

BĀU	= *Bṛhadāraṇyaka Upaniṣad*
BhGī	= *Bhagavadgītā*
BrSū	= *Brahmasūtra*
MīSū	= *Mīmāṃsāsūtra*
TU	= *Taittirīya Upaniṣad*
US	= *Upadeśasāhasrī*
YS	= *Yogasūtra*

Bh, signifying a commentary *(bhāṣya)*, may be added to another abbreviation to indicate a commentary on that work. For example, *BrSūBh* = *Brahmasūtrabhāṣya*, Śaṅkara's commentary on the *Brahmasūtra*.

2. For a general introduction to Śaṅkara's philosophy the reader may consult Paul Deussen, *The System of Vedānta*, or Eliot Deutsch, *Advaita Vedānta: A Philosophical Reconstruction*.

3. *Pañcadaśī* XI. Prior to Vidyāraṇya the relation of karma and knowledge *(jñāna)* had been treated by Vācaspatimiśra and Prakāśātman. While Vācaspati sees karma as a remote auxiliary of knowledge *(ārādupakāraka)*, Prakāśātman sees it as a proximate auxiliary *(sannipatyopakāraka)*. See J. F. Staal, *Advaita and Neo-Platonism*, pp. 94 f.

4. V. V. Gokhale, "The Vedānta Philosophy Described by Bhavya in His Mādhyamakahṛdaya"; see especially *kārikā* 15.

5. *BhGī* V.4.

6. *Nyāyasūtra* IV.2.26.

7. See, for example, Maharishi Mahesh Yogi in the preface to his *Bhagavad Gita*, pp. 11–15. Jan Gonda (*Die Religionen Indiens*, 2:83) refers to Śaṅkara as "the great champion of the unity of Hinduism."

8. Daniel H. H. Ingalls notes ("The Study of Śaṃkarācārya," p. 13) that Buddhism was already on the wane when Śaṅkara wrote his commentaries. As will be discussed in the present study, it is not the Buddhists, but, primarily, the Mīmāṃsakas and the Sāṃkhyas against whom Śaṅkara directs his attack.

9. Thus, according to Śaṅkara, the fruit of the horse sacrifice can be attained by those not entitled to perform it (only kings are so entitled) simply by meditating on it; *BĀUBh* I.1.1, intro.

10. Paul Hacker has pioneered the effort to determine the authentic works of Śaṅkara in his articles "Śaṅkarācārya and Śaṅkarabhagavatpāda: Preliminary Remarks Concerning the Authorship Problem" and "Eigentümlichkeiten der Lehre und Terminologie Śaṅkaras." The results of these investigations have been applied by Sengaku Mayeda to works ascribed to Śaṅkara but not dealt with by Hacker; see Mayeda's studies listed in the bibliography.

11. It is unclear whether this is equivalent to reaching the world of Brahman *(brahmaloka)*, of which Śaṅkara speaks elsewhere as the final station on the path of the gods *(devayāna)*; see *BrSūBh* III, *pādas* 2 and 3.

12. See *BrSūBh* III.1.8–24.

13. *The Brahmasūtrabhāṣya: Text with Foot-notes and Variants, etc.*, ed. N. R. Āchārya, I.1.4, p. 14:4–9.

14. Ibid., p. 14:9–22.

15. Ibid., p. 17:3–4.

16. Ibid., p. 18:4–8.

17. *brahma veda brahmaiva bhavati; ānandaṃ brahmaṇo vidvān na bibheti kutaścana.* Ibid., p. 15:1–2.

18. Ibid., pp. 18:10–19:1.

19. Ibid., p. 19:13–15. In translating passages from Śaṅkara's works I have consulted the translations of George Thibaut, Swāmī Mādhavānanda, Swāmī Gambhīrānanda, and Swāmī Jagadānanda. Practical considerations have precluded printing the Sanskrit text for all the passages I translate. I generally provide those which are especially difficult or in which key terms and concepts appear for the first time (in the order of my exposition).

20. *īśā vāsyam ityādayo mantrāḥ karmasu aviniyuktāḥ, teṣām akarmaśeṣasyātmano yāthātmyaprakāśakatvāt. yāthātmyaṃ cātmanaḥ śuddhatvāpāpaviddhatvaikatvanityatvāśarīratvasarvagatatvādi vakṣyamāṇam. . . . na hy evaṃlakṣaṇam ātmano yāthātmyam utpādyaṃ vikāryam āpyaṃ saṃskāryam. Īśāvāsyopaniṣatsaṭīkāśaṅkarabhāṣyopetā*, I, pp. 1–2.

21. . . . *nānātmalābhavad aprāptaprāptilakṣaṇa ātmalābho labdhṛlabdhavyayor bhedābhāvāt. yatra hy ātmano 'nātmā labdhavyo bhavati, tatrātmā labdhā, labdhavyo 'nātmā. sa cāprapta utpādyādikriyāvyavahitaḥ. . . . ayaṃ tu tadviparīta ātmā. ātmatvād eva notpādyādikriyāvyavahitaḥ. Bṛhadāraṇyakopaniṣad Ānandagirikṛtaṭīkāsaṃvalitaśaṅkarabhāṣyasametā*, I.4.7, p. 144.

22. At least, Śaṅkara does everything he can to avoid giving an explanation in his system. D. H. H. Ingalls accuses him of hedging a philosophical issue in his article "Śaṃkara on the Question: Whose Is Avidyā?" But a positive account of error can easily lead to paradox (see in this regard Plato's *Theatetus*). That error is "indescribable" *(anirvācanīya)* becomes an explicit philosophical theory with Maṇḍanamiśra; see L. Schmithausen, *Maṇḍanamiśra's Vibhramavivekaḥ*.

23. . . . *vidyayā tadapohanamātram eva lābho nānyaḥ kadācid apy upapadyate. tasmād ātmalābhe jñānād arthāntarasādhanasyānarthakyaṃ vakṣyāmaḥ. BĀUBh* I.4.7, p. 145.

24. Hacker ("Śaṅkara der Yogin und Śaṅkara der Advaitin," p. 126) refers to the denial found at *BrSūBh* II.1.3: "Neither by the knowledge of Sāṃkhya independent of the Veda nor by the path of yoga is the highest good to be attained; for the scripture rejects any means to the highest good other than the Vedic knowledge of the unity of the self" (*na sāṃkhyajñānena vedanirapakṣeṇa yogamārgeṇa vā niḥśreyasam adhigamyata iti. śrutir hi vaidikād ātmaikatvavijñānād anyan niḥśreyasasādhanaṃ vārayati*. . . , p. 183:19–20). But this remark occurs in a discussion about the material cause of the universe in which Śaṅkara is intent on refuting the Sāṃkhya view that the material cause of things is an unconscious prime matter *(pradhāna)*. Since the yoga system borrows its metaphysics from the Sāṃkhya here, it stands or falls with the latter—but, Śaṅkara adds, only concerning this particular point. Insofar as they are not contradicted by a portion of scripture, there is room for yoga and Sāṃkhya (*yena tv aṃśena na virudhyete teneṣṭam eva sāṃkhyayogasmṛtayoḥ sāvakāśatvam*, 24–25). Since Śaṅkara acknowledges the authority of yoga as "a means of [conveying] perfect vision" *(saṃyagdarśanābhyupāya)* in the same passage (p. 183:4), we may assume that he means to accept yoga *practice* here.

25. *Upāsana* entails viewing the absolute under a particular divine aspect —for example, the meditation on Brahman as the golden person within the sun, whose name is Ud, described in *Chāndogya Upaniṣad* I.6.6–7.9 (discussed by Śaṅkara *BrSūBh* I.1.20–21). Yogic concentration *(nirodha)*, on the other hand, is the complete cessation of mental activity (according to *YS* I.2), during which there is no object of consciousness.

26. . . . *syāc cittavṛttinirodhasya vedavākyajanitād ātmavijñānād arthāntaratvāt. tantrāntareṣu ca kartavyatayāvagatatvād vidheyatvam. . . . na, mokṣasādhanatvenānavagamāt. na hi vedānteṣu brahmātmavijñānād anyat paramapuruṣārthasādhanatvena avagamyate. BĀUBh* I.4.7, p. 136.

27. It is implicit in the thesis of Hacker ("Śaṅkara der Yogin") that Śaṅkara was originally a yogin who in his mature philosophy rejected yoga in favor of a radical monistic illusionism. Hacker for the most part neglects the preparatory importance of spiritual practice in Śaṅkara's later system. More explicitly, Vetter (*Brahmasiddhiḥ*, pp. 18–21) sees in the *Brahmasiddhi* of Maṇḍanamiśra an effort to mend the rift between Advaita and Hindu tradition caused by Śaṅkara's emphasis on renunciation *(sannyāsa)* and, at the same time, in Śaṅkara's notion that knowledge derives immediately from what is known and is not something to be carried out, his most original contribution to Vedānta soteriological epistemology. Vetter also uses Śaṅkara's apparent rejection of yoga to explain his switch from idealism in his *Māṇḍūkya-*

kārikābhāṣya to realism in his *BrSūBh* ("Zur Bedeutung des Illusionismus bei Śaṅkara," pp. 416 f.). Thus the two foremost Vedānta scholars of recent times have, in an effort to make Śaṅkara stand out as an individual in the history of Indian philosophy, tended to emphasize his conflict with his own religious milieu and hence his reservations about accepted spiritual practice.

28. Swami Satchidanandendra Saraswati, *The Vision of Atman*, p. 27.

29. *BrSūBh* I.1.4, p. 21:16–19.

30. Ibid., IV.3.14, p. 498:19–21.

31. Ibid., I.1.4, p. 20:3; see, in general, II.3.40.

32. Compare *BrSūBh* I.1.4, p. 18:7: "*Mokṣa* is the state of being Brahman" *(brahmabhāvaś ca mokṣah).*

33. Ibid., I.4.23.

34. Ibid., II.1.14, p. 197:6–7.

35. Ibid., I.2.18.

36. Ibid., I.1.3.

37. Ibid., II.1.14, pp. 200:23–202:3.

38. Ibid., I.1.2, p. 8:5–8.

39. Ibid., IV.1.1, p. 460:10–12.

40. See Vetter, *Brahmasiddhiḥ*, pp. 119–121. In what follows we consider the discussion at *BrSūBh* IV.1.1–2, where the same view is anticipated by the opponent as a possible objection to *his* (not Śaṅkara's) position that the Vedic text need be heard only once: *athocyate na kevalaṃ vākyaṃ kaṃcid arthaṃ sākṣātkartuṃ śaknoty ato yuktyapekṣaṃ vākyam anubhāvayiṣyati brahmātmatvam iti*, p. 461:8–10.

41. For example, the metaphysical notion that cause and effect are identical. This idea clarifies those scriptural passages which suggest to Śaṅkara that the world, which is the effect of Brahman, is not different from it (as in *Chāndogya Upaniṣad* IV.1.4). For Śaṅkara's interesting views on the employment of reasoning in the context of theological discussion, see *BrSūBh* I.1.2, II.1.6, II.1.11, discussed in my "Reason, Revelation and Idealism in Śaṅkara's Vedānta."

42. *BrSūBh* IV.1.2, p. 462:17–23; compare the discussion by Vetter, *Studien zur Lehre und Entwicklung Śaṅkaras*, pp. 117–129.

43. It is not denied that liberation proceeds from understanding the truth of the Veda. Precisely that is granted. But what is involved in such understanding? Is it tantamount to the mere ability to recite the phrase "I am Brahman"? Certainly by the term *brahmātmāvagati* Śaṅkara means more than that.

44. *BrSūBh* IV.1.2, p. 461:6–8.

45. "The Ideal of Renunciation," p. 300.

46. *niścitaṃ ca jñānaṃ puruṣārthasādhanam iṣyate "yasya syād addhā na vicikitsāsti"; "saṃśayātmā vinaśyati" iti śrutismṛtībhyām*, *BĀUBh* I.4.10, p. 159; *api ca saṃyagjñānān mokṣa iti sarveṣāṃ mokṣavādīnām*

abhyupagamaḥ, *BrSūBh* II.1.11, p. 193:24–25. See especially the discussion in which the latter remark occurs.

The false interpretation considered here is a serious fault because it makes Vedānta into an absurd contemplation of the absolute in the face of a world utterly opposed to it. Śaṅkara manifestly does not consider it in such a way. For him Vedānta is self-verifying. The scripture reveals its object to one without him having to imagine it, and that constitutes its authority. In this respect the point that knowledge of Brahman is not a "fanciful combination" (*saṃpat*, as in certain meditations; *BrSūBh* I.1.4, p. 15:18) is important, as is the much quoted remark that "the fact that a sentence is a description of a thing or a description of an action is not the cause of its authority or lack of authority, but rather that it gives rise to precise and fruitful knowledge *(niścitaphalavadvijñānotpādakatvam)*; in that case a sentence has authority, otherwise not" (*BĀUBh* I.4.7, p. 138). (It is the Mīmāṃsaka, of course, who insists that a sentence has validity only if it expresses an action.) The paradigm for such knowledge is the knowledge that the snake one thinks one sees is really a rope.

The transformation of Vedānta into a *faith* by certain Neohinduistic writers is probably due to the influence of Christianity. In classical Hindu theology faith plays a relatively minor role. See in this regard Hacker's treatment of Vivekananda's Vedānta in "Der religiöse Nationalismus Vivekānandas"; see also his article "Über den Glauben in der Religionsphilosophie des Hinduismus."

47. *teṣu hi satsu, prāg api dharmajijñāsāyā ūrdhvaṃ ca śakyate brahma jijñāsāyituṃ jñātuṃ ca, na viparyaye*; *BrSūBh* I.1.1, p. 5:6–8. The material dealt with in this section has also been discussed by Richard De Smet, "The Theological Method of Śaṃkara," chap. 4.

48. That is, the *vivekākhyāti* or *sattvapuruṣānyathākhyāti*, also referred to as "the highest meditation" (*paraṃ prasaṃkhyānam*, *YSBh* II.2). This discrimination is clearly an important step on the way to liberation. It is the "means to escape" *(hānopāya)*—that is, to the final state of the isolation *(kaivalya)* of the *puruṣa* from the *guṇas* (see the discussion in *YS* II.25–27). It is not equivalent to that final state, but one must subdue it *(nirunaddhi)*, too, in order for the latter to arise (*YSBh* I.2).

49. *abhyāsavairāgyābhyāṃ tannirodhaḥ*, *YS* I.12. The mental flow *(cittanadī)* tends toward two directions, Vyāsa explains—toward what is good, that is, *kaivalya (yā . . . kaivalyaprāgbharā . . . sā kalyāṇavahā)*, or toward what is bad, that is, *saṃsāra (saṃsāraprāgbharā . . . pāpavahā)*. *Vairāgya* clogs up *(khilīkriyate)* the flow toward worldly objects. *Abhyāsa* opens up the flow toward discrimination.

50. *YSBh* I.15.

51. *cittasyāvṛttikasya praśāntavāhitā sthitiḥ tadarthaḥ prayatnaḥ* [= *abhyāsaḥ*]; *YSBh* I.13.

52. *yathā prāvṛṣi tṛṇāṅkurasyodbhavena tadbījasattānumīyate tathā mokṣamārgaśravaṇena yasya romaharṣāśrupātau dṛṣyete tatrāpy asti viśeṣadarśanabījam apavargabhāgīyaṃ karmābhinirvārtitam ity anumīyate. tasyātmabhāvabhāvanā svābhāvikī pravartate:* "As one infers the existence of a grass seed from the emergence of a sprout in the rainy season, so one infers that karma conducive to release is present, which will serve as the seed of the [final] discriminating vision, from the fact that one cries [for joy] and one's hair bristles upon hearing about the path to liberation. For such a person the contemplation of one's state is automatic." *YSBh* IV.25.

53. It is to be noted that Śaṅkara's attitude toward yoga in the *Brahmasūtrabhāṣya*, his most important work, is in general favorable. He seems to have written the *BrSūBh* in an atmosphere of respect for yoga techniques and doctrines. At III.2.24, for example, he says that the yogin perceives the self in a state of complete mental calmness *(saṃrādhana)*. Elsewhere he refers to the ability of yogins to animate several bodies at the same time and maintains in general that such powers are to be taken seriously (I.3.27, p. 121:21–22; I.3.33, p. 135:12–13). Regarding Śaṅkara's proximity to yoga on matters of philosophical doctrine in his later works, Hacker has made several observations ("Śaṅkara der Yogin," pp. 136–146), only a few of which can be mentioned. That both Śaṅkara and the yoga system do not differentiate the mind but ascribe all of its functions (mind, intellect, ego) to one organ (the *antaḥkaraṇa* or the *citta*) is well known (see, for example, Hermann Jacobi, "Über das ursprüngliche Yogasystem"). Hacker notes further that the natural but false attribution of mental states to the self rather than the mind is, specifically, for both a "superimposition" *(adhyāropaṇā)*. Ignorance *(avidyā)* is the main cause of bondage for yoga as well as for Śaṅkara. The application of the means for removing ignorance (in yoga, the observances, meditation, and so forth; in Vedānta, knowledge) is described in each system as a kind of therapy. Hacker shows that Śaṅkara even depends on yoga in developing typically Advaitin doctrines. The theory of the self-luminousness of the self (*BĀUBh* IV.3.7), for example, which represents in the final analysis a step beyond yoga psychology, depicts the mind as assuming the character of *sarvārthakaraṇa*, "organ for all" (as in *YS* IV.23), by virtue of the self's illumining it.

54. *tasmād evaṃvic chānto dānta uparatas titikṣuḥ samāhito bhutvātmany evātmānaṃ paśyati*; *BĀU* IV.4.23.

55. *śānto bahyendriyavyāpārata upaśāntas tathā dānto 'ntaḥkaraṇatṛṣṇāto nivṛttaḥ:* "One is calm who has ceased from the activity of the external senses; one is controlled who has eliminated the thirst of the inner organ." *BĀUBh* IV.4.23, p. 700.

56. For *nirodha* of the fluctuations of the mind is accompanied by *nirodha* of the senses: "Supreme control exists when, the mind being subdued, the senses are subdued without dependence on any further effort to subdue them,

as when one sense overcomes another" (*paramā tv iyaṃ vaśyatā yac cittanirodhe niruddhānīndriyāṇi netarendriyajayavat prayatnakṛtam upāyāntaram apekṣante yoginā iti*, *YSBh* II.55). In Vedānta literature after Śaṅkara, the referents of *śama* and *dama* are not fixed; see, for example, the *Vedāntasāra* of Sadānanda.

57. Śaṅkara: *titikṣur dvandvasahiṣṇuḥ*, *BĀUBh* IV.4.23, p. 700; *YSBh* II.32: *tapo dvandvasahanam.*

58. *samāhito indriyāntaḥkaraṇacalanarūpād vyāvṛtyaikāgryarūpeṇa samāhitaḥ*; ibid. Compare Sadānanda, *Vedāntasāra*, p. 2.

59. For a post-Śaṅkaran account of these concepts see *Sarvavedāntasiddhāntasārasaṃgraha*, vv. 94 ff.

60. *etam eva pravrājino lokam icchantaḥ pravrājanti.*

61. *BĀUBh* IV.4.22, p. 691.

62. *etad ha sma vai tat pūrve vidvāṃsaḥ prajāṃ na kāmayante kiṃ prajayā kariṣyāmo yeṣām no 'yam ātmāyaṃ loka iti.* Note that Śaṅkara renders all three Vedic particles *ha sma vai* with the single particle *kila* (p. 692). Regarding Śaṅkara's uncertain command of Vedic Sanskrit see Wilhelm Rau, "Bemerkungen zu Śaṃkaras Bṛhadāraṇyakopaniṣadbhāṣya."

63. *BĀUBh* IV.4.22, p. 694.

64. An example of an *apūrvavidhi* is the injunction, "One who desires heaven ought to sacrifice" *(svargakāmo yajeta)*, which establishes the need to sacrifice in the first place. An example of a *niyamavidhi* is, "He pounds the rice grains" *(vrīhīn avahanti)*, which declares that the rice to be used in the sacrifice is to be husked, not with the nails, but by being pounded on a millstone. Thus it restricts one to a certain known alternative. See P. V. Kane, *History of Dharmaśāstra* 5:1229 f.

65. *kathaṃ punar upāsanasya pakṣaprāptir yāvatā pāriśeṣyād ātmajñānasmṛtisantatiḥ nityaivety abhihitam. bāḍham. yady apy evaṃ śarīrārambhakasya karmaṇo niyataphalatvāt saṃyagjñānaprāptāv apy avaśyambhāvinī pravṛttir vāgmanaḥkāyānām. labdhavṛtteḥ karmaṇo balīyastvāt. mukteṣvādipravṛttivat. tena pakṣe prāptaṃ jñānapravṛttidaurbalyam. tasmāt tyāgavairāgyādisādhanabalāvalambena ātmavijñānasmṛtisantatir niyantavyā bhavati. . . . BĀUBh* I.4.7, pp. 140 f. Compare Śaṅkara's problematic gloss of *BĀUBh* III.5.1: "Thus let the Brahman, after doing away with learnedness *(pāṇḍitya)* [or, according to Śaṅkara's paraphrase, having completely achieved self-knowledge: *ātmavijñānaṃ niravaśeṣaṃ kṛtvā*] live as a child *(bālyena tiṣṭhāset)*. Having done away with both the state of childhood and learnedness, he becomes a sage *(muni)*. Having done away with wisdom *(mauna)* and the opposite of wisdom *(amauna)*, he becomes a Brahman." According to his more straightforward treatment of this passage in his *BrSūBh* (III.4.7)—which nevertheless squares with that of his *BĀUBh*—wisdom *(mauna)*, "preeminence of knowledge" *(jñānātiśaya)*, is meant to be

enjoined for the sannyāsin who is already in possession of self-knowledge *(vidyāvataḥ sannyāsinaḥ)*. This is appropriate in case, "due to the influence of the vision of differences, one has not [truly] achieved knowledge" *(yasmin pakṣe bhedadarśanaprābalyān na prāpnoti, tasminn eṣa vidhir iti*; p. 455:17). Śaṅkara's proximity to Maṇḍanamiśra regarding the need for a meditative intensification of the initial insight into the truth of the self has been overlooked by recent investigators. See Vetter, *Brahmasiddhiḥ*, pp. 119 ff., and Vetter's introductory remarks, pp. 17–21.

66. *sarvakriyoparama eva ātmalokasādhanaṃ mukhyam antaraṅgam*; *BĀUBh* IV.4.22, p. 692.

67. *tam etaṃ vedānuvacanena brāhmaṇā vividiṣanti yajñena dānena tapasānāśakena. etam eva viditvā munir bhavati.*

68. *karmabhiḥ saṃskṛtā hi viśuddhātmanaḥ śaknuvanty ātmānam upaniṣatprakāśitam apratibandhena veditum. tathā hy ātharvaṇe viśuddhasattvas tatas tu taṃ paśyate niṣkalaṃ dhyāyamānaḥ iti. smṛtiś ca jñānam utpadyate puṃsāṃ kṣayāt pāpasya karmaṇaḥ ityādih. BĀUBh* IV.4.22, p. 689.

69. *Kāmyakarma*, as opposed to *nityakarma*, is a rite performed for worldly prosperity (sons, wealth, and the like) or heaven.

70. *vedānuvacanayajñadānatapaḥśabdena sarvam eva nityaṃ karmopalakṣyate. evaṃ kāmyavarjitaṃ nityaṃ karmajātaṃ sarvam ātmajñānotpattidvāreṇa mokṣasādhanatvaṃ pratipadyate. evaṃ karmakāṇḍenāsya ekavākyatāvagatiḥ. BĀUBh* IV.4.22, p. 690.

71. *evaṃ eva ātmaikatvajñāne 'pi kvacij janmāntarakṛtaṃ karma nimittaṃ bhavati. yathā prajāpateḥ. kvacit tapo nimittaṃ, tapasā brahma vijijñāsasva iti śruteḥ. kvacid ācāryavān puruṣo vedo, śraddhāval labhate jñānam, tad vidhi praṇipātena, ācāryād haiva, draṣṭavyaḥ śrotavyaḥ ityādiśrutismṛtibhya ekāntajñānalābhanimittatvam. śraddhāprabhṛtīṇām adharmādinimittaviyogahetutvāt. vedāntaśravaṇamanananididhyāsanānāṃ ca sākṣājjñeyaviṣayatvāt. pāpādipratibandhakṣaye cātmamanasoḥ bhūtārthajñānanimittasvābhāvyāt. tasmād ahetutvaṃ na jātu jñānasya śraddhāpraṇipātādīnām iti. BĀUBh* I.4.2, p. 101.

72. *Taittirīyopaniṣad Ānandagirikṛtaṭīkāsaṃvalitaśaṅkarabhāṣyopetā*, p. 3.

73. Ibid., p. 36.

74. Ibid., p. 39:16.

75. *yathāprāptam eva kārakāstitvam upādāyopāttaduritakṣayārthaṃ karmāṇi vidadhac chāstraṃ mumukṣūṇām phalārthināṃ ca phalasādhanam, na kārakāstitve vyāpriyate. upacitaduritapratibandhasya hi vidyotpattir nāvakalpate. tatkṣaye ca vidyotpattiḥ syāt tataś cāvidyānivṛttis tata ātyantikaḥ saṃsāroparamaḥ.* Ibid., p. 40.

76. *virodhād eva ca vidyā mokṣaṃ prati na karmāṇy apekṣate. svātmalābhe tu pūrvopacitapratibandhāpanayadvāreṇa vidyāhetutvaṃ prati-*

padyante karmāṇi nityānīti. . . . evaṃ cāvirodhaḥ karmavidhiśrutīnām. ataḥ kevalāyā eva vidyāyāḥ paraṃ śreya iti siddham. Ibid., p. 41. See also the discussion of the purifying function of Vedic learning, truthfulness, righteousness, and so forth, I.11, p. 31.

77. The notions of *apūrva-* and *niyamavidhi* are but two examples. For another example: the false dilemma posed at *BrSūBh* I.1.1—that an investigation of Brahman cannot be undertaken if Brahman is known, for then it would be superfluous; nor can it be undertaken if it is not known, for then there would be no object to investigate—is a variation on *MīSūBh* I.1.1. A systematic comparison of the *MīSūBh* and the *BrSūBh* would yield many insights into the ideological background of the latter. See De Smet, pp. 197–217.

78. *MīSūBh* II.1.6.

79. Ibid., II.1.8.

80. This matter is confused by the later Vedānta usage of *ārādupakāraka*, "remote auxiliary," to refer to karma. In Mīmāṃsā a remote auxiliary is a subsidiary ritual which produces an intermediate *apūrva.*

81. In other words, one does not accomplish something by attempting the opposite.

82. *BrSūBh* IV.1.2, p. 463:14–17.

83. *BrSūBh* III.4.26. Compare Kumārila's doctrine that knowledge is dependent on external factors for its origin but self-established with respect to its own characteristics *(svaguṇeṣu)* once it has arisen—cited by Śāntarakṣita in his *Tattvasaṃgraha*, vv. 2848 ff.

84. *BrSūBh* III.4.33, p. 449:12–18.

85. Ibid., III.4.52, pp. 458:26–459:6.

86. *TUBh* I.12, p. 41.

87. Ibid., p. 42.

88. Ibid.

89. Only members of the twice-born castes are qualified to study the Veda. The student shows reverence to the Vedānta guru by giving him fuel for his sacrificial fire.

90. *US (gadyaprabandha)* I.2 and 4.

91. I am indebted to Jerry Jarvis for this analogy.

92. See Madeleine Biardeau, "Quelques reflexions sur l'apophatisme de Śaṅkara."

93. *na hi vastuto muktāmuktatvaviśeṣo 'sti. ātmano nityaikarūpatvāt. kiṃtu tadviṣayāvidyāpohyate śāstropadeśajanitavijñānena. prāk tadupadeśaprāpteḥ tadarthaś ca prayatna upapadyata eva. BĀUBh* IV.4.6, pp. 663 f. Compare *BrSūBh* II.1.14, p. 198:17–18.

94. On various occasions the philosophical ramifications of this double way of talking become the theme of Śaṅkara's discussion. At *BrSūBh* II.1.14 Śaṅkara admits in effect that his own theory, because it assumes a distinction

between teacher and student, is to be relegated to the sphere of untruth, but he still insists on its ability to produce enlightenment—for, he says, a person can awaken from a dream by dreaming he was bitten by a snake! The comparative philosopher will recognize similarities between Śaṅkara and Wittgenstein on this point. (*Tractatus Logico-Philosophicus* 6.54: "My propositions serve as elucidations in the following way: anyone who understands me eventually recognizes them as nonsensical, when he has used them—as steps—to climb up beyond them. [He must, so to speak, throw away the ladder after he has climbed it.]")

95. One might object, for example, that Śaṅkara's commentaries do not always represent his views. For sometimes, it seems, he is constrained by the text on which he is commenting, which he must respect as revelation and interpret piously in accord with an accepted tradition of exegesis. (See Hacker, "Notes on the Māṇḍūkyopaniṣad and Śaṅkara's Āgamaśāstravivaraṇa," p. 115.) Śaṅkara's acceptance of karma, yoga, and *upāsana* may in fact represent only a concession to Brahmanical tradition; they are not essential to his own system. This would seem to be the case especially for his *TUBh*, where the content of his discussion seems dictated by the strong pronouncements in favor of religious practice of the Upaniṣad itself. Moreover, the latter text probably belongs to the earliest of Śaṅkara's Vedānta works, prior to which he may well have written a commentary on the *Yogasūtra* as an adherent of the yoga school (Hacker, "Śaṅkara der Yogin," pp. 125, 129–136). The *TUBh*, that is, with its adoption of karma, may be simply a carry-over from an earlier yoga phase which Śaṅkara, in such works as the *BĀUBh* and *BrSūBh*, later outgrew. Finally, one might charge that Śaṅkara's recourse to a theory of two truths is not a sincere philosophical consideration but an expedient to escape the various difficulties he causes for himself by expounding his system in connection with religious texts which contradict it on many points—that is, the theory of two truths is just a "garbage disposal of philosophical problems" (Vetter, "Illusionismus bei Śaṅkara," pp. 421–423).

None of these observations constitutes a serious objection, in my opinion. To begin with the last, an interpretation that is unable to take an author at his word seems dubious indeed. To do so in the present case is simply to preclude serious discussion of what has been considered Śaṅkara's most important philosophical idea: that the world is an illusion. Nor, to return to the first objection, does the fact that Śaṅkara's remarks sometimes appear dictated by the text warrant rejecting them as not his own. There are many degrees of divergence or coincidence between a commentary and its text. *TUBh* I, although it always takes its cue from the Upaniṣad, contains much material that is incidental to the text; in any case, it is hardly a word-for-word gloss. Moreover, the discussion of *TUBh* I coincides in many respects with that of the *BĀUBh* and statements of the *US*, as we have seen. And it is to be noted that at *BĀU* IV.4.22 and I.4.2 Śaṅkara goes out of his way to recommend various kinds of spiritual practice, even in plain opposition to the prima facie meaning of the Upaniṣad. With regard, finally, to the objection that the *TUBh* is not to be considered an example of Śaṅkara's mature thought, we may, while agreeing, still notice the continuity between the *TUBh* and later works. In order to see that a certain (undated) work of a particular author was composed prior to another, one does not necessarily have to see that the author reversed himself.

Chapter 2

1. K. Tynan, "Profiles: Tom Stoppard," *The New Yorker*, 19 December 1977, p. 96.

2. See especially J. F. Staal, "Negation and the Law of Contradiction in Indian Thought," and his discussion of the *catuṣkoti* in *Exploring Mysticism*, pp. 35–46.

3. By B. K. Matilal, for example, in *Epistemology, Logic and Grammar in Indian Philosophical Analysis*.

4. See the various studies in Steven T. Katz, ed., *Mysticism and Philosophical Analysis*, most of which have critical reference to W. T. Stace, *Mysticism and Philosophy*. For a bibliography see P. G. Moore, "Recent Studies of Mysticism."

5. Thus Staal on the denial of the principle of contradiction: "The difficulty is not . . . that Aristotle's principle is a law of thought, which might be thrown overboard by anyone who prefers to engage in activities other than thinking. The difficulty is rather that this principle makes explicit the function of the particle 'not,' of which the occurrence, when used in any other way, makes no sense. Of course, we may avoid using 'not' altogether. But if we make use of 'not,' it is perverse to use it in such a manner as to conflict with its proper function. That is not what words are for. Such precisely is the reason that any violation of the principle of noncontradiction is irrational" (*Exploring Mysticism*, pp. 36 f.).

6. *BrSūBh* I.1.5, p. 25:4–5.

7. Ibid., I.1.5, p. 25:13–17.

8. *tad aikṣata bahu syāṃ prajāyeyeti tat tejo 'sṛjata.*

9. *BrSūBh* I.1.5, p. 27:3–4.

10. Therefore Brahman can properly serve as the subject of the verb "thinks" in the Upaniṣad verse. This observation perhaps clarifies the Sāṃkhya objection about a lack of independence: he is trying to prevent the Vedāntin from utilizing *Chāndogya Upaniṣad* VI.2.3 for his purposes, by arguing that if Brahman is identical with its own activity then it is not a grammatical *kartṛ*.

11. *tattvānyatvābhyām anirvacanīye nāmarūpe avyākṛte*, *BrSūBh* I.1.5, p.

27:13. Here I am following the not uncontroversial interpretation of these terms offered by Hacker, "Eigentümlichkeiten der Lehre and Terminologie Śaṅkaras," pp. 261–264.

12. *BrSūBh* I.1.5, p. 27:19–20.

13. *savitṛprakāśavad brahmaṇo jñānasvarūpanityatve jñānasādhanāpekṣānupapatteḥ*, ibid., p. 27:18.

14. *BĀU* II.4.12.

15. *kūṭasthanitya evāyaṃ vijñānaghana ātmā nāsyocchedaprasaṅgo 'sti. mātrādibhis tv asya bhūtendriyalakṣaṇābhir avidyākṛtābhir asaṃsargo vidyayā bhavati. saṃsargābhāve ca tatkṛtasya viśeṣavijñānasyābhavān na pretya saṃjñāstīty uktam iti. BrSūBh* I.4.22, p. 172:25–26.

16. *na vā are 'haṃ mohaṃ bravīmi, avināśī vā are 'yam ātmānucchittidharmā.* The last half of this passage is not to be found in the corresponding verse *BĀU* II.4.13.

17. These two verses also diverge somewhat in wording.

18. *BĀU* II.4.14.

19. To be precise, it is the agent suffix which indicates the element of knowledge according to Śaṅkara: *vijñānadhātur eva kevalaḥ . . . kartṛvacenena tṛcā nirdiṣṭaḥ*; *BrSūBh* I.4.22, p. 173:10–11.

20. *jño nityacaitanyo 'yam ātmā*, p. 280:12, thus extraordinarily taking the *jña* of the *sūtra* to indicate a substance rather than an agent. See Thibaut, *The Vedānta Sūtras of Bādarāyaṇa with the Commentary by Śaṅkara*, 1:liv.

21. *yasmād eva notpadyate param eva brahmāvikṛtam upādhisaṃparkāj jīvabhāvenāvatiṣṭhate*, *BrSūBh* II.3.18, p. 280:13.

22. *tad eva cet paraṃ brahma jīvas tasmāj jīvasyāpi nitycaitanyasvarūpatvam agnyauṣṇyaprakāśavad iti gamyate*, *BrSūBh* II.3.18, p. 280:16–18.

23. *yad vai tan na paśyati paśyan vai tan na paśyati, na hi draṣṭur dṛṣṭer viparilopo vidyate 'vināśitvāt. na tu tad dvitīyam asti tato 'nyad vibhaktaṃ yat paśyet.*

24. See especially "Vedānta-Studien: 1. Bemerkungen zum Idealismus Śaṅkaras" and "Śaṅkara's Conception of Man."

25. *kiṃjyotir ayaṃ puruṣaḥ.*

26. *ātmeti kāryakaraṇasvāvayavasaṃghātavyatiriktaṃ kāryakaraṇāvabhāsakam ādityādibāhyajyotirvat svayam anyenānavabhāsyamānam abhidhīyate jyotir*, *BĀUBh* IV.3.6, p. 551.

27. *yo 'yaṃ vijñānamayaḥ prāṇeṣu hṛdyantarjyotiḥ puruṣaḥ.*

28. *prāṇeṣu prāṇebhyo vyatirikta ity arthaḥ*, *BĀUBh* IV.3.7, p. 560.

29. *vijñānaprāyo buddhivijñānopādhisaṃparkāvivekād vijñānamaya ity ucyate*, ibid., p. 559.

30. *pāraṃparyeṇa sūkṣmasthūlatāratamyāt*; ibid., p. 561.

31. Ibid., p. 562.

32. See p. 559. Only insofar as it is made distinct by the light of the intellect

is an object of the senses perceived *(buddhivijñānālokaviśiṣṭam eva hi sarvaṃ viṣayajātam upalabhyate)*. The sense organs are mere channels *(dvāramātrāṇi)* for the intellect.

33. In discussing *BrSū* II.3.40 Śaṅkara develops an analogy for the agency of the self in relation to the organs of the relative human person. It is like a carpenter in relation to the tools he uses. With reference to the particular tools he employs in cutting wood and so on, a carpenter can be considered an agent. But with reference to the work that the tools perform he is not—or, as Śaṅkara puts it, "he is not an agent through his own body" *(svaśarīreṇa tv akartaiva)*. Likewise, the self is an agent only with reference to the employment of the mind and senses but not with reference to the work they perform —not in itself. And just as a carpenter can lay down his tools, the self can through knowledge put aside the senses and "be content in a state of complete serenity" *(sukhī bhavati saṃprasādasthāyām)*. *BrSūBh* II.3.40, p. 293: 9–20.

34. *Critique of Pure Reason*, trans. Norman Kemp Smith, A341.

35. At A346, Kant structures his argument somewhat differently. The "I that thinks" does not even count as a concept. We are unable to apprehend it because it is what must be presupposed whenever one apprehends anything. "We can assign no other basis for [the paralogisms] than the simple, and in itself completely empty, representation 'I'; and we cannot even say that this is a concept, but only that it is a bare consciousness which accompanies all concepts. Through this I or he or it (the thing) which thinks, nothing further is represented than a transcendental subject of the thoughts = X. It is known only through the thoughts which are its predicates, and of it, apart from them, we cannot have any concept whatsoever, but can only revolve in a perpetual circle, since any judgment upon it has always already made use of its representation."

36. *svabhāvato viṣayaviṣayānīndriyāṇi. na brahmaviṣayāni. BrSūBh* I.1.2, p. 8:21–22. See Chapter 1, p. 11, regarding the culminating intuition of Brahman.

37. At *BrSūBh* I.1.4, p. 20:2–6, Śaṅkara specifically denies that the self is the "object of the idea 'I' " *(ahaṃpratyayaviṣaya)*. See, however, Hacker's remarks in "Śaṅkara's Conception of Man," p. 124.

38. See, for example, *Gauḍapādīyakārikābhāṣya* III.3, where Śaṅkara plays down the idea of the *kārikā* that a knowing *relation* between the self and itself does exist. The verse reads: *akalpakam ajaṃ jñānaṃ jñeyābhinnaṃ pracakṣate/brahmajñeyam ajaṃ nityam ajenājaṃ vibudhyate.* Śaṅkara glosses the last few words as follows: "By the knowledge that comprises the essence of the self, the essence of the self which is the unborn object of knowledge knows by itself, like the sun which is in essence eternal light. The meaning is that because it is a homogeneous mass of eternal consciousness it does

not depend on any other knowledge in order to know" *(tenātmasvarūpeṇājena jñānenājaṃ jñeyam ātmatattvaṃ svayam eva vibudhyate avagacchati, nityaprakāśasvarūpa iva savitā. nityavijñānaikarasaghanatvān na jñānāntaram apekṣata ity arthaḥ). Sagauḍapādīyakārikātharvavedīyamāṇḍūkyopaniṣad Ānandagirikṛtaṭīkāsaṃvalitaśāṅkarabhāṣyasametā*, p. 142. With regard to the general point, see Vetter, "Erfahrung des Unerfahrbaren bei Śaṅkara," pp. 45–49.

39. It is odd that Paul Deussen, who first introduced Śaṅkara to the European world and evaluated his philosophy critically from a Kantian standpoint, did not pose the question whether Śaṅkara's theory of the self is a rational psychology in the precise Kantian sense. Had he done so he would have realized that Śaṅkara is not guilty of the sort of "transcendent" use of the categories which Kant attacks in his discussion of the paralogisms and that Kant simply did not share the vision of the self Śaṅkara appears to have achieved, not through an improper "dialectical" use of reason, but through direct experience.

40. *The System of Vedānta*, p. 90, n. 54.

41. "Cit and Noûs, or the Concept of Spirit in Vedāntism and Neoplatonism," pp. 320–327.

42. *The Subject of Consciousness*, p. 48.

43. *Analysis of the Phenomena of the Human Mind*, 1:255 ff.; quoted in Evans, pp. 48 f.

44. See *The Concept of Mind*, pp. 156–163.

45. Evans, pp. 45–48.

46. Ibid., p. 41.

47. As in the sentence, "Animals have consciousness, but not plants." The word "fruit," which was mentioned as the standard of a generic term, may also be used without an article—to refer collectively to all the various fruits displayed for sale at the market, for example. But it is not thereby a mass term; using it thus without an article, one does not believe that the fruit one picks up from one bin will be indistinguishable from that from another. It may seem to the reader that these remarks are valid only for the concept of consciousness in English, but it will be shown that they also apply to the Sanskrit notion of consciousness.

48. The last stipulation is meant to define an active/passive relationship between subject and object of consciousness.

49. See Jean-Paul Sartre, *Being and Nothingness*, pp. 10 f.

50. For a list of such expressions see Hacker, "Śaṅkara der Yogin," p. 138. A thorough linguistic analysis of the actual use of these words in classical Sanskrit cannot be attempted here. Hacker makes the interesting suggestion in another article ("Die Idee der Person im Denken von Vedānta-Philosophen," p. 33) that the various cognitive words Śaṅkara employs to describe the self can

be ordered on a scale of increasing abstractness. Concerning the meaning of *cit, caitanya* (spirit, *Geist*) in general see Hacker, "Cit and Noûs."

51. *BrSūBh* II.3.18, p. 280:8–12.

52. *Essays in Radical Empiricism*, p. 4.

53. Ibid., p. 7.

54. Ibid.

55. *Philosophical Studies*, p. 17.

56. Ibid., p. 18.

57. Ibid., p. 20.

58. Thus James is accurately restating Moore's view when he writes, "The usual view is that by mental subtraction we can separate the two factors of experience . . . not isolating them entirely, but distinguishing them enough to know that they are two." "Does Consciousness Exist?" p. 7.

59. Hacker ("Idealismus Śaṅkaras," pp. 240 f.) demonstrates that the opponent of the *mahāpūrvapakṣa* of Rāmānuja's *Śrībhāṣya* is not Śaṅkara himself, though certainly one of his followers, that is, an Advaitin.

60. *na ca nirviṣayā saṃvit kācid asti, anupalabdheḥ* (*Śrībhāṣya*, ed. Vasudev Shastri Abhyankar, p. 36:10–11). The occasion for this remark is the denial that consciousness is eternal. If consciousness were eternal, Rāmānuja argues, then certain *objects* would appear to be eternal because the object of an act of consciousness exists necessarily as long as the consciousness of it (p. 36:4–7). It is ostensibly to prevent an escape from this objection that Rāmānuja denies that there can be a consciousness without an object.

61. See *US* II.93 *(gadyaprabandha)*.

62. *Śrībhāṣya* I.1.1, p. 36:16–18.

63. *arthāntarānubhavasyārthāntarābhāvasya cānubhūtārthāntarāsmaraṇahetutvābhāvāt*, ibid., p. 37:4–5.

64. *tathā hy asya kartuḥ sthiratvaṃ kartṛdharmasya saṃvedanākhyasya sukhaduḥkhāder ivotpattisthitinirodhaś ca pratyakṣam īkṣyante. kartṛsthairyaṃ tāvat sa evāyam arthaḥ pūrvaṃ mayānubhūta iti pratyabhijñāsiddham. ahaṃ jānāmy aham ajñāsiṣaṃ jñātur eva mamedānīṃ jñānaṃ naṣṭam iti ca saṃvidutpattyādayaḥ pratyakṣasiddhā iti kutas tadaikyam. evaṃ kṣaṇabhaṅginyāḥ saṃvida ātmatvābhyupagame pūrvedyur dṛṣṭam idam aparedyur idam aham adarśam iti pratyabhijñā ca na ghaṭate. anyenānubhūtasya na hy anyena pratyabhijñānasaṃbhavaḥ. kiṃcānubhūter ātmatvābhyupagame tasyā nityatve 'pi pratisandhānāsaṃbhavas tadavasthaḥ. pratisandhānaṃ hi pūrvaparakālasthāyinam anubhavitāram upasthāpayati nānubhūtimātram. . . . svasaṃbandhaviyoge tu jñaptir eva na sidhyati. chettuś chedyasya cābhāve chedanāder asiddhivat. ato 'ham artho jñātaiva pratyagātmeti niścitam.* Ibid., pp. 39:15–41:2.

65. G. K. Pletcher, "Mysticism, Contradiction, and Ineffability."

66. See the sources cited in note 4. Stace in particular, drawing mainly on

the studies of R. C. Zaehner, Evelyn Underhill, William James, Rudolf Otto, and D. T. Suzuki, names paradoxicality as one of the characteristics of "the universal core of mystical experience" which he believes to represent a single experience shared by mystics throughout history in all parts of the world. See Stace, especially chap. 2 and chap. 3 (sec. 5), the latter dealing with Śaṅkara. As noted previously, Stace—a philosopher, not a scholar—has come under severe attack by historians of religion for oversimplifying complex data. See P. G. Moore, "Recent Studies," pp. 149 ff.

67. See Stace, chap. 5, where he discusses the theories cited here, eventually rejects them, and presents his own view.

68. Ibid., p. 164.

69. Ibid., p. 174.

70. Ibid., pp. 270–276.

71. Paul Henle, "Mysticism and Semantics."

72. Pletcher, p. 205, italics added. Pletcher goes on to defend the somewhat controversial presupposition of this position—that one can be aware of a proposition that one cannot express.

73. Stace's recommendation is of course absurd—a fact that investigators in this area, including Pletcher, have not stressed sufficiently. It should suffice to point out that Aristotle (*Metaphysics*, Γ, 4) showed that the presupposition of the principle of noncontradiction is necessary for rational discourse. There is no way that the principle of noncontradiction can *meaningfully* be denied. The same view has been put forward by modern logicians, who have demonstrated that a contradiction implies any statement whatsoever (including the denial of the very same contradiction). It might seem profound to suggest, as Stace does, that one might step back from the perspective of logic and view its principles as rules that one can choose to go along with or not, just as one can choose to play checkers or chess. But insofar as that suggestion is to have any meaning it must be made within the perspective in which the law of noncontradiction holds—and is therefore necessarily false. All of Stace's efforts to get around this fact (chap. 5, sec. 6) are to be judged futile.

74. *bhāvasādhano jñānaśabdo, na tu jñānakartṛ*, *TUBh* II.1, p. 49. My interpretation of *bhāva* as the meaning of the verbal root—that is, an action—follows L. Renou, *Terminologie grammaticale du Sanskrit*, pt. 2, p. 51. Since the *bhāva* expressed by the verbal root is not considered *absolutely* eternal *(kūṭasthanitya)*, Śaṅkara seems well justified when he later qualifies its application to Brahman as merely figurative. I am indebted to Professor Vetter for clarification of this point.

75. *yatra nānyad vijānāti sa bhūmā . . . atha yatrānyad vijānāti tad alpam.*

76. *eka evātmā jñeyatvena jñātṛtveṇa cobhayathā bhavatīti*; *TUBh* II.1, p. 49.

77. *na hi niravayavasya yugapad jñeyajñātṛtvopapattiḥ*; ibid.

78. Thus in the *BrSūBh* it occurs as a premise in various exegetical arguments. The being that consists of mind *(manomayaḥ)* mentioned at *Chāndogya Upaniṣad* III.14, for example, must be the highest self as distinct from the lower self (the individual soul), because it is spoken of as an object to be attained, and the designation of a single entity as both object and agent is not proper (*na . . . ekasya karmakartṛvyapadeśaḥ yuktaḥ*; *BrSūBh* I.2.4, p. 66: 14–15). Similarly the "bridge of the immortal" *(amṛtasya setuḥ)*, spoken of at *Muṇḍaka Upaniṣad* II.2.5 as an object to be known *(tam evaikaṃ jānatha ātmānam)*, is thus designated as the highest Brahman qua different from the individual soul, insofar as the one is what is to be known and the other is the knower (*bhedavyapadeśaḥ . . . jñeyajñātṛbhāveṇa*; *BrSūBh* I.3.5, p. 96:24). A discussion of the same matter in the *Bṛhadāraṇyaka Upaniṣad* commentary, though from a somewhat different perspective, has been noted by Hacker (see "Śaṅkara der Yogin," pp. 133 f.). With reference to the bliss that Brahman is identified with in *BĀU* III.9.28 *(vijñānam ānandaṃ brahma)*, Śaṅkara denies that it is a *feeling* of happiness, the kind of happiness that can be experienced *(saṃvedyaṃ sukham)*; for in the absence of a body and organs of sensation there is no experience or consciousness *(vijñāna)*, and the state of bliss talked about in the text is supposed to arise only upon liberation from the body *(mokṣa)*—that is, upon the cessation of one's existence as an embodied self. If one were to *experience* the bliss of Brahman as oneself, then its identity, unequivocally affirmed by scripture, would be contradicted *(atha brahmānandam anyaḥ san mukto vedayate pratyagātmānaṃ ca, aham asmy ānandasvarūpa iti, tadaikatvavirodhaḥ)*. Rather than experiencing Brahman's bliss, the individual soul merges in it completely, like a handful of water thrown into the ocean. It does not continue to exist separately so that one might possibly *know* it *(na pṛthaktveṇa vyavatiṣṭhate ānandātmakabrahmavijñānāya)*. See also *BĀUBh* I.4.7, p. 123:6–7.

79. The passage under consideration has been previously handled by Olivier Lacombe, *L'Absolu selon le Vedānta*, pp. 79–86, and Richard De Smet, "The Theological Method of Śaṃkara," pp. 268–292.

80. *tajjñānaṃ bhavati yad anyebhyo nirdhāritam*, *TUBh* II.1, p. 49.

81. For the sources of this theory, see Madeleine Biardeau, "La définition dans la pensé indienne."

82. *lakṣaṇārthapradhānāni viśeṣaṇāni na viśeṣaṇapradhānāny eva*; *TUBh* II.1, p. 49.

83. *śūnyārthataiva prāptā satyādivākyasya*; ibid., p. 50.

84. *satyādyarthair arthavattve tu tadviparītadharmavadbhyo viśeṣyebhyo brahmaṇo viśeṣyasya niyantṛtvam upapadyate*; ibid., p. 50.

85. *ātmavijñānāvabhasāś ca te vijñānaśabdavācyāś ca dhātvarthabhūtāḥ*; ibid., p. 51.

86. *tathāpi tadābhāsavācakena buddhidharmaviṣayeṇa jñānaśabdena tal lakṣyate na tūcyate*; ibid., p. 52.

87. *evaṃ satyādiśabdā itaretarasaṃnidhāv anyonyaniyamyaniyāmakāḥ santaḥ satyādiśabdavācyāt tannivartakā brahmaṇo lakṣaṇārthāś ca bhavantīty ataḥ siddhaṃ yato vāco nivartante aprāpya manasā saha*; ibid., p. 52.

88. The passage discussed should be compared to *BĀUBh* I.4.7, pp. 142 f., where Śaṅkara says that the word and the concept "self" do not really apply to the self *(ātmaśabdapratyayoḥ ātmatattvasya paramārthato 'viṣayatva-)*. In contrast the Mīmāṃsā resolves to rely only on the ordinary use of words. Thus *MīSūBh* I.1.1: *loke yeṣv artheṣu prasiddhāni padāni, tāni sati saṃbhave tadarthāny eva sutreṣv iti avagantavyam* ("It is to be kept in mind that, so far as possible, the words of the *sūtras* have precisely the same meaning they have in ordinary usage").

89. It should not go unnoticed that Śaṅkara accepts the principle of non-contradiction in general. This has been pointed out by J. F. Staal ("Negation and the Law of Contradiction," pp. 62 f.) in connection with Śaṅkara's insistence that the truth about an established thing (*bhūtavastu*, in this case Brahman) depends on the thing *(vastutantra)* and is not a matter of option *(vikalpa)*, as in the case of what is to be accomplished through the performance of action (*BrSūBh* I.1.2, p. 8:5–19); and it is directly stated by Śaṅkara in his refutation of Jainism (*BrSūBh* II.2.33, p. 253:5–6).

90. Only by ignoring Śaṅkara's hints that he is *not* using words in the usual way was I able to construct the contradiction for his theory in Section 2 in the first place.

91. To put the matter somewhat differently: Śaṅkara sacrifices the advantage he gained against his opponent when he said (in effect) that words are able to denote objects by virtue of their own meaning, by suggesting in this case, for Brahman, that they are not being used as intended. See the discussion by De Smet, who is very much awake to this problem. He attempts to solve it for Śaṅkara by appealing to the (later) Advaitin theory of implication *(lakṣaṇā)*. See, in general, his chap. 3.

92. J. G. Fichte, *Sämmtliche Werke*, ed. I. H. Fichte, I:99 n.

93. Ibid., p. 275. Two forces might fall together on the same line, but insofar as they remain distinct, as centripetal and centrifugal forces are by definition, they will not move in the same *direction*.

94. Fichte's idea of self-consciousness has been judged absurd with particular finality by Jakob Barion, who writes, with recourse to Kerler and Heimsoeth: "In the case of every intellectual activity, and certainly the intellectual intuition of the 'Absolute I' must be that, we have to distinguish the act of knowledge and the intended object, which is different from it. To be sure, it is valid that I as the object which is thought am dependent on myself as the one who is thinking. But both are not yet identical thereby. . . . Every intellectual

act is referred to an object and it cannot be referred to itself, because it is then ipso facto not the same act. This identity maintained by Fichte is therefore quite unthinkable; it suffers from an immanent contradiction" (*Die intellektuelle Anschauung bei J. G. Fichte und Schelling und ihre religionsphilosophische Bedeutung*, pp. 41 f.). Ulrich Pothast, more recently, has critically explored the antinomy contained in Fichte's assumption of the self-apprehension of the I as the precondition for its own existence (*Über einige Fragen zur Selbstbeziehung*, pp. 39–48). If the I exists only insofar as it knows itself, how can it exist to be known by itself if that must already be the case in order for it to exist? Note that this is a different problem than that of the self-knowledge of the I, the identity of subject and object. There have been several attempts to get around these absurdities and their consequences for Fichte's system as a whole. (Thus Barion, p. 42: "Therein lies the great importance of this error, that . . . the [paradoxical] identity is asserted of the Absolute I, the source of all being and happening. If this identity becomes untenable, then the whole foundation for the speculation of Fichte collapses.") All these attempts have rested on the interpretation of the Absolute Ego as an unreachable ideal, a *thought* rather than an actuality—not a metaphysical principle which generates the world but a fundamental tendency in human consciousness to be arrived at by analysis. W. Janke argues forcefully for this thesis in *Fichte: Sein und Reflexion*; see also W. E. Wright, "Self and Absolute in the Philosophy of Fichte." The trouble with this approach is that, being really unthinkable, Fichte's self-consciousness fails even as a thought! Regarding the problems of self-reflexivity in this context, Hacker's article "Cit and Noûs" deserves attention.

95. See in this regard Hugo Mynell, "On Understanding the Unintelligible."

96. That is, in fact, St. Thomas's position with regard to our knowledge of God. St. Thomas, in a way very similar to Śaṅkara, restricts the application of predicates to the Divine Being. The word "wisdom," for example, does not apply to God in exactly the same sense as it applies to His creatures. For we know creatures to be wise only by means of the senses which God altogether transcends. On the other hand, it is not true of Him in an entirely different sense either, for His creatures reflect His essence. "Wisdom," rather, applies *analogically* (compare Śaṅkara, *upacārāt*, *TUBh*, p. 51:15) to God *and* His creatures: it applies analogically to God in the order of naming, because we learn the meaning of that predicate by knowing His creatures; but it also applies analogically to His creatures in the order of being, in that they ultimately derive their wisdom from Him (see *Summa Theologica*, I, Q13, 3–6). For St. Thomas God is perfectly knowable only upon death and salvation, when man is freed from the senses. Approximate knowledge of Him in this life provided by natural theology performs the important function of buttressing *faith*, on which salvation depends. For Śaṅkara, however, perfect knowledge

of the ultimate is possible in this life and is in fact the *cause* of salvation and freedom from the senses. For a selected bibliography of the vast contemporary analytical philosophical literature on religious language, one may consult B. Mitchell, ed., *The Philosophy of Religion.*

97. This is precisely what is overlooked by Vetter in his study of Śaṅkara's *Heilslehre*, "Erfahrung des Unerfahrbaren bei Śaṅkara." Vetter traces a development from a primarily negative soteriology (in the *Gauḍapādīyakārikābhāṣya*)—which merely abstracts from the self all notions that have been falsely superimposed on it—to a more positive method (in the *US*, especially *padaprabandha* 18) which relates the self to empirical states of consciousness. Vetter suggests that the changeover to a modified *via positiva* constitutes an improvement: "It is thus not the insight into nonidentity with the object [the body, mind, and senses of the individual person] that liberates in this case. . . . The knowledge that is necessary here must no longer consist just in the direct removal of the false identification; it can also be an indirect perception of the self by means of the always present reflection [of pure consciousness in the psyche]. . . . One no longer simply argues the snake out of existence; one can now concern himself with seeing the rope, which alone is capable of expelling once and for all the opinion that there is a snake" (pp. 56 f.). But Vetter fails to recognize that the concept "consciousness" *(Geistigkeit)* as applied to the self remains problematic in spite of its relation to empirical consciousness. His extended treatment of this theme in *Studien zur Lehre und Entwicklung Śaṅkaras* does not rectify this oversight.

98. *Mysticism and Philosophy*, pp. 31–38. This thesis has been defended also by Evelyn Underhill *(Mysticism)* and Ninian Smart ("Interpretation and Mystical Experience," among other studies).

99. *Mysticism and Philosophy*, p. 31.

100. Ibid., pp. 34 f.

101. Compare S. Katz, "Language, Epistemology, and Mysticism," in *Mysticism and Philosophical Analysis*, ed. S. Katz, pp. 33–46.

102. Ibid., pp. 26–32; see also P. G. Moore, "Mystical Experience, Mystical Doctrine, Mystical Technique," in Katz, *Mysticism and Philosophical Analysis*, pp. 108–112.

103. Bruce Garside, "Language and the Interpretation of Mystical Experience," p. 93.

104. Ibid., p. 94.

105. Ibid., p. 96.

106. Ibid., p. 95.

107. See Robert Gimello, "Apophatic and Kataphatic Discourse in Mahāyāna: A Chinese View." Gimello documents the Chinese (Hua-yen) effort to supplement the "relentless nay-saying" of Nāgārjuna with a system of affirmative principles to be used in meditation.

108. Ibid., p. 99; italics added.

109. Ibid., p. 102. But Stace, too, is aware of this. See *Mysticism and Philosophy*, pp. 204 f.

110. This point has been anticipated by Streng: "A religious statement . . . while articulating a 'truth,' itself provides the *means of apprehending* Truth by the way it structures the possibilities of apprehension. The symbolic expression is recognized as a limiting mechanism for revealing the religious vision and cannot be considered an outer manifestation of a parallel inner structure; rather, it is a crystallization of certain features of a potential in human experience" (*Emptiness*, p. 177). See, in general, his discussion on pp. 175–180.

111. This is vividly brought to light by a passage from Helen Keller (cited by Hans Hörmann, *Psycholinguistics*, p. 276) in which she describes the moment of realization—brought on by the shock of water splashed in her face—that the patterns traced on the palm of her hand by her teacher were signs, that is, words, referring to things:

> I knew then that "w-a-t-e-r" meant the wonderful cool something that was flowing over my hand. That living word awakened my soul, gave it light, hope, joy, set it free! There were barriers still, it is true, but barriers that could in time be swept away.
>
> I left the well house eager to learn. Everything had a name, and each name gave birth to a new thought. As we returned to the house every object which I touched seemed to quiver with life. That was because I saw everything with the strange, new sight that had come to me. . . . I learned a great many words that day . . . words that were to make the world blossom for me.

The thesis that words create or illumine objects for us is supported by psychological studies, such as that of Glucksberg and Weisberg ("Verbal Behavior and Problem Solving") and those of Glanzer mentioned by Hörmann (see in general his chap. 15). It was also widely subscribed to among classical Indian philosophers; see M. Biardeau, *Theorie de la connaissance et philosophie de la parole dans le brahmanisme classique*, pp. 315–329.

This is not to say that thinking is in no way a part of verbal learning (for Piaget has proved that it is). Nor is a version of Whorf's hypothesis being presented here—that one's language determines the specific structure of reality. Something more basic is being asserted: that a language of whatever sort is necessary for one to be aware of reality at all. It has been argued, further, by Wilfrid Sellars (in such studies as "Language as Thought and Communication") that the world comes into being not just when one uses words but when one uses words as *language*—that is, when one is aware of the rules for their use and is using them properly.

112. Therefore an investigation of it is possible, since we know what is to be investigated, but not superfluous, since it is not *completely* known. *BrSūBh* I.1.1, p. 6:7–23.

113. *yogāṅgānuṣṭhānād aśuddhikṣaye jñānadīptir āvivekakhyāteḥ*; *YS* II.28.

114. For a concise summary of this theory see Erich Frauwallner, *Geschichte der indischen Philosophie*, 1:419–424.

115. *YS* I.3 implies that *samādhi* is a state of self-consciousness: *tadā draṣṭuḥ svarūpe 'vasthānam* ("Then the seer abides in his essence").

116. Sureśvara's *Naiṣkarmyasiddhi*, ed. G. A. Jacob, I.48, p. 30.

117. Ibid., I.52, p. 32.

118. See Hacker's discussion, *Untersuchungen über Texte des frühen Advaitavāda: 1: Die Schüler Sankaras*, pp. 89–95.

119. *The Bhāmatī of Vācaspati*, ed. and trans. S. S. Suryanarayaṇa Sastri and C. Kunhan Raja, p. 72.

120. Ibid., p. 73.

121. Sadānanda (fifteenth century), for another example, explicitly mentions the *aṣṭāṅgas* in his discussion of *savikalpa* and *nirvikalpa samādhi*. He associates *samādhi* with the more immediate means *śravaṇa*, *manana*, and *nididhyāsana*, thus lending it more importance than it has for Śaṅkara. See *Vedāntasāra*, pp. 12–14.

122. The negative aspects of Śaṅkara's theology should not obscure the fact that he is presenting a real conceptual scheme. In general, as P. G. Moore reminds us, "If mystics are using language at all responsibly then even what they say about the indescribable types or aspects of experience may at least serve to define them in relation to a known class of experiences. Thus when St. John of the Cross calls 'ineffable' the experience of 'the touch of the substance of God in the substance of the soul,' he is nonetheless communicating something of the experience by defining it in terms of the categories 'substance,' 'touch,' and so on. Similarly, his statement that the delicacy of delight felt in this experience is 'impossible of description' . . . at least defines the experience within the class of 'delights impossible of description,' which is far from being empty or meaningless to non-mystics" ("Mystical Experience," p. 105). The mystic directs our attention to something beyond empirical space. He points it out by telling us that it is the one thing that cannot be pointed to. While Brahman, for Śaṅkara, cannot be directly described, it can be circumscribed; certainly the cosmology he develops in the second and third *adhyāyas* of the *BrSūBh*, for example, provides a great deal of positive information about it.

It is Vetter's achievement *(Studien zur Lehre und Entwicklung Śaṅkaras)* to have worked out the details and evolution of the method of reflection which leads to the final comprehension of the *mahāvākya* in Śaṅkara's writings. Although I have concentrated here on the steps that lead up to this, a full picture of Śaṅkara's path to salvation emerges only when this, too, is taken into account.

123. The notion of precognitive knowledge plays a central role in the religious philosophy of Abraham Heschel. In *God in Search of Man*, Heschel writes: "Knowledge does not come into being only as the fruit of thinking. Only an extreme rationalist or solipsist would claim that knowledge is produced exclusively through the combination of concepts. Any genuine encounter with reality is an encounter with the unknown, is an intuition in which an awareness of the object is won, a rudimentary, *preconceptual* knowledge. Indeed, no object is truly known, unless it was first experienced in its unknown-ness" (p. 115). "Thus, the certainty of the realness of God does not come about as a corollary of logical premises, as a leap from the realm of logic to the realm of ontology, from an assumption to a fact. It is, on the contrary, a transition from an immediate apprehension to a thought, from a preconceptual awareness to a definite assurance, from being overwhelmed by the presence of God to an awareness of His existence. What we attempt to do in the act of reflection is to raise that preconceptual awareness to the level of understanding. . . . (p. 121).

124. *Buddhism: Its Essence and Development*, p. 20.

125. Ibid.

126. See the survey by Lambert Schmithausen, "Zur Struktur der erlösenden Erfahrung im indischen Buddhismus." Each of the systems Schmithausen discusses involves extensive preparation through meditative procedures and—except for perhaps the Yogācāra—culminates in a specific insight, typically regarding the Four Noble Truths.

127. See Gerhard Oberhammer's discussion of the *Yuktidīpikā (Strukturen yogischer Meditation)* and David Bastow's treatment of the classical Sāṃkhya system ("An Attempt to Understand Sāṃkhya-Yoga").

Chapter 3

1. *Was Heisst Denken?*, pp. 36 f., translated by J. Glenn Gray (*What Is Called Thinking?*, pp. 92 f.).

2. Fichte is noted for his relentless efforts to bring his ideas to the general public. Thus he wrote, besides the introductory works under consideration here, *A Report, Clear as the Sun, for the General Public on the Real Essence of the Latest Philosophy: An Attempt to Compel the Reader to Understand (Sonnenklarer Bericht an das grössere Publikum über das eigentliche Wesen der neueren Philosophie: Ein Versuch den Leser zum Verstehen zu zwingen)* in 1801. Under introductions to the *WL* one should also include four popular works of somewhat broader scope: *The Vocation of Man* (*Die Bestimmung des Menschen*, 1800); *On the Nature of the Scholar* (*Über das Wesen des Gelehrten*, 1805); *The Way to the Blessed Life, or the Doctrine of Religion* (*Die*

Anweisung zum seligen Leben, oder auch die Religionslehre, 1806); and *Addresses to the German Nation (Reden an die deutsche Nation,* 1807–1808). The most important technical presentations of the *WL* are: *The Foundation of the Entire Theory of Science (Die Grundlage der gesammten Wissenschaftslehre,* 1794); *The Theory of Science According to a New Method (Die Wissenschaftslehre 1798, nova methodo;* in the *Nachlass); Exposition of the Theory of Science, 1801 (Darstellung der Wissenschaftslehre, aus dem Jahre 1801); The Theory of Science, Presented in 1804 (Die Wissenschaftslehre, vorgetragen im Jahre 1804;* in the *Nachlass); The Theory of Science in its General Outline (Die Wissenschaftslehre in ihrem allgemeinen Grundrisse,* 1810); *The Facts of Consciousness* of 1810–1811 *(Die Tatsachen des Bewusstseins);* and *The Facts of Consciousness* of 1813 *(Nachlass).*

3. The *Wissenschaftslehre* was enthusiastically applauded by Fichte's students when he first presented it at Jena and then, later, by Reinhold. But it was vehemently attacked by a group of philosophers who called themselves "the Kantists" in a series of publications in *Annalen der Philosophie,* edited by Ludwig Heinrich von Jakob of Halle.

4. I:422. Volume and page references are to *J. G. Fichtes Sämmtliche Werke,* ed. I. H. Fichte, and *J. G. Fichtes Nachgelassene Werke,* also edited by Fichte's son and numbered consecutively as vols. IX, X, and XI. All passages have been checked against *J. G. Fichte: Gesamtausgabe der Bayrischen Akademie der Wissenschaften* (Akad. Ausg.), ed. R. Lauth and H. Jacob, which has preserved the pagination of I. H. Fichte. Translations of passages from the *First* and *Second Introductions* and the *GWL* are taken, with minor adaptations, from Peter Heath and John Lachs, *Fichte: Science of Knowledge (Wissenchaftslehre) with First and Second Introductions;* otherwise the translations are my own.

5. I:433 f.

6. I:434.

7. I:96. For a discussion of the term "positing" see John Lachs's preface to *Fichte: Science of Knowledge,* pp. xiii f.

8. I:97. "Die natürliche Antwort darauf ist: *ich* war nicht; denn ich war nicht Ich." Compare with the *First Introduction,* I:435 f.: "The intellect as such *observes itself;* and this self-observation is directed immediately upon its every feature. The nature of intelligence consists in this *immediate* unity of being and seeing. What is in it, and what it is in general, it is *for itself,* and it is that, qua intellect, only insofar as it is that for itself. . . . A thing, to be sure, is supposed to have a diversity of features, but as soon as the question arises: '*For whom,* then, is it to have them?' no one who understands the words will answer: 'For itself'; for we must still subjoin in thought an intellect *for* which it exists. The intellect is, by contrast, necessarily what it is for itself, and requires nothing subjoined to it in thought. By being posited as intellect, that

for which it exists is already posited with it. In the intellect, therefore—to speak figuratively—there is a double series, of being and of seeing, of the real and of the ideal; and its essence consists in the inseparability of these two . . . while the thing has only a single series, that of the real. . . ."

9. I:98.

10. It comes before substance. See *First Introduction*, I:440; *Second Introduction*, I:499.

11. I:98.

12. See, for example, I:459, quoted on pages 75f.

13. See I:471 f.

14. I:463.

15. I:466.

16. See Frederick Copleston, *History of Philosophy*, vol. 7, pt. 1, *Fichte to Hegel*, pp. 60–62. On p. 62 he states: "It is not claimed that we intuit the pure ego as a spiritual substance or entity transcending consciousness but simply as an activity within consciousness, which reveals itself to reflection." Thus, also, Daniel Breazeale ("Fichte's *Aenesidemus* Review and the Transformation of German Idealism," p. 562): "Intellectual intuition . . . is not a form of *consciousness* at all. . . . Neglect of this important point is responsible for the widespread (romantic) misinterpretation of 'intellectual intuition' as a privileged *faculty* of philosophical knowledge. Fichte's actual view is that the structure of I-hood (the I's presence to itself as an absolute self-positing) has the *form* of an intellectual intuition. This is something that the philosopher learns by means of abstraction and reflection; it is not discovered *by* intellectual intuition."

17. I:464.

18. I:427.

19. I:428.

20. I:459.

21. I:464 f.: "If it has to be admitted that there is no immediate isolated consciousness of intellectual intuition, how does the philosopher then arrive at the knowledge and isolated presentation of the same? I answer: by . . . an inference from the obvious facts of consciousness. The inference . . . is as follows: I propose to think of some determinate thing or other, and the required thought ensues; I propose to do some determinate thing or other, and the presentation of its occurrence ensues. This is a fact of consciousness. Were I to view it by the laws of merely sensory consciousness, it would contain no more than has just been given, a sequence of particular presentations; this sequence in the time series is all I would be conscious of, and all I could assert. I could say only: I know that the presentation of that particular thought, with the indication that it was to occur, was immediately followed in time by a presentation of the same thought, with the indication that it actually was occurring;

that presentation of that particular phenomenon, as one that was to happen, was immediately followed by its presentation as really taking place; I could not, however, enunciate the utterly different proposition, that the first presentation contains the *real ground* of the second; that through thinking the first, the second *came about* for me. . . . Yet I make the latter assumption and cannot abandon it without abandoning myself. How do I arrive at this? There is no basis for it in the sensory ingredients referred to; hence it is a special consciousness, and yet not an immediate consciousness, or intuition, relating to a material, static existent, but an intuition of sheer activity, not static but dynamic; not a matter of being, but of life."

22. I:424 f.

23. I:428.

24. I:279.

25. I:459. Fichte sums up this matter in the *First Introduction*, I:448: "The course of this idealism runs . . . from something that occurs in consciousness, albeit only as the result of a free act of thought, to the entirety of experience. What lies between these two is its proper field. This latter is not a fact of consciousness and does not lie within the compass of experience; how could anything that did so ever be called philosophy, when philosophy has to exhibit the ground of experience, and the ground lies necessarily outside of what it grounds?"

26. I:463.

27. I:429.

28. I:493.

29. I:497.

30. I:503.

31. II:607.

32. Reading *nach* instead of *noch*—the latter being suggested in the Akad. Ausg. Recall that, according to Fichte, there can be no consciousness without self-consciousness. A philosophical objection cannot be raised without performing the act of intellectual intuition.

33. I:504 f.

34. I:506.

35. I:507; italics in the original.

36. IX:3.

37. IX:4; italics in the original. Fichte adds that this point, "which was not completely clear to Kant," became clear to Fichte himself "only in the lengthy exposition of this teaching [the *WL*] and after close acquaintance with the opposed way of thinking."

38. IX:4.

39. IX:5.

40. IX:6.

41. V:412 f.

42. *Nachgelassene Schriften*, ed. Hans Jacob, vol. 2, *Die Wissenschaftslehre 1798, nova methodo*, p. 364. See the Akad. Ausg.; the text is corrupt. See also the *First Introduction*, I:435 f.

43. *YS* 1.1.2 and 3.

44. The most notable exception is Reinhard Lauth; see his article "Fichtes Gesamtidee der Philosophie."

45. See I:488 f.

46. See I:477.

47. I:441. Hence Fichte's justification for calling his system "transcendental idealism" (ibid.).

48. I:446; italics omitted.

49. I refer the reader especially to the work by Wolfgang Janke: *Fichte: Sein und Reflexion.* One may also profitably consult Max Wundt, *Fichte-Forschungen*, and Richard Kroner, *Von Kant bis Hegel*, as well as the more recent study by Dieter Henrich, "Fichtes ursprüngliche Einsicht." W. E. Wright's dissertation, "Self and Absolute in the Philosophy of Fichte," is the best study we have in English. Frederick Copleston's account of the *WL* in his *History of Philosophy*, while it contains some inaccuracies, is also on the whole quite helpful.

50. I:275. See Chapter 2, p. 53 and note 95, regarding the insuperable problems associated with this idea.

51. I:264 f.

52. The idea of a self-limiting absolute which forgets its supreme stature and behaves as though it were an individual self is central to the system of Kāśmīrī Śaivism in Indian philosophy. If we were interested here in comparative *metaphysics*, this, and not Advaita Vedānta, would be the logical choice to set beside the *Wissenschaftslehre.* See in general J. C. Chatterji, *Kashmir Shaivism.*

53. I:453 f. See also I:448: Idealism sees "the whole [system of experience] take form before its eyes."

54. See I:444–447.

55. This is anticipated in the so-called practical deduction of the *GWL* (pt. III). There has been some debate about whether Fichte's later philosophy, beginning with the *Darstellung der Wissenschaftslehre, aus dem Jahre 1801*, is just a reformulation of his earlier WL or an altogether different system. See W. Janke, *Fichte: Sein und Reflexion*, pp. 207–222. I prefer to follow Fichte's own assurances (for example, in the preface to his *Way to the Blessed Life*) that his outlook does not change in any fundamental way.

56. V:516–518.

57. V:512: "Absolute Being deposits itself in this, its *Dasein*, as this absolute freedom and autonomy of apprehending itself *(sich selber zu nehmen)* and as

this independence from its own inner Being. It does not create some freedom outside itself but it itself *is*, in this portion of form [that is, in this formal mode of existence] its very own freedom outside itself. And in this respect it indeed divides Itself—in its *Dasein*—from Itself—in its Being, and thrusts itself out from itself in order to return, enlivened, back into itself."

58. V:464 ff.

59. V:470.

60. V:472. See *Die Staatslehre*, IV:536: "Understanding *(Verstehen)* means seeing the law according to which a certain entity *(Sein)* comes into being—*genetic* knowledge."

61. II:311.

62. II:315 f.

63. II:316.

64. Ibid.

65. Echoes and ramifications of this experience are to be found in many of Fichte's works. Throughout *The Way to the Blessed Life* he speaks of how, when the truth is attained, the world of ordinary experience is reduced to an empty illusion *(leerer Schein)* (see, for example, V:448, 450). The blessed life is also clearly a kind of emancipation: "Everything that the moral-religious person wants and continuously does has for him no value at all in and of itself . . . but it has value for him because it is the immediate appearance of God which he assumes in him, this particular individual" (V:535). The enlightened person is above obligation. He has no individual purpose; the Absolute acts *through* him. Thus, in effect, for Fichte, as for Śaṅkara, merit or demerit do not accrue to one's deeds. Moreover, "the religious person is forever removed from the possibility of doubt and uncertainty" (V:549). He is confident of whatever he strives to achieve, for his will flows undistorted and undisturbed from the godhead. "Nothing which goes on around him dismays him" (ibid.)—for, in harmony with the force of evolution, he is in harmony with the whole divinely created world. Therefore, "there is no fear in him about the future, for the absolutely Divine carries him toward it; no remorse about the past; for to the extent that he was not in God he was nothing, and that is now gone . . ." (V:550). The ultimate, cosmic Will facilitates and supports his actions: "Work and effort have disappeared for him; his whole life *(Erscheinung)* flows pleasantly and easily from within . . ." (ibid.).

66. Cited by Otto, *Mysticism East and West*, p. 64.

67. Ibid., p. 80.

68. *Play of Consciousness*, p. 193. The identity of the saint is not given.

69. *Ramakrishna: Prophet of New India*, ed. Swāmī Nikhilānanda, p. 11.

70. In *The Way to the Blessed Life* Fichte characterizes authentic mysticism as "the true religion, the comprehension of God in the spirit and in truth" (V:428). Considering the charge of mysticism, he declares: "We admit the

entire accusation and confess, not without a happy and uplifting feeling, that in this sense of the word our teaching is certainly mysticism" (ibid.). Yet Fichte exercises discretion in this matter. In *Characteristics of the Present Age* (*Grundzüge des gegenwärtigen Zeitalters*, 1804–1805) he disapproves of the writings of Jacob Boehme.

71. *Die Thatsachen des Bewusstseins*, 1813, IX:569.

72. It seems that Fichte achieved his own illumination while reading the works of Kant. He writes in a letter to Johanna Rahn (later to become his wife) in the winter of 1790: "My scheming spirit has now found rest, and I thank Providence that, shortly before all my hopes were frustrated, I was placed in a position which enabled me to bear disappointment with cheerfulness. A circumstance which seemed the result of mere chance led me to give myself up entirely to the study of the Kantian philosophy—a philosophy that restrains the imagination which was always too powerful with me, gives reason the sway, and raises the soul to an indescribable elevation above all earthly concerns. I have accepted a noble morality, and instead of occupying myself with outward things, I employ myself more with my own being. This has given me a peace such as I have never before experienced" (*Briefwechsel*, Fichte to Johanna Rahn, 5 Sept. 1790; translated by William Smith, *The Popular Works of Johann Gottlieb Fichte*, 1:33). See also Fichte's letter to his friend Achelis, *Briefwechsel*, 29 Nov. 1790.

73. VII:281.

74. VII:284.

75. VII:287.

76. VII:298.

77. VII:400.

78. VII:404.

79. VII:407 f. This is reminiscent of the Buddhist practice of "mindfulness." See the *Satipatthānasutta*, *Dīghanikāya* 31.

80. VII:289.

81. VII:405.

82. VII:290 f.

83. Huxley seems close to an appreciation of this point in his study *The Perennial Philosophy*, for he writes in the preface: "The Perennial Philosophy is primarily concerned with the one, divine Reality substantial to the manifold world of things and lives and minds. But the nature of this one Reality is such that it cannot be directly and immediately apprehended except by those who have chosen to fulfill certain conditions, making themselves loving, pure in heart and poor in spirit. . . . It is only by making physical experiments that we can discover the intimate nature of matter and its potentialities. And it is only by making psychological and moral experiments that we can discover the intimate nature of mind and its potentialities" (pp. viii f.). Yet the rest of

the book consists of a survey of the basic doctrines of the perennial philosophy under such headings as "The Nature of the Ground," "Self-Knowledge," "Grace and Free Will," and "Good and Evil."

84. *Individuals*, p. 9.

85. See *BrSūBh* 1.1.2, p. 8:5–19. Knowledge of Brahman is *vastutantra*, dependent on a thing, not on human notions. It admits of no options *(vikalpa)*.

86. See Ludwig Wittgenstein, *Philosophical Investigations*, I:27 ff.

87. Certainly Plato views the orderliness of the soul as ensuing not just from the study of science but also from such disciplines as gymnastics and music. The apprehension of the Good by means of dialectic depends on taming the passions and developing the personality holistically—that is, cultivating all faculties at once, in harmony with each other. On the basis of this maturity of spirit, philosophical knowledge can then be gained through the skillful employment of the faculty of reason alone.

88. *BrSūBh* I.3.28.

89. *BrSūBh* II.1.6, p. 188:22.

90. *naiṣā tarkena matir āpaneyā proktānyenaiva sujñānāya preṣṭha*; *BrSūBh* II.1.6, p. 188:12–14.

91. *BrSūBh* II.1.11, pp. 192:23–193:5.

92. Thus, perhaps, Descartes' *cogito*. The ontological argument for the existence of God can also be seen in this way, as is indeed suggested by the attitude *Credo, ut intelligam*. According to Peter Moore, "the mystic is not like one who infers the existence of fire from the appearance of smoke when he has no independent rule of inference justifying the link between the two, but like one who 'infers' smoke from the visual sensing of smoke—that is, like one who sees the smoke directly. While it is certainly the case that some mystical claims are presented as inferences (valid or invalid as the case may be), others no less certainly refer to perceptions of objects or realities immediately apprehended" ("Experience, Doctrine, and Technique," p. 125).

93. We find Śaṅkara himself sometimes asserting, in reply to skeptical objections, that *mokṣa* is indeed real. Thus *BrSūBh* II.1.14, p. 199:22–24; I.1.4, p. 21:15–25.

94. Thus, perhaps, the forms or ideas for Plato and "simples" for Descartes, whose necessary connections with other simples are revealed directly by "natural light" or "mental vision."

Chapter 4

1. I:468 f.

2. See Kant's own disclaimer, which appeared in the *Intelligenzblatt der Allgemeinen Literaturzeitung*, 28 August 1799 (included in Fichte's *Briefwechsel*, vol. 2, no. 386). But see also Fichte's rationalization of Kant's state-

ment in his letter to Schelling, September 1799 (vol. 2, no. 397). Kant himself practically admits to not having actually read the *GWL*.

3. I:470 f.

4. V:437 f.

5. *Was Heisst Denken?*, hereafter abbreviated *WHD*. All quotations from this work are from the translation by J. Glenn Gray, *What Is Called Thinking?*, to be cited alongside the German edition as *WCT*.

6. Thus *WHD*, p. 9 (*WCT*, p. 21): "We shall never learn what 'is called' swimming, for example, or what it 'calls for,' by reading a treatise on swimming. Only the leap into the river tells us what is called swimming. The question 'What is called thinking?' can never be answered by proposing a definition of the concept *thinking*, and then diligently explaining what is contained in that definition. In what follows we shall not think *about* what thinking is. We remain outside that mere reflection which makes thinking its object. Great thinkers, first Kant and then Hegel, have understood the fruitlessness of such reflection. That is why they had to attempt to reflect their way out of such reflection."

7. *WHD*, p. 61 (*WCT*, pp. 45 f.).

8. *WHD*, p. 55 (*WCT*, p. 25): "Indeed, what is most thought-provoking is even closer to us than the most palpable closeness of our everyday handiwork —and yet it withdraws."

9. *WHD*, p. 5 (*WCT*, p. 9).

10. This thought, that something subtle and elusive is at the heart of things, is central to Taoism. Hence one of the homely sayings of Lao Tzu:

> We put thirty spokes together and call it a wheel;
> But it is on the space where there is nothing that the usefulness of the wheel depends.
> We turn clay to make a vessel;
> But it is on the space where there is nothing that the usefulness of the vessel depends.
> We pierce doors and windows to make a house;
> And it is on these spaces where there is nothing that the usefulness of the house depends.
> Therefore just as we take advantage of what is, we should recognize the usefulness of what is not.

(*The Way and Its Power*, trans. Arthur Waley, chap. 11, p. 155; for a more scientific statement see chap. 14, p. 159.) Heidegger's interest in and (limited) knowledge of Asian philosophy is documented in the papers presented at a symposium sponsored by the Department of Philosophy of the University of Hawaii, 17–21 November 1969, at Honolulu, and published in *Philosophy East and West* 20, no. 3 (July 1970). See especially Elisabeth Hirsch, "Martin

Heidegger and the East." Hirsch cites the well-known anecdote which has Heidegger say of D. T. Suzuki: "If I understand this man correctly, this is what I have been trying to say in all my writings." Hirsch also points out important doctrinal differences between Heidegger and Śaṅkara (pp. 257–259). One should keep in mind, however, that Heidegger himself conceived the encounter between Oriental and European philosophy not in the form of a comparison but in the form of a dialogue between the *languages* of East and West, to bring out the different ways in which they speak. See J. L. Mehta's contribution to the symposium, "Heidegger and the Comparison of Indian and Western Philosophy."

11. *WHD*, p. 6 (*WCT*, p. 9).

12. See *WHD*, p. 41 (*WCT*, p. 101), concerning the reckoning of time.

13. *WHD*, p. 64 (*WCT*, p. 66); see also *WHD*, pp. 69 f. (*WCT*, pp. 72 f.).

14. *WHD*, p. 27 (*WCT*, pp. 61 f.).

15. See Richard Rorty, for example, whose views are discussed later in this chapter.

16. *WHD*, p. 30 (*WCT*, p. 74).

17. *WHD*, p. 24 (*WCT*, p. 57).

18. Cited by Heidegger, *WHD*, p. 31 (*WCT*, p. 83).

19. *WHD*, p. 32 (*WCT*, p. 84). "Representation *(Vorstellen)* has no longer the character of an apprehension of what is present, in the unhiddenness of which this apprehension itself belongs, with its own mode of presence. In representation there is nothing more of the opening oneself for, but only a grabbing and grasping of. . . . Here it is not what is presented that has its sway; it is the attitude of attacking that prevails" ("Die Zeit des Weltbildes," in *Holzwege*, p. 100).

20. See the passage from *WHD* translated above, pp. 68f.

21. *Über den Humanismus*, pp. 34 f.; English translation: "Letter on Humanism," in *Martin Heidegger: Basic Writings*, ed. and trans. David F. Krell, p. 228.

22. See *WHD*, p. 85 (*WCT*, p. 121).

23. The Taoist philosopher Chuang Tzu speaks of "the empty chamber where brightness is born" (*The Complete Works of Chuang Tzu*, trans. Burton Watson, p. 58).

24. Even nonbeing depends on a "free space" to present itself: "What nihilates illumines itself as the negative" (*Humanismus*, p. 43; "Humanism," p. 237).

25. In *Gelassenheit* Heidegger attempts to articulate this Openness as a "region" *(Gegend)* which "shelters" things and which is the place where things "return to themselves": "A region gathers *(gegnet)*, just as if nothing were happening, each to each and each to all into an abiding, while resting in itself" (pp. 41 f.).

26. "Das Ende der Philosophie und die Aufgabe des Denkens," in *Zur Sache des Denkens*, p. 74; English translation: "The End of Philosophy and the Task of Thinking," in *Basic Writings*, p. 386.

27. "In what way does the thinking of Being stand to theoretical and practical behavior? It exceeds all contemplation because it cares for the light in which a seeing, as *theoria*, can first live and move" (*Humanismus*, p. 45; "Humanism," p. 239). Thus Heidegger came to evaluate critically the "fundamental ontology" of *Being and Time:* " 'Ontology' itself . . . whether transcendental or precritical, is subject to criticism, not because it thinks the Being of beings and thereby reduces Being to a concept, but because it does not think the truth of Being and so fails to recognize that there is a thinking more rigorous than the conceptual. In the poverty of its first breakthrough, the thinking that tries to advance thought into the truth of Being brings only a small part of that wholly other dimension to language. This language is still faulty insofar as it does not yet succeed in retaining the essential help of phenomenological seeing and in dispensing with the inappropriate concern with 'science' and 'research.' But in order to make the attempt at thinking recognizable and at the same time understandable for existing philosophy, it could at first be expressed only within the horizon of that existing philosophy and its use of current terms. In the meantime I have learned to see that these very terms were bound to lead immediately and inevitably into error" (*Humanismus*, pp. 41 f.; "Humanism," pp. 235 f.). In "Heidegger's Topology of Being," Otto Pöggeler discusses the consequences for Heidegger's philosophy of ceasing to be connected primarily with assertion, by asking: "When philosophy is related to a . . . happening, what manner of speaking, what 'logic,' does it have to follow?" (p. 113).

28. *Humanismus*, p. 30 ("Humanism," p. 223).

29. *Humanismus*, pp. 9 f. ("Humanism," p. 199).

30. *WHD*, p. 61 (*WCT*, p. 45).

31. "Ende der Philosophie," p. 61 ("End of Philosophy," p. 373).

32. The theme and method of meditative thinking *(besinnliches Denken)* are dealt with and practiced with particular intensity in *Gelassenheit*; English translation: *Discourse on Thinking*, trans. John M. Anderson and E. Hans Freund. See especially pp. 15 and 49–52 (*Discourse*, pp. 46 and 72–74).

33. Being is never divorced from language for Heidegger; for, in a sense, *it is language:* "Thinking in its saying merely brings the unspoken word of Being to language. The usage 'bring to language' employed here is now to be taken quite literally. Being comes, lighting itself, to language" (*Humanismus*, p. 45; "Humanism," p. 239). Moreover, language *is* Being insofar as words bestow presence.

34. See J. L. Mehta's treatment, *Martin Heidegger: The Way and the Vision*, pp. 430–444. Note, however, Mehta's confession in the preface of his

book (p. xiv) that he felt compelled to change its title from *The Philosophy of Martin Heidegger* when Heidegger himself ironically suggested that he had no such thing as a "philosophy."

35. "Ende der Philosophie," p. 66 ("End of Philosophy," pp. 378 f.).

36. In *Being and Time*, on the other hand, we find Heidegger engaged in a more or less constructive program. There he still speaks of conceptually formulating, "bringing to a concept," the sense of Being. Philosophy is still taken up by the analyses proper to a "science of Being as such." This task involves, among other things, inventing a new language appropriate for expressing the modalities of the *Existenzial*. See Mehta, *The Way and the Vision*, pp. 53–55.

37. See especially the essays ". . . dichterisch wohnet der Mensch" and "Bauen, Wohnen, Denken" in *Vorträge und Aufsätze*, translated by Albert Hofstadter in *Poetry, Language, Thought*. For a general discussion of this theme see Werner Marx, "The World in Another Beginning: Poetic Dwelling and the Role of the Poet."

38. Egon Vietta (*Die Seinsfrage bei Martin Heidegger*, pp. 93 f.) suggests that, because they are shaped by the purpose actually to *think* Being, Heidegger's writings may be able to serve as universal means to a higher truth: "Indian princes in particular have ever again sought for a religion which should be equally valid for all men and above all creeds. The quest of a religion for which all dogmatic differences become untenable engages every thoughtful east Asiatic. The East also knows the sage for whom various religious communities coexist as of equal value in the eyes of God. But in Oriental thinking the sages themselves have not been able to find a way of realizing this demand in thought. For that reason, we may suggest, at least as a question, whether Heidegger's philosophizing does not offer such a way. Heidegger's thinking is world historical, very much as the thinking of Plato and Kant has determined the course of Western history." Mehta, however, after quoting this passage (p. 464, n. 96), suggests in turn (pp. 464–469) that, because of the importance of Being in human history and the fact that all philosophical traditions must necessarily have reference to it, the particularly direct encounter with the unthought depth of thought achieved in the Orient may, after all is said and done, have importance for Western attempts to recover it.

39. To suggest this is, of course, to call into question the validity, or at least the literal importance, of Heidegger's idea of the historicity of philosophical attitudes, including his own—that is, the thinking of any epoch is a unique expression of the particular "disposition" *(Geschick)* of Being at that time. Heidegger's emphasis on historicity discourages attempts to see the same idea, even the same "dynamic," reappearing in different guises throughout a developing tradition.

40. Heidegger exhibits other characteristics of a transformative philosopher which, unfortunately, cannot be entered into here. To mention just one of

these, he conceives of philosophy as merely pointing things out instead of *proving*: "From the Sciences to Thinking there is no bridge but only a leap. It brings us not only to another side but to a wholly different locality. What it opens up can never be proved, if proving means deriving, on the basis of suitable assumptions, propositions about some state of affairs by means of chains of deductive inference. . . . To that which lets itself be known only in such a way that in its self-concealment it manifests itself, we can also come (be equal) only so that we point to it and, with that, enjoin our own selves to let that which shows itself appear in its own unhiddenness. This simple pointing is a distinctive mark of [authentic] thinking, the way to that which it is given to man to think, once and for time to come. Everything permits of being proved, that is, of being derived from suitable assumptions. But very little is amenable to pointing, to being emancipated into arrival by being pointed to, and this is also very seldom." *Vorträge und Aufsätze*, p. 134; quoted by Mehta, *The Way and the Vision*, p. 21, n. 6.

41. And yet in this it has only been true to its own special character as schematic thinking. Although Being is a "possibility from which philosophy must start," philosophy cannot comprehend it without ceasing to be philosophy. See "Ende der Philosophie," p. 65 ("End of Philosophy," p. 377).

42. Rorty openly acknowledges his debt to Heidegger.

43. *Philosophy and the Mirror of Nature*, pp. 138 ff.

44. Ibid., chap. 5; also p. 177.

45. Rorty develops this idea in connection with discussions of the theories of Descartes, Locke, and Kant which I am unable to go into here. See his chaps. 1 and 3.

46. *Mirror of Nature*, p. 163.

47. It was Sellars's important achievement to have shown how this happens. See Rorty's discussion, *Mirror of Nature*, pp. 188–191.

48. Ibid., p. 360.

49. See Rorty's discussion of Sartre in this connection, *Mirror of Nature*, pp. 360–362.

50. Ibid., p. 367. I do not think that this characterization fits Freud or Marx very well, whom Rorty wishes to include among edifying philosophers.

51. See *Mirror of Nature*, pp. 371 f., regarding Heidegger and Wittgenstein.

52. Ibid., p. 359.

53. *Bildung* is also a term Fichte used to refer to his educational program. Its meaning was considerably altered when Dilthey employed it in a *geisteswissenschaftliche* context. Gadamer's use of the term presupposes Dilthey's.

54. *Mirror of Nature*, p. 359.

55. Ibid., pp. 162 f.

56. "Overcoming the Tradition: Heidegger and Dewey," p. 284.

57. Rorty draws attention to this fact in his earlier essay "Overcoming the

Tradition," where it serves as a major difference between Heidegger and Dewey. He does not emphasize it as he should in *Philosophy and the Mirror of Nature*. Thus in the latter work Heidegger, placed next to such figures as Kuhn and Wittgenstein, is made to appear more of a philosophical anarchist than he really is.

58. *WHD*, p. 128 (*WCT*, pp. 211 f.).

59. Here Rorty fails to show how for Heidegger the notion of representation expresses the Greek preoccupation with reality as continuous presence *(Anwesenheit)* and is thus intimately tied up with time. This realization is central to *Being and Time*.

60. Again, Rorty shows in "Overcoming the Tradition" that he knows this full well; yet, eager to include Heidegger in the camp of the edifying philosophers, he glosses over it in *Mirror of Nature*. See his discussion in the former essay (pp. 298 f.) of Heidegger's revulsion against treating the history of philosophy as a series of mere *Weltanschauungen*, as if one were "to choose among them as we choose our favorite pictures."

61. See Habermas's discussion of Fichte in this regard, *Erkenntnis und Interesse*, pp. 253–258.

62. Just as Fichte, in proclaiming the *Wissenschaftslehre* the fulfillment of critical philosophy, misunderstood Kant going the other way! While Kant was in fact intent on solving certain problems regarding the validity of scientific knowledge, Fichte mistook him to be trying primarily to give a complete account of experience.

63. Rorty's version of the history of Western philosophy, moreover, may have to be revised when one takes fully into account the fact that many of the issues of Western philosophy are also issues in Asian philosophy—including epistemological skepticism. In the case of Asian philosophy the latter problem is hardly called forth by the concern to justify scientific knowledge. It has to do, rather, with ascertaining the nature of human existence in general.

64. I am, in other words, proposing a rethinking of the notion of absolute truth as not involving a unique content to be universally assented to. A truth can be absolute without being fixed.

65. The paradigm is William James, as in *A Pluralistic Universe*. In determining whether the transformative philosopher is inclined to "freeze conversation" one would do well to consider the example of Śaṅkara. Śaṅkara, to be sure, believed that there was only one correct way to view things. At the same time, however, he was committed to defending that view against all possible objections. Śaṅkara, moreover, wrote as if he knew that there is never an end to the objections and that a philosophical defense is a continuous, open-ended affair. Thus, while the truth exists objectively, independently of our realizing it according to him, he gives the impression that it exists *for us* only as long as it stands unrefuted. His strategy in argument, finally, reflects a certain acknowl-

edgment of the absence of a common field of discourse on which to settle matters; for he is intensely polemical. If opponents cannot be brought over to his side, then at least they can be made to shut up. Hence the frequently heard complaint that Śaṅkara is "unfair." It would seem, however, that this is a kind of stifling of conversation that Rorty would approve of. For further discussion of Śaṅkara's method see my "Reason, Revelation and Idealism in Śaṅkara's Vedānta."

66. *Mirror of Nature*, p. 360.

67. Thus Rorty's definition of "wisdom" as, especially, "the practical wisdom necessary to participate in a conversation" (p. 372).

68. Note Rorty's rather provocative suggestion (p. 394) that if philosophy were to become purely edifying, "one's self-identification as a philosopher [would] be purely in terms of the books one reads and discusses, rather than in terms of the problems one wishes to solve."

69. See "Overcoming the Tradition," pp. 293–297. Once again, Rorty gives us in this essay every reason *not* to classify Heidegger as an edifying philosopher.

70. *Mirror of Nature*, p. 366.

71. Ibid., p. 369.

72. Ibid., p. 381.

73. Transformative trends in philosophy have been systematically overlooked due to the general assumption among scholars that what a philosopher says is, or can be made, commensurable with one's own point of view—which assumption, in turn, no doubt stems from the influence of traditional philosophy. Hence the hermeneuticist's emphasis on the disparity between different fields of discourse is a welcome corrective. The present study has, I hope, demonstrated how drastic this disparity can be. For an attempt to study Spinoza from the transformative point of view, see Jon Wetlesen, *The Sage and the Way: Spinoza's Ethics of Freedom.*

74. *Mirror of Nature*, pp. 361, 375 f.

75. Ibid., p. 377.

76. See J. Barion, *Die intellektuelle Anschauung bei J. G. Fichte*, pp. 16 ff. Kant's tract is directed immediately at J. C. Schlosser, one of Jacobi's disciples. Some have taken it to be an attack on Fichte, but Barion points out that Fichte himself did not view it as such.

77. For it assumes the affection of the senses by things beyond appearances —things-in-themselves—which are in principle unknowable and to which causality cannot apply.

78. See Barion, pp. 10 f.

79. I:472.

80. I:460.

81. I:461.

82. I:91 ff.
83. I:96.
84. I:95.
85. Fichte provides another, rather interesting defense based on the identification of the intellectual intuition with the moral will (the categorical imperative)—namely, self-consciousness is the only proper basis for knowledge, because one must enact it in order to act rightly: "I cannot go beyond this standpoint [of the necessity of the intellectual intuition] because I *should not* go beyond it. Thus transcendental idealism shows itself to be at once the sole obligatory way of thinking in philosophy as well as the way of thinking in which speculation and the moral law are most intimately combined. I *should* proceed from the pure self in my thinking and conceive it as absolutely self-active, as determining things, not as determined by them" (*Second Introduction*, I:467).
86. And when Śaṅkara suggests, as in the introduction to his *BrSūBh*, that the supreme knowledge conveyed by the Veda overrules other independent means of knowledge *(pramāṇas)*—that is, perception, inference, and so forth.
87. *Humanismus*, p. 41 ("Letter on Humanism," p. 235).
88. As worked out by John Dewey in *Reconstruction in Philosophy*, especially chaps. 2 and 3.

Bibliography

Sanskrit Texts and Translations

Frauwallner, Erich, ed. and trans. *Materialien zur ältesten Erkenntnislehre der Karmamīmāṃsā*. Österreichische Akademie der Wissenschaften, Philosophisch-Historische Klasse, Sitzungsberichte, vol. 259, Abhandlung 2. Vienna: Hermann Böhlaus, 1968.

Gambhīrānanda, Swāmī, trans. *Eight Upaniṣads with the Commentary of Śaṅkarācārya*. 2 vols. Calcutta: Advaita Ashrama, 1957.

Jagadananda, Swami, trans. and ed. *A Thousand Teachings of Sri Sankaracharya*. Madras: Sri Ramakrishna Math, 1941.

Mādhavānanda, Swāmī, trans. *Bṛhadāraṇyaka Upaniṣad with the Commentary of Śaṅkarācārya*. Calcutta: Advaita Ashrama, 1934.

Patañjali. *Pātañjalayogadarśana*. Edited by Svāmi Sri Brahmalīna Muni. Kashi Sanskrit Series, no. 201. Varanasi: Chowkhambha Sanskrit Series Office, 1970.

Rāmānuja. *Śrībhāṣya*. Edited by Vasudev Shastri Abhyankar. Bombay Sanskrit and Prakrit Series, no. 68. Bombay, 1914–1916.

Sadānanda. *Vedāntasāra*. Edited and translated by M. Hiriyanna. Poona: Oriental Book Agency, 1962.

Śaṅkara. *Īśāvāsyopaniṣatsaṭīkāśaṅkarabhāṣyopetā*. Ānandāśrama Sanskrit Series, no. 5. Poona, 1910.

______. *Bṛhadāraṇyakopaniṣad Ānandagirikṛtaṭīkāsaṃvalitaśaṅkarabhāṣyasametā*. Ānandāśrama Sanskrit Series, no. 15. Poona, 1914.

______. *Taittirīyopaniṣad Ānandagirikṛtaṭīkāsaṃvalitaśaṅkarabhāṣyopetā*. Ānandāśrama Sanskrit Series, no. 12. Poona, 1929.

______. *Sagauḍapādīyakārikātharvavedīyamāṇḍūkyopaniṣad Ānandagirikṛtaṭīkāsaṃvalitaśāṅkarabhāṣyasametā*. Ānandāśrama Sanskrit Series, no. 10. Poona, 1936.

______. *The Brahmasūtrabhāṣya: Text with Foot-notes and Variants, etc.* Edited by Nārāyan Rām Āchārya. Bombay: Nirṇaya Sāgar Press, 1948.

Śaṅkara [?]. *Sarvavedāntasiddhāntasārasaṃgraha*. Śrīraṅgam: Sri Vani Vilas Press, 1912.

Śāntarakṣita. *Tattvasaṃgraha*. 2 vols. Edited by Swami Dwarikadas Shastri. Bauddha Bharati Series, no. 2. Varanasi, 1968.

Schmithausen, Lambert, ed. and trans. *Maṇḍanamiśra's Vibhramavivekaḥ*.

Österreichische Akademie der Wissenschaften, Philosophisch-Historische Klasse, Sitzungsberichte, vol. 247, Abhandlung 1. Vienna: Hermann Böhlaus, 1965.

Sureśvara. *Naiṣkarmyasiddhi.* Edited by G. A. Jacob. Revised by M. Hiriyanna. Bombay Sanskrit and Prakrit Series, no. 38. Bombay, 1925.

Thibaut, George, trans. *The Vedānta Sūtras of Bādarāyaṇa with the Commentary by Śaṅkara.* 2 vols. 1890–1896. Reprint. New York: Dover, 1962.

Vācaspati. *The Bhāmatī of Vācaspati.* Edited and translated by S. S. Suryanarayaṇa Sastri and C. Kunhan Raja. Madras: Theosophical Publishing House, 1933.

Vetter, Tilmann, trans. and ed. *Maṇḍanamiśra's Brahmasiddhiḥ.* Österreichische Akademie der Wissenschaften, Philosophisch-Historische Klasse, Sitzungsberichte, vol. 262, Abhandlung 2. Vienna: Hermann Böhlaus, 1969.

Vidyāraṇya. *Pañcadaśī.* Edited and translated by Hari Prasad Shastri. London: Shanti Sadan, 1954.

Fichte's Works

Fichte, Johann Gottlieb. *Nachgelassene Werke.* Edited by I. H. Fichte. 3 vols. Bonn, 1834.

———. *Sämmtliche Werke.* Edited by I. H. Fichte. 8 vols. Berlin, 1845.

———. *Briefwechsel: Kritische Gesamtausgabe.* Edited by Hans Schulz. 2 vols. Leipzig, 1925.

———. *Nachgelassene Schriften.* Edited by Hans Jacob. 2 vols. Berlin, 1937.

———. *J. G. Fichte: Gesamtausgabe der Bayrischen Akademie der Wissenschaften.* Edited by R. Lauth and H. Jacob. 17 vols. Stuttgart–Bad Canstatt: Fromann, 1965–.

Heath, Peter, and Lachs, John, trans. *Fichte: Science of Knowledge (Wissenschaftslehre) with First and Second Introductions.* New York: Appleton-Century-Crofts, 1970.

Heidegger's Works

Anderson, John M., and Freund, E. Hans, trans. *Discourse on Thinking.* New York: Harper & Row, 1966.

Gray, J. Glenn, trans. *What Is Called Thinking?* New York: Harper & Row, 1968.

Heidegger, Martin. *Über den Humanismus.* Frankfurt: Klostermann, 1949.

———. *Holzwege.* 5th ed. (First published 1950.) Frankfurt, Klostermann, 1972.

———. *Was Heisst Denken?* Tübingen: Niemeyer, 1954.

———. *Vorträge und Aufsätze.* Pfullingen: Neske, 1954.

______. *Unterwegs zur Sprache.* Pfullingen: Neske, 1959.

______. *Gelassenheit.* Pfullingen: Neske, 1959.

______. *Zur Sache des Denkens.* Tübingen: Niemeyer, 1969.

Hofstadter, Albert, trans. *Poetry, Language, Thought.* New York: Harper & Row, 1971.

Krell, David F., trans. *Martin Heidegger: Basic Writings.* New York: Harper & Row, 1977.

Other Sources

Aquinas, St. Thomas. *Introduction to St. Thomas Aquinas.* Edited by A. Pegis. New York: Random House, 1948.

Barion, Jakob. *Die intellektuelle Anschauung bei J. G. Fichte und Schelling und ihre religions-philosophische Bedeutung.* Abhandlungen zur Philosophie und Psychologie der Religion, no. 22. Würzburg: C. J. Becker, 1929.

Bastow, David. "An Attempt to Understand Sāṃkhya-Yoga." *Journal of Indian Philosophy* 5(1978):191–207.

Biardeau, Madeleine. "La définition dans la pensée indienne." *Journal Asiatique* 245(1957):375–384.

______. "Quelques reflexions sur l'apophatisme de Śaṅkara." *Indo-Iranian Journal* 2(1959):81–101.

______. *Theorie de la connaissance et philosophie de la parole dans le brahmanisme classique.* Paris: Mouton, 1964.

Breazeale, Daniel. "Fichte's *Aenisidemus* Review and the Transformation of German Idealism." *Review of Metaphysics* 34(1981):545–568.

Chatterji, J. C. *Kashmir Shaivism.* 1914. Reprint. Srinagar: Research and Publication Department, Government of Jammu and Kashmir, 1962.

Conze, Edward. *Buddhism: Its Essence and Development.* New York: Philosophical Library, 1951.

Copleston, Frederick. *A History of Philosophy.* Vol. 7, pt. 1: *Fichte to Hegel.* Garden City: Image Books, 1965.

Descartes, René. *Philosophical Works of Descartes.* Edited by E. Haldane and G. R. T. Ross. 2 vols. Cambridge: Cambridge University Press, 1970.

De Smet, Richard. "The Theological Method of Śaṃkara." Ph.D. dissertation, Pontifical Georgian University, 1953.

Deussen, Paul. *The System of Vedānta.* Translated by C. Johnston. 1912. Reprint. New York: Dover, 1973.

Deutsch, Eliot. *Advaita Vedānta: A Philosophical Reconstruction.* Honolulu: University Press of Hawaii, 1969.

Dewey, John. *Reconstruction in Philosophy.* Boston: Beacon Press, 1957.

Evans, C. O. *The Subject of Consciousness.* London: Allen & Unwin, 1970.

Frauwallner, Erich. *Geschichte der indischen Philosophie.* 2 vols. Salzburg: Otto Müller, 1953.

Gale, R. "Mysticism and Philosophy." *Journal of Philosophy* 57(1960):471-481.

Garside, Bruce. "Language and the Interpretation of Mystical Experience." *International Journal for Philosophy of Religion* 3(1972):93-102.

Gimello, Robert. "Apophatic and Kataphatic Discourse in Mahāyāna: A Chinese View." *Philosophy East and West* 26(1976):117-136.

Glucksberg, S., and Weisberg, R. W. "Verbal Behavior and Problem Solving." *Journal of Experimental Psychology* 72(1966):659-664.

Gokhale, V. V. "The Vedānta Philosophy Described by Bhavya in His Mādhyamakahṛdaya." *Indo-Iranian Journal* 2(1958):165-180.

Gonda, Jan. *Die Religionen Indiens.* 2 vols. Stuttgart: Kohlhammer, 1963.

Habermas, Jürgen. *Erkenntnis und Interesse.* Frankfurt: Suhrkamp, 1968.

Hacker, Paul. "Śaṅkarācārya and Śaṅkarabhagavatpāda: Preliminary Remarks Concerning the Authorship Problem." *New Indian Antiquary* 9(1947):175-186.

______. "Vedānta-Studien: 1. Bemerkungen zum Idealismus Śaṅkaras." *Welt des Orients* 3(1948):240-249.

______. "Eigentümlichkeiten der Lehre und Terminologie Śaṅkaras: Avidyā, Nāmarūpa, Māyā, Īśvara." *Zeitschrift der deutschen morgenländischen Gesellschaft* 100(1950):246-286.

______. *Untersuchungen über Texte des frühen Advaitavāda: 1. Die Schüler Śaṅkaras.* Wiesbaden: Franz Steiner, 1950.

______. "Über Den Glauben in der Religionsphilosophie des Hinduismus." *Zeitschrift für Missionskunde und Religionswissenschaft* 38(1954):51-66.

______. "Die Idee der Person im Denken von Vedānta-Philosophen." *Studia Missionalia* 13(1963):30-52.

______. "Śaṅkara der Yogin und Śaṅkara der Advaitin: Einige Beobachtungen." In Oberhammer (1968-1969), pp. 119-148.

______. "Śaṅkara's Conception of Man." *Studia Missionalia* 19(1970):123-131.

______. "Der religiöse Nationalismus Vivekānandas." *Evangelische Missions-Zeitschrift* 28(1971):1-15.

______. "Notes on the Māṇḍūkyopaniṣad and Śaṅkara's Āgamaśāstravivaraṇa." In *India Maior: Congratulation Volume Presented to J. Gonda*, edited by J. Ensink and P. Gaeffke. Leiden: Brill, 1972.

______. "Cit and Noûs, or the Concept of Spirit in Vedāntism and Neoplatonism." In *Kleine Schriften*, pp. 320-337.

______. *Kleine Schriften.* Edited by L. Schmithausen. Wiesbaden: Franz Steiner, 1978.

Henle, Paul. "Mysticism and Semantics." *Philosophy and Phenomenological Research* 9(1949):416-422.

Henrich, Dieter. "Fichtes ursprüngliche Einsicht." In *Subjektivität und Metaphysik: Festschrift für Wolfgang Cramer*, edited by D. Henrich. Frankfurt: Klostermann, 1966.

Heschel, Abraham. *God in Search of Man*. New York: World, 1959.

Hirsch, Elisabeth. "Martin Heidegger and the East." *Philosophy East and West* 20(1970):247–263.

Hörmann, Hans. *Psycholinguistics*. Berlin: Springer, 1971.

Huxley, Aldous. *The Perennial Philosophy*. New York: Harper & Row, 1945.

Ingalls, Daniel H. H. "The Study of Śaṃkarācārya." *Annals of the Bhandarkar Oriental Research Institute* 33(1952):1–14.

______. "Śaṃkara on the Question: Whose Is Avidyā?" *Philosophy East and West* 3(1953):69–72.

Jacobi, Hermann. "Über das ursprüngliche Yogasystem." In *Kleine Schriften*, edited by B. Kölver. Wiesbaden: Franz Steiner, 1970.

James, William. *Essays in Radical Empiricism and A Pluralistic Universe*. New York: Dutton, 1971.

Janke, Wolfgang. *Fichte: Sein und Reflexion: Grundlagen der kritischen Vernunft*. Berlin: De Gruyter, 1970.

Kane, P. V. *History of Dharmaśāstra*. 5 vols. Poona: Bhandarkar Oriental Research Institute, 1962.

Kant, Immanuel. *Critique of Pure Reason*. Translated by Norman Kemp Smith. London: Macmillan, 1964.

Katz, Steven T., ed. *Mysticism and Philosophical Analysis*. Oxford: Oxford University Press, 1978.

Kockelmans, Joseph, ed. *On Heidegger and Language*. Evanston, Ill.: Northwestern University Press, 1972.

Kroner, Richard. *Von Kant bis Hegel*. Tübingen: Mohr, 1921.

Lacombe, Olivier. *L'Absolu selon le Védānta*. Paris: Guenther, 1937.

Lauth, Reinhard. "Fichtes Gesamtidee der Philosophie." *Philosophisches Jahrbuch* 71(1963):252–270.

Mahesh, Maharishi. *The Bhagavad Gita*. Baltimore: Penguin, 1969.

Marx, Werner. "The World in Another Beginning: Poetic Dwelling and the Role of the Poet." In Kockelmans, pp. 235–250.

Matilal, B. K. *Epistemology, Logic and Grammar in Indian Philosophical Analysis*. The Hague: Mouton, 1971.

Mayeda, Sengaku. "The Authenticity of the Bhagavadgītābhāṣya Ascribed to Śaṅkara." *Wiener Zeitschrift für die Kunde Süd- und Ostasiens* 9(1965): 173–183.

______. "On the Author of the Māṇḍūkyopaniṣad- and the Gauḍapādīya-Bhāṣya." *Adyar Library Bulletin* 31(1967):73–94.

______. "Śaṅkara's Authorship of the Kenopaniṣadbhāṣya." *Indo-Iranian Journal* 10(1967):33–53.

Mehta, J. L. "Heidegger and the Comparison of Indian and Western Philosophy." *Philosophy East and West* 20(1970):303–317.

———. *Martin Heidegger: The Way and the Vision.* Honolulu: University Press of Hawaii, 1976.

Mill, James. *Analysis of the Phenomena of the Human Mind.* Edited by J. S. Mill. 2 vols. London, 1869.

Mitchell, Basil, ed. *The Philosophy of Religion.* Oxford: Oxford University Press, 1971.

Moore, G. E. *Philosophical Studies.* London: Routledge & Kegan Paul, 1922.

Moore, Peter. "Recent Studies of Mysticism." *Religion: Journal of Religion and Religions* 3(1975):146–156.

———. "Mystical Experience, Mystical Doctrine, Mystical Technique." In Katz, pp. 101–131.

Muktananda, Swami. *Play of Consciousness.* New York: Harper & Row, 1978.

Mynell, Hugo. "On Understanding the Unintelligible." *Analysis* 34(1973–1974):108–112.

Nikhilānanda, Swāmī, ed. *Ramakrishna: Prophet of New India.* New York: Harper and Bros., 1942.

Oberhammer, Gerhard. *Strukturen yogischer Meditation.* Österreichische Akademie der Wissenschaften, Philosophisch-Historische Klasse, Sitzungsberichte, vol. 322. Veröffentlichungen der Kommission für Sprachen und Kulturen Indiens, no. 13. Vienna, 1977.

Oberhammer, Gerhard, ed. *Beiträge zur Geistesgeschichte Indiens: Festschrift für Erich Frauwallner. Wiener Zeitschrift für die Kunde Süd- und Ostasiens* 12–13 (1968–1969).

———. *Transzendenzerfahrung: Vollzugshorizont des Heils: Das Problem in indischer und christlicher Tradition.* Publications of the De Nobili Research Library, no. 5. Vienna, 1978.

Otto, Rudolf. *Mysticism East and West.* Translated by B. L. Bracey and R. C. Payne. New York: Macmillan, 1932.

Pletcher, G. K. "Mysticism, Contradiction, and Ineffability." *American Philosophical Quarterly* 10(1973):201–212.

Pöggeler, Otto. "Heidegger's Topology of Being." In Kockelmans, pp. 107–135.

Pothast, Ulrich. *Über einige Fragen zur Selbstbeziehung.* Frankfurt: Klostermann, 1971.

Prabhavānanda, Swāmī. "The Ideal of Renunciation." In *Vedanta for Modern Man,* edited by Christopher Isherwood. New York: Collier, 1962.

Rau, Wilhelm. "Bemerkungen zu Śaṃkaras Bṛhadāraṇyakopaniṣadbhāṣya." *Padeuma: Mitteilungen zur Kulturkunde* 7(1960):294–299.

Renou, Louis. *Terminologie grammaticale du Sanskrit.* 3 pts. Paris, 1942.

Rorty, Richard. "Overcoming the Tradition: Heidegger and Dewey." *Review of Metaphysics* 30(1976):280–305.

______. *Philosophy and the Mirror of Nature.* Princeton: Princeton University Press, 1979.

Ryle, Gilbert. *The Concept of Mind.* New York: Barnes & Noble, 1949.

Saraswati, Swami Satchidanandendra. *The Vision of Atman.* Holenarsipur: Adhyatma Prakasha Karyalaya, 1970.

Sartre, Jean-Paul. *Being and Nothingness.* Translated by H. Barnes. New York: Washington Square Books, 1966.

Schmithausen, Lambert. "Zur Struktur der erlösenden Erfahrung im indischen Buddhismus." In Oberhammer (1978), pp. 97–119.

Sellars, Wilfrid. "Language as Thought and Communication." *Philosophy and Phenomenological Research* 29(1969):506–527.

Smart, Ninian. "Interpretation and Mystical Experience." *Religious Studies* 1(1965):75–87.

Smith, William. "Memoir of J. G. Fichte." In *The Popular Works of Johann Gottlieb Fichte*, ed. W. Smith. 2 vols. London: Trubner, 1889.

Staal, J. F. *Advaita and Neo-Platonism.* Madras: University of Madras Press, 1961.

______. "Negation and the Law of Contradiction in Indian Thought." *Bulletin of the School of Oriental and African Studies* 25(1962):52–71.

______. *Exploring Mysticism.* Berkeley: University of California Press, 1975.

Stace, W. T. *Mysticism and Philosophy.* New York: Lippincott, 1960.

Strawson, P. F. *Individuals.* London: Methuen, 1959.

Streng, Frederick. *Emptiness: A Study in Religious Meaning.* Nashville: Abingdon, 1967.

Taber, John. "Reason, Revelation and Idealism in Śaṅkara's Vedānta." *Journal of Indian Philosophy* 9(1981):283–307.

Tynan, K. "Profiles: Tom Stoppard." *The New Yorker*, 19 December 1977, pp. 41–111.

Underhill, Evelyn. *Mysticism.* New York: Meridian Books, 1955.

Vetter, Tilmann. "Zur Bedeutung des Illusionismus bei Śaṅkara." In Oberhammer (1968–1969), pp. 407–423.

______. "Erfahrung des Unerfahrbaren bei Śaṅkara." In Oberhammer (1978), pp. 45–69.

______. *Studien zur Lehre und Entwicklung Śaṅkaras.* Publications of the De Nobili Research Library, no. 6. Vienna, 1979.

Vietta, Egon. *Die Seinsfrage bei Martin Heidegger.* Stuttgart: Schwab, 1950.

Waley, Arthur, trans. *The Way and Its Power.* London: Allen & Unwin, 1934.

Watson, Burton, trans. *The Complete Works of Chuang Tzu.* New York: Columbia University Press, 1968.

Wetlesen, Jon. *The Sage and the Way: Spinoza's Ethics of Freedom.* Atlantic Heights, N.J.: Humanities Press, 1979.

Wittgenstein, Ludwig. *Tractatus Logico-Philosophicus.* London: Kegan Paul, Trench, and Trubner, 1922.

______. *Philosophical Investigations.* New York: Macmillan, 1953.

Wright, William E. "Self and Absolute in the Philosophy of Fichte." Ph.D. dissertation, Vanderbilt University, 1971.

Wundt, Max. *Fichte-Forschungen.* Stuttgart: Fromann, 1929.

Index

absolute, 56; in Fichte's philosophy, 87, 88, 96, 166 n.65; in Kāshmīrī Śaivism, 165 n.52; in Śaṅkara's philosophy, 54–55, 96. *See also* Absolute I; Brahman; self
Absolute I (Absolute Ego, Absolute Self), 73; criticized, 156–157 n.94; as first principle of human knowledge, 74, 134–135; manifestation of, 84–86; as selfhood, 78; and universal Will, 87. *See also* absolute; self
Advaitin: doctrines of Śaṅkara, 144 n.53; theory of implication, 156 n.91. *See also* Vedānta, Advaita
afflictions *(kleśas)*, 62
agent: self as, according to Śaṅkara, 7, 151 n.33; according to Fichte, 73; of knowledge, 33, 44, 47–48, 49, 50
agent suffix, 150 n.19
Aitareyopaniṣadbhāṣya (Śaṅkara), 8
apūrva, 21
Aquinas, St. Thomas, 157 n.96
Aristotle, 154 n.73
asceticism. *See* austerity
āśramas (stages of Hindu life), 22–23
ātman. *See* self
attrition of impurities, 63
austerity *(tapas)*, 14, 18, 23–24, 25, 55, 62–63
Ayer, A. J., 27

Barion, Jakob, 156–157 n.94, 175 n.76
Being (Being of beings), 105, 107, 110–111, 115, 123, 124
Bhagavad Gītā, 5–6
Bhagavadgītābhāṣya (Śaṅkara), 7
Bhāmatī (Vācaspati), 63
bhāva (action), 154 n.74
Bhavya, 6
blessedness: nature of, according to Fichte, 82; absolute as, 96
bliss, 96, 155 n.78
brahmajijñāsā (investigation of Brahman). *See* Brahman, prerequisites of investigation of
Brahman, 7; as bliss, 155 n.78; as cause of universe, 11, 30–31; familiarity with, 60–61; as inactive, 96; knowledge of, as identical with self, 8–9, 11, 12, 13, 17, 21–22, 55, 168 n.85; as knowledge (consciousness), 33, 47–52, 61; omniscience of, 30–31; prerequisites of investigation of, 13–14, 26, 55, 60–61; world of, 140 n.11. *See also* absolute; self
Brāhmaṇas, 7, 19
Brahmasiddhi (Maṇḍanamisra), 141 n.27
Brahmasūtrabhāṣya (Śaṅkara), 7, 29–30, 34, 144 n.53, 148 n.95. I.1.1: 13–14, 60, 147 n.77; I.1.4: 7–8, 10, 142 n.32, 143 n.46, 151 n.37, 168 n.93; I.1.5: 30–31, 33, 34; I.4.19–22: 31–33; II.1.6 and 11: 101 n.41, 142–143 n.101; II.3.18: 33–34, 41; III.4.26, 32 and 52: 22; IV.1.1 and 2: 11–12, 21–22
Bṛhadāraṇyaka Upaniṣad: IV.4.22 and 23: 14–15, 17; II.4: 31–33; IV.3: 34–35
Bṛhadāraṇyakopaniṣadbhāṣya (Śaṅkara), 8, 19, 148 n.95. I.4.2: 18–19, 22, 148–149 n.95; I.4.7: 8–9, 16–17, 143 n.46, 156 n.88; III.5.1: 145–146 n.65; IV.3.6: 6 and 7: 34, 35–36, 144 n.53; IV.4.22 and 23: 14, 15–18, 148 n.95
Buddhism, 6, 65

calculating, 107, 124. *See also* thinking, authentic
calmness *(śama)*, 14, 23, 145 n.56
categorical imperative: and goal of education, 92; as principle of morality, 87–88; as principle of universal Will, 86–87

Production Notes

This book was designed by Roger Eggers. Composition and paging were done on the Quadex Composing System and typesetting on the Compugraphic Unisetter by the design and production staff of University of Hawaii Press.

The text and display typeface is Compugraphic Caledonia.

Offset presswork and binding were done by Vail-Ballou Press, Inc. Text paper is Writers R Offset, basis 50.